Building RESTful Web Services with Go

Learn how to build powerful RESTful APIs with Golang that scale gracefully

Naren Yellavula

BIRMINGHAM - MUMBAI

Building RESTful Web Services with Go

First published: December 2017

Production reference: 1261217

Published by Packt Publishing Ltd.
Livery Place
35 Livery Street
Birmingham
B3 2PB, UK.

ISBN 978-1-78829-428-7

www.packtpub.com

Credits

Author
Naren Yellavula

Reviewer
Anshul Joshi

Commissioning Editor
Aaron Lazar

Acquisition Editor
Denim Pinto

Content Development Editor
Sreeja Nair

Technical Editor
Rutuja Vaze

Copy Editors
Dhanya Baburaj
Safis Editing

Project Coordinator
Sheejal Shah

Proofreader
Safis Editing

Indexer
Rekha Nair

Graphics
Jason Monteiro

Production Coordinator
Nilesh Mohite

About the Author

Naren Yellavula—fondly called by the developer community as Naren Arya—started his programming career in the funniest way. He ditched mechanical engineering for computer science after watching The Matrix for the first time. With dreams of coding a mini world, he continuously sharpened his practical skills. Initially, he built few a mobile applications. Then, he completely moved into the space of full stack development. He always believed that computers and software can help make this world a better place. He wrote 120+ development articles on various open source technologies, including Go and Python. He is also one of the few young speakers at the PyCon India conference (he spoke at Bangalore in 2015 and Delhi in 2017). With detailed knowledge of web scraping and REST APIs, he dived into multiple domains such as cloud telephony and cloud-based web services. On this journey, he bathed in a lot of design decisions. He currently works as a software engineer for Citrix R&D, India. Naren is a great fan of Go personally because of the speed and intuitiveness of the language. In his spare time, he tries to educate the youth in programming and software development. He loves reading nonfiction most of the time, and Victorian and Russian fiction sometimes.

Acknowledgments

I would like to thank my grandmother, Tayamma, for raising me to be helpful to others by sharing my knowledge in every possible way. She was the one who always taught me how to put in serious effort with 100% dedication, and not worry much about results. Therefore, I dedicate this book to her, to my inspiration.

I also cannot understate the support given by my father, Venkataiah Yellavula; mother, ShobaRani Dasyam; and lovely younger brother Saikiran, who understood the value of the time I spent on this book and always encouraged me with their positive wishes. I am grateful to my mentor, Chandrashekar MuniBudha, Solutions Architect, Amazon Web Services, whom I am deeply indebted to. I also thank Ashwin Baskaran, Senior Director, Citrix, who encouraged and pushed me forward in all possible ways. Thank you!

I cannot name everyone here; the list is so big. However, I sincerely thank all my friends who always wished success for this book.

About the Reviewer

Anshul Joshi is a data scientist with experience in recommendation systems, predictive modeling, neural networks, and high-performance computing. His research interests encompass deep learning, artificial intelligence, and computational physics. Most of the time, he can be found exploring GitHub or trying anything new he can get his hands on. His blog can be found at `https://anshuljoshi.com/`.

www.PacktPub.com

For support files and downloads related to your book, please visit www.PacktPub.com.

Did you know that Packt offers eBook versions of every book published, with PDF and ePub files available? You can upgrade to the eBook version at www.PacktPub.com and as a print book customer, you are entitled to a discount on the eBook copy. Get in touch with us at service@packtpub.com for more details.

At www.PacktPub.com, you can also read a collection of free technical articles, sign up for a range of free newsletters and receive exclusive discounts and offers on Packt books and eBooks.

https://www.packtpub.com/mapt

Get the most in-demand software skills with Mapt. Mapt gives you full access to all Packt books and video courses, as well as industry-leading tools to help you plan your personal development and advance your career.

Why subscribe?

- Fully searchable across every book published by Packt
- Copy and paste, print, and bookmark content
- On demand and accessible via a web browser

Customer Feedback

Thanks for purchasing this Packt book. At Packt, quality is at the heart of our editorial process. To help us improve, please leave us an honest review on this book's Amazon page at https://www.amazon.com/dp/1788294289.

If you'd like to join our team of regular reviewers, you can email us at customerreviews@packtpub.com. We award our regular reviewers with free eBooks and videos in exchange for their valuable feedback. Help us be relentless in improving our products!

Table of Contents

Preface

Initially, SOAP-based web services became more popular with XML. Then, since 2012, REST picked up the pace and gulped SOAP in whole. The rise of a new generation of web languages, such as Python, JavaScript (Node.js), and Go, showed a different approach to web development compared to the traditional ones, such as ASP.NET and Spring. Since this decade, Go has become more and more popular due to its speed and intuitiveness. Less verbose code, strict type checking, and support for concurrency make Go a better choice for writing any web backend. Some of the best tools, such as Docker and Kubernetes, are written in Go. Google uses Go a lot in its daily activities. You can see a list of Go-using companies at `https://github.com/golang/go/wiki/GoUsers`.

For any internet company, the web development department is crucial. Data that the company accumulates needs to be served to the clients in form of an API or web service. Various clients (browser, mobile application, and server) consume API every day. REST is an architectural pattern that defines resource consumption in the form of methods.

Go is a better language to write web servers. It is the responsibility of an intermediate Go developer to know how to create RESTful services using the constructs available in the language. Once the basics are understood, the developer should learn other things, such as testing, optimizing, and deploying services. This book is an attempt to make the reader comfortable with developing web services.

Experts think that in the near future, as Python is moving into the Data Science space and competing with R, Go can emerge as the single go-to language in the web development space by competing with NodeJS. This book is not a cookbook. However, it offers many tips and tricks throughout your journey. By the end of the book, the reader will be comfortable with REST API development through a multitude of examples. They will also come to know about the latest practices, such as protocol buffers/gRPC/API Gateway, which will move their knowledge to the next level.

What this book covers

Chapter 1, *Getting Started with REST API Development*, discusses the fundamentals of REST architecture and verbs.

Chapter 2, *Handling Routing for Our REST Services*, describes how to add routing to our API.

Chapter 3, *Working with Middleware and RPC*, is about working with middleware handlers and basic RPC.

Chapter 4, *Simplifying RESTful Services with Popular Go Frameworks*, presents quick prototyping API with frameworks.

Chapter 5, *Working with MongoDB and Go to Create REST API*, explains how to use MongoDB as the database for our API.

Chapter 6, *Working with Protocol Buffers and gRPC*, shows how to use Protocol buffers and gRPC to obtain performance boost over HTTP/JSON.

Chapter 7, *Working with PostgreSQL, JSON, and Go*, explains the benefits of PostgreSQL and a JSON store for creating APIs.

Chapter 8, *Building a REST API Client in Go and Unit Testing*, presents techniques for building client software and API testing with unit tests in Go.

Chapter 9, *Scaling Our REST API Using Microservices*, is about breaking our API service into microservices using Go Kit.

Chapter 10, *Deploying Our REST Services*, shows how we can deploy services built on Nginx and monitor them using supervisord.

Chapter 11, *Using an API Gateway to Monitor and Metricize REST API*, explains how to make our services production grade by adding multiple APIs behind API Gateway.

Chapter 12, *Handling Authentication for Our REST Services*, discusses securing our API with basic authentication and JSON Web Tokens (JWT).

What you need for this book

For this book, you need a laptop/PC with Linux (Ubuntu 16.04), macOS X, or Windows installed. We will use Go 1.8+ as the version of our compiler and install many third-party packages, so a working internet connection is required.

We will also use Docker in the final chapters to explain concepts of API Gateway. Docker V17.0+ is recommended. If Windows users have problems with the native Go installation for any examples, use Docker for Windows and run Ubuntu container, which gives more flexibility; refer to `https://www.docker.com/docker-windows` for more details.

Before diving into the book, refresh your language basics at `https://tour.golang.org/welcome/1`.

Even though these are the basic requirements, we will guide you through the installations wherever required.

Who this book is for

This book is for all the Go developers who are comfortable with the language and seeking to learn REST API development. Even senior engineers can enjoy this book, as it has many cutting-edge concepts, such as microservices, protocol buffers, and gRPC.

Developers who are already familiar with REST concepts and stepping into the Go world from other platforms, such as Python and Ruby, can also benefit a lot.

Conventions

In this book, you will find a number of text styles that distinguish between different kinds of information. Here are some examples of these styles and an explanation of their meaning.

Code words in text, database table names, folder names, filenames, file extensions, pathnames, dummy URLs, user input, and Twitter handles are shown as follows: "Name the preceding program as `basicHandler.go`."

A block of code is set as follows:

```
{
  "ID": 1,
  "DriverName": "Menaka",
  "OperatingStatus": true
}
```

Any command-line input or output is written as follows:

```
go run customMux.go
```

New terms and **important words** are shown in bold. Words that you see on the screen, for example, in menus or dialog boxes, appear in the text like this: "It returns message saying **Logged In successfully**."

Warnings or important notes appear in a box like this.

Tips and tricks appear like this.

Reader feedback

Feedback from our readers is always welcome. Let us know what you think about this book-what you liked or disliked. Reader feedback is important for us as it helps us develop titles that you will really get the most out of.

To send us general feedback, simply e-mail feedback@packtpub.com, and mention the book's title in the subject of your message.

If there is a topic that you have expertise in and you are interested in either writing or contributing to a book, see our author guide at www.packtpub.com/authors .

Customer support

Now that you are the proud owner of a Packt book, we have a number of things to help you to get the most from your purchase.

Downloading the example code

You can download the example code files for this book from your account at http://www.packtpub.com. If you purchased this book elsewhere, you can visit http://www.packtpub.com/support and register to have the files e-mailed directly to you.

You can download the code files by following these steps:

1. Log in or register to our website using your e-mail address and password.
2. Hover the mouse pointer on the **SUPPORT** tab at the top.
3. Click on **Code Downloads & Errata**.
4. Enter the name of the book in the **Search** box.
5. Select the book for which you're looking to download the code files.
6. Choose from the drop-down menu where you purchased this book from.
7. Click on **Code Download**.

You can also download the code files by clicking on the **Code Files** button on the book's webpage at the Packt Publishing website. This page can be accessed by entering the book's name in the **Search** box. Please note that you need to be logged in to your Packt account.

Once the file is downloaded, please make sure that you unzip or extract the folder using the latest version of:

- WinRAR / 7-Zip for Windows
- Zipeg / iZip / UnRarX for Mac
- 7-Zip / PeaZip for Linux

The code bundle for the book is also hosted on GitHub at `https://github.com/PacktPublishing/Building-RESTful-Web-Services-with-Go`. We also have other code bundles from our rich catalog of books and videos available at `https://github.com/PacktPublishing/`. Check them out!

Downloading the color images of this book

We also provide you with a PDF file that has color images of the screenshots/diagrams used in this book. The color images will help you better understand the changes in the output. You can download this file from `https://www.packtpub.com/sites/default/files/downloads/BuildingRESTfulWebServiceswithGo_ColorImages.pdf`.

Errata

Although we have taken every care to ensure the accuracy of our content, mistakes do happen. If you find a mistake in one of our books-maybe a mistake in the text or the code-we would be grateful if you could report this to us. By doing so, you can save other readers from frustration and help us improve subsequent versions of this book. If you find any errata, please report them by visiting http://www.packtpub.com/submit-errata, selecting your book, clicking on the **Errata Submission Form** link, and entering the details of your errata. Once your errata are verified, your submission will be accepted and the errata will be uploaded to our website or added to any list of existing errata under the Errata section of that title.

To view the previously submitted errata, go to https://www.packtpub.com/books/content/support and enter the name of the book in the search field. The required information will appear under the **Errata** section.

Piracy

Piracy of copyrighted material on the Internet is an ongoing problem across all media. At Packt, we take the protection of our copyright and licenses very seriously. If you come across any illegal copies of our works in any form on the Internet, please provide us with the location address or website name immediately so that we can pursue a remedy.

Please contact us at copyright@packtpub.com with a link to the suspected pirated material.

We appreciate your help in protecting our authors and our ability to bring you valuable content.

Questions

If you have a problem with any aspect of this book, you can contact us at questions@packtpub.com, and we will do our best to address the problem.

1
Getting Started with REST API Development

A web service is a communication mechanism defined between different computer systems. Without web services, custom peer-to-peer communication becomes cumbersome and platform specific. It is like a hundred different kinds of things that the web needs to understand and interpret. If computer systems align with the protocols that the web can understand easily, it is a great help.

A web service is a software system designed to support interoperable machine-to-machine interaction over a network, **World Wide Web Consortium (W3C)**, `https://www.w3.org/TR/ws-arch/`.

Now, in simple words, a web service is a road between two endpoints where messages are transferred smoothly. Here, this transfer is usually one way. Two individual programmable entities can also communicate with each other through their own APIs. Two people communicate through language. Two applications communicate through the **Application Programming Interface (API)**.

The reader might be wondering; what is the importance of the API in the current digital world? The rise of the **Internet of Things (IoT)** made API usage heavier than before. Consciousness about the API is growing day by day, and there are hundreds of APIs that are being developed and documented all over the world every day. Notable major businesses are seeing futures in the **API as a Service (AAAS)**. A bright example is **Amazon Web Services (AWS)**. It is a huge success in the cloud world. Developers write their own applications using the REST API provided by the AWS.

A few more hidden use cases are from travel sites like Ibibo and Expedia, which fetch real-time prices by calling the APIs of third-party gateways and data vendors. Web services are often charged these days.

Topics to be covered in this chapter are:

- The different Web Services available
- Representational State Transfer (REST) architecture in detail
- Introduction to Single Page Applications (SPA) with REST
- Setting up a Go project and running a development server
- Building our first service for finding Roman numerals
- Using Gulp to auto-compile Go code

Types of web services

There are many types of web services which have evolved over time. Prominent ones are :

- SOAP
- UDDI
- WSDL
- REST

Out of these, **SOAP** became popular in the early 2000s, when XML was on the top wave. The XML data format is used by various distributed systems to communicate with each other. SOAP is too complex to implement. Criticizers of SOAP point out how bulky the SOAP HTTP request is.

A SOAP request usually consists of these three basic components:

- Envelope
- Header
- Body

Just to perform an HTTP request and response cycle, we have to attach a lot of additional data in SOAP. A sample SOAP request looks like this:

```
POST /StockQuote HTTP/1.1
Host: www.stockquoteserver.com
Content-Type: text/xml; charset="utf-8"
Content-Length: nnnn
SOAPAction: "Some-URI"

<SOAP-ENV:Envelope
  xmlns:SOAP-ENV="http://schemas.xmlsoap.org/soap/envelope/"
  SOAP-ENV:encodingStyle="http://schemas.xmlsoap.org/soap/encoding/">
  <SOAP-ENV:Body>
      <m:GetLastTradePrice xmlns:m="Some-URI">
          <symbol>DIS</symbol>
      </m:GetLastTradePrice>
  </SOAP-ENV:Body>
</SOAP-ENV:Envelope>
```

This is a standard example of SOAP from the W3C standard (https://www.w3.org/TR/2000/NOTE-SOAP-20000508/). If we observe carefully, it is in XML format, with special tags specifying the envelope and body. Since XML operates on a lot of namespaces to function, additional information comes into play.

REST API

The name **Representational state transfer (REST)** was coined by Roy Fielding from the University of California. It is a very simplified and lightweight web service compared to SOAP. Performance, scalability, simplicity, portability, and modifiability are the main principles behind the REST design.

The REST API allows different systems to communicate and send/receive data in a very simple way. Each and every REST API call has a relation between an HTTP verb and the URL. The resources in the database in an application can be mapped with an API endpoint in the REST.

When you are using a mobile app on your phone, your phone might be secretly talking to many cloud services to retrieve, update, or delete your data. REST services have a huge impact on our daily lives.

REST is a stateless, cacheable, and simple architecture that is not a protocol but a pattern.

Characteristics of REST services

These are the main properties that make REST simple and unique compared to its predecessors:

- **Client-server based architecture:** This architecture is most essential for the modern web to communicate over HTTP. A single client-server may look naive initially, but many hybrid architectures are evolving. We will discuss more of these shortly.
- **Stateless:** This is the most important characteristic of a REST service. A REST HTTP request consists of all the data needed by the server to understand and give back the response. Once a request is served, the server doesn't remember if the request has arrived after a while. So the operation will be a stateless one.
- **Cacheable:** Many developers think a technology stack is blocking their web application or API. But in reality, their architecture is the reason. The database can be a potential tuning piece in a web application. In order to scale an application well, we need to cache content and deliver it as a response. If the cache is not valid, it is our responsibility to bust it. REST services should be properly cached for scaling.
- **Scripts on demand:** Have you ever designed a REST service which serves the JavaScript files and you execute them on the fly? This code on demand is also the main characteristic REST can provide. It is more common to request scripts and data from the server.
- **Multiple layered system:** The REST API can be served from multiple servers. One server can request the other, and so forth. So when a request comes from the client, request and response can be passed between many servers to finally supply a response back to the client. This easily implementable multi-layered system is always a good strategy for keeping the web application loosely coupled.
- **Representation of resources:** The REST API provides the uniform interface to talk to. It uses a **Uniform Resource Identifier** (**URI**) to map the resources (data). It also has the advantage of requesting a specific data format as the response. The Internet Media Type (MIME type) can tell the server that the requested resource is of that particular type.

- **Implementational freedom:** REST is just a mechanism to define your web services. It is an architectural style that can be implemented in multiple ways. Because of this flexibility, you can create REST services in the way you wish to. Until it follows the principles of REST, your server has the freedom to choose the platform or technology.

 Thoughtful caching is essential for the REST services to scale.

REST verbs and status codes

REST verbs specify an action to be performed on a specific resource or a collection of resources. When a request is made by the client, it should send this information in the HTTP request:

- REST verb
- Header information
- Body (optional)

As we mentioned previously, REST uses the URI to decode its resource to be handled. There are quite a few REST verbs available, but six of them are used frequently. They are as follows:

- GET
- POST
- PUT
- PATCH
- DELETE
- OPTIONS

If you are a software developer, you will be dealing with these six most of the time. The following table explains the operation, target resource, and what happens if the request succeeds or fails:

REST Verb	Action	Success	Failure
GET	Fetches a record or set of resources from the server	200	404
OPTIONS	Fetches all available REST operations	200	-
POST	Creates a new set of resources or a resource	201	404, 409
PUT	Updates or replaces the given record	200, 204	404
PATCH	Modifies the given record	200, 204	404
DELETE	Deletes the given resource	200	404

The numbers in the **Success** and **Failure** columns of the preceding table are HTTP status codes. Whenever a client initiates a REST operation, since REST is stateless, the client should know a way to find out whether the operation was successful or not. For that reason, HTTP has status codes for the response. REST defines the preceding status code types for a given operation. This means a REST API should strictly follow the preceding rules to achieve client-server communication.

All defined REST services have the following format. It consists of the host and API endpoint. The API endpoint is the URL path which is predefined by the server. Every REST request should hit that path.

A trivial REST API URI: `http://HostName/API endpoint/Query(optional)`

Let us look at all the verbs in more detail. The REST API design starts with the defining of operations and API endpoints. Before implementing the API, the design document should list all the endpoints for the given resources. In the following section, we carefully observe the REST API endpoints using PayPal's REST API as a use case.

GET

A GET method fetches the given resource from the server. To specify a resource, GET uses a few types of URI queries:

- Query parameters
- Path-based parameters

In case you didn't know, all of your browsing of the web is done by performing a GET request to the server. For example, if you type www.google.com, you are actually making a GET request to fetch the search page. Here, your browser is the client and Google's web server is the backend implementer of web services. A successful GET operation returns a 200 status code.

Examples of path parameters:

Everyone knows **PayPal**. PayPal creates billing agreements with companies. If you register with PayPal for a payment system, they provide you with a REST API for all your billing needs. The sample GET request for getting the information of a billing agreement looks like this: /v1/payments/billing-agreements/agreement_id.

Here, the resource query is with the path parameter. When the server sees this line, it interprets it as *I got an HTTP request with a need for agreement_id from the billing agreements*. Then it searches through the database, goes to the billing-agreements table, and finds an agreement with the given agreement_id. If that resource exists it sends the details to copy back in response (200 OK). Or else it sends a response saying resource not found (404).

Using GET, you can also query a list of resources, instead of a single one like the preceding example. PayPal's API for getting billing transactions related to an agreement can be fetched with /v1/payments/billing-agreements/transactions. This line fetches all transactions that occurred on that billing agreement. In both, the case's data is retrieved in the form of a JSON response. The response format should be designed beforehand so that the client can consume it in the agreement.

Examples of query parameters are as follows:

- Query parameters are intended to add detailed information to identify a resource from the server. For example, take this sample fictitious API. Let us assume this API is created for fetching, creating, and updating the details of the book. A query parameter based GET request will be in this format:

  /v1/books/?category=fiction&publish_date=2017

- The preceding URI has few query parameters. The URI is requesting a book from the book's resource that satisfies the following conditions:
  - It should be a fiction book
  - The book should have been published in the year 2017

    Get all the fiction books that are released in the year 2017 is the question the client is posing to the server.

Path vs Query parameters—When to use them? It is a common rule of thumb that Query parameters are used to fetch multiple resources based on the query parameters. If a client needs a single resource with exact URI information, it can use Path parameters to specify the resource. For example, a user dashboard can be requested with Path parameters and fetch data on filtering can be modeled with Query parameters.

Use Path parameters for a single resource and Query parameters for multiple resources in a GET request.

POST, PUT, and PATCH

The POST method is used to create a resource on the server. In the previous book's API, this operation creates a new book with the given details. A successful POST operation returns a 201 status code. The POST request can update multiple resources: /v1/books.

The POST request has a body like this:

```
{"name" : "Lord of the rings", "year": 1954, "author" : "J. R. R. Tolkien"}
```

This actually creates a new book in the database. An ID is assigned to this record so that when we GET the resource, the URL is created. So POST should be done only once, in the beginning. In fact, *Lord of the Rings* was published in 1955. So we entered the published date incorrectly. In order to update the resource, let us use the PUT request.

The PUT method is similar to POST. It is used to replace the resource that already exists. The main difference is that PUT is idempotent. A POST call creates two instances with the same data. But PUT updates a single resource that already exists:

```
/v1/books/1256
```

with body that is JSON like this:

```
{"name" : "Lord of the rings", "year": 1955, "author" : "J. R. R. Tolkien"}
```

1256 is the ID of the book. It updates the preceding book by year:1955. Did you observe the drawback of PUT? It actually replaced the entire old record with the new one. We needed to change a single column. But PUT replaced the whole record. That is bad. For this reason, the PATCH request was introduced.

The PATCH method is similar to PUT, except it won't replace the whole record. PATCH, as the name suggests, patches the column that is being modified. Let us update the book 1256 with a new column called ISBN:

```
/v1/books/1256
```

with the JSON body like this:

```
{"isbn" : "0618640150"}
```

It tells the server, *Search for the book with id 1256. Then add/modify this column with the given value.*

 PUT and PATCH both return the 200 status for success and 404 for not found.

DELETE and OPTIONS

The DELETE API method is used to delete a resource from the database. It is similar to PUT but without any body. It just needs an ID of the resource to be deleted. Once a resource gets deleted, subsequent GET requests return a 404 not found status.

Responses to this method are *not cacheable* (in case caching is implemented) because the DELETE method is idempotent.

The OPTIONS API method is the most underrated in the API development. Given the resource, this method tries to know all possible methods (GET, POST, and so on) defined on the server. It is like looking at the menu card at a restaurant and then ordering an item which is available (whereas if you randomly order a dish, the waiter will tell you it is not available). It is best practice to implement the OPTIONS method on the server. From the client, make sure OPTIONS is called first, and if the method is available, then proceed with it.

Cross-Origin Resource Sharing (CORS)

The most important application of this OPTIONS method is **Cross-Origin Resource Sharing** (CORS). Initially, browser security prevented the client from making cross-origin requests. It means a site loaded with the URL www.foo.com can only make API calls to that host. If the client code needs to request files or data from www.bar.com, then the second server, bar.com, should have a mechanism to recognize foo.com to get its resources.

This process explains the CORS:

1. foo.com requests the OPTIONS method on bar.com.
2. bar.com sends a header like Access-Control-Allow-Origin: http://foo.com in response to the client.
3. Next, foo.com can access the resources on bar.com without any restrictions that call any REST method.

If bar.com feels like supplying resources to any host after one initial request, it can set Access control to * (that is, any).

The following is the diagram depicting the process happening one after the other:

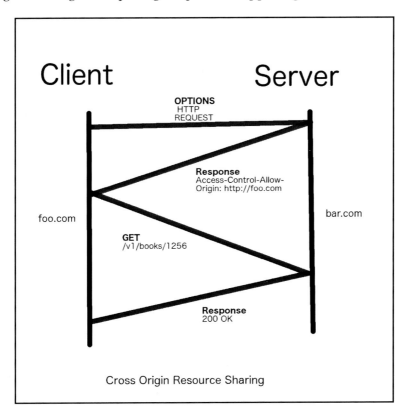

Cross Origin Resource Sharing

Types of status codes

There are a few families of status codes. Each family globally explains an operation status. Each member of that family may have a deeper meeting. So a REST API should strictly tell the client what exactly happened after the operation. There are 60+ status codes available. But for REST, we concentrate on a few families of codes.

2xx family (successful)

200 and 201 fall under the success family. They indicate that an operation was successful. Plain **200** (**Operation Successful**) is a successful CRUD Operation:

- **200** (**Successful Operation**) is the most common type of response status code in REST
- **201** (**Successfully Created**) is returned when a POST operation successfully creates a resource on the server
- **204** (**No content**) is issued when a client needs a status but not any data back

3xx family (redirection)

These status codes are used to convey redirection messages. The most important ones are **301** and **304**:

- **301** is issued when a resource is moved permanently to a new URL endpoint. It is essential when an old API is deprecated. It returns the new endpoint in the response with the 301 status. By seeing that, the client should use the new URL in response to achieving its target.
- The **304** status code indicates that content is cached and no modification happened for the resource on the server. This helps in caching content at the client and only requests data when the cache is modified.

4xx family (client error)

These are the standard error status codes which the client needs to interpret and handle further actions. These have nothing to do with the server. A wrong request format or ill-formed REST method can cause these errors. Of these, the most frequent status codes API developers use are **400**, **401**, **403**, **404**, and **405**:

- **400** (**Bad Request**) is returned when the server cannot understand the client request.
- **401** (**Unauthorized**) is returned when the client is not sending the authorization information in the header.
- **403** (**Forbidden**) is returned when the client has no access to a certain type of resources.

- 404 (**Not Found**) is returned when the client request is on a resource that is nonexisting.
- 405 (**Method Not Allowed**) is returned if the server bans a few methods on resources. GET and HEAD are exceptions.

5xx family (server error)

These are the errors from the server. The client request may be perfect, but due to a bug in the server code, these errors can arise. The commonly used status codes are **500**, **501**, **502**, **503**, and **504**:

- 500 (**Internal Server Error**) status code gives the development error which is caused by some buggy code or some unexpected condition
- 501 (**Not Implemented**) is returned when the server is no longer supporting the method on a resource
- 502 (**Bad Gateway**) is returned when the server itself got an error response from another service vendor
- 503 (**Service Unavailable**) is returned when the server is down due to multiple reasons, like a heavy load or for maintenance
- 504 (**Gateway Timeout**) is returned when the server is waiting a long time for a response from another vendor and is taking too much time to serve the client

For more details on status codes, visit this link: https://developer.mozilla.org/en-US/docs/Web/HTTP/Status

Rise of REST API with Single Page Applications

You need to understand why **Single Page Applications** (**SPA**) are the hot topic today. Instead of building the UI in a traditional way (request web pages), these SPA designs make developers write code in a totally different way. There are many MVC frameworks, like AngularJS, Angular2, React JS, Knockout JS, Aurelia, and so on, to develop web UIs rapidly, but the essence of each of them is pretty simple. All MVC frameworks help us to implement one design pattern. That design pattern is *No requesting of web pages, only REST API.*

The modern web frontend development has advanced a lot since 2010. In order to exploit the features of **Model-View-Controller** (**MVC**) architecture, we need to consider the frontend as a separate entity which talks to the backend only using the REST API (most preferably, REST JSON).

Old and new ways of data flow in SPA

All websites go through the following steps:

1. Request a web page from the server.
2. Authenticate and show the Dashboard UI.
3. Allow the user to modify and save.
4. Request as many web pages from the server as needed to show individual pages on the site.

But in the SPA, the flow is quite different:

1. Request the HTML template/s to the browser in one single go.
2. Then, query the JSON REST API to fill a model (data object).
3. Adjust the UI according to the data in the model (JSON).
4. When users modify the UI, the model (data object) should change automatically. For example, in AngularJS, it is possible with two-way data binding. Finally, make REST API calls to notify the server about changes whenever you want.

In this way, communication happens only in the form of the REST API. The client takes care of logically representing the data. This causes systems to move from **Response Oriented Architecture** (**ROA**) to **Service Oriented Architecture** (**SOA**). Take a look at the following diagram:

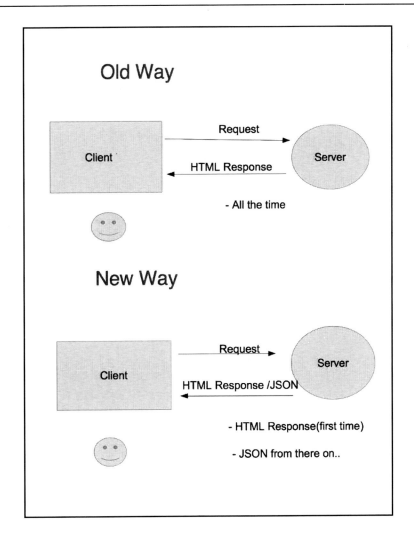

 SPA reduces the bandwidth and improves the site performance.

Why Go for REST API development?

REST services are trivial in the modern web. SOA (which we discuss in more detail later) created an activity space for REST services to take web development to the next level. **Go** is a programming language from the house of Google for solving the bigger problems they have. It has been eight-plus years since its first appearance. It matured along the way with a developer community jumping in and creating huge scale systems in it.

 Go is the darling of the web. It solves bigger problems in an easy way.

One can choose Python or JavaScript (Node) for their REST API development. The main advantage of Go lies in its speed and compile-time error detection. Go is proved to be faster than dynamic programming languages in terms of computational performance by various benchmarks. These are the three reasons why a company should write their next API in Go:

- To scale your API for a wider audience
- To enable your developers to build robust systems
- To invest in the future viability of your projects

You can look at the neverending online debates for more information about REST services with Go. In later chapters, we try to build the fundamentals of designing and writing the REST services.

Setting up the project and running the development server

This is a building series book. It assumes you already know the basics of Go. If not, no worries. You can jump start and learn them quickly from Go's official site at `https://golang.org/`. Go uses a different way of developing projects. Writing a standalone, simple program doesn't bother you much. But after learning the basics, people try to advance a step further. For that reason, as a Go developer, you should know how Go projects are laid out and the best practices to keep your code clean.

Make sure you have done the following things before proceeding:

- Install Go compiler on your machine
- Set GOROOT and GOPATH environment variables

There are many online references from which you can get to know the preceding details. Depending on your machine type (Windows, Linux, or macOS X), set up a working Go compiler. We see more details about GOPATH in the following section.

Demystifying GOPATH

GOPATH is nothing but the current appointed workspace on your machine. It is an environment variable that tells the Go compiler about where your source code, binaries, and packages are placed.

The programmers coming from a Python background may know the Virtualenv tool to create multiple projects (with different Python interpreter versions) at the same time. But at a given time, one activates the environment and develops his project. Similarly, you can have any number of Go projects on your machine. While developing, set the GOPATH to one of your projects. The Go compiler now activates that project.

It is a common practice to create a project under the home directory and set the GOPATH environment variable like this:

```
>mkdir /home/naren/myproject
export GOPATH=/home/naren/myproject
```

Now we install external packages like this:

```
go get -u -v github.com/gorilla/mux
```

Go copies the project called mux into the currently activated project myproject.

For Go get, use the -u flag to install updated dependencies of the external package and -v to see the verbose details of installation.

A typical Go project has the following structure, as mentioned on the official Go website:

```
bin/
    hello                   # command executable
pkg/
    linux_amd64/            # this will reflect your OS and architecture
        github.com/user/
            stringutil.a  # package object
src/
    github.com/user/
        hello/
            hello.go      # command source
        stringutil/
            reverse.go    # package source
```

Let us understand this structure before digging further:

- `bin`: Stores the binary of our project; a shippable binary which can be run directly
- `pkg`: Contains the package objects; a compiled program which supplies package methods
- `src`: The place for your project source code, tests, and user packages

In Go, all the packages which you import into your main program have an identical structure, `github.com/user/project`. But who creates all these directories? Should the developer do that? Nope. It is the developer's responsibility to create directories for his/her project. It means he/she only creates the directory `src/github.com/user/hello`.

When a developer runs the following command, the directories bin and package are created if they did not exist before. `.bin` consists of the binary of our project source code and `.pkg` consists of all internal and external packages we use in our Go programs:

```
go install github.com/user/project
```

Building our first service – finding the Roman numeral

With the concepts we have built upto now, let us write our first basic REST service. This service takes the number range (1-10) from the client and returns its Roman string. Very primitive, but better than Hello World.

Design:

Our REST API should take an integer number from the client and serve back the Roman equivalent.

The block of the API design document may look like this:

HTTP Verb	PATH	Action	Resource
GET	/roman_number/2	show	roman_number

Implementation:

Now we are going to implement the preceding simple API step-by-step.

 Code for this project is available at `https://github.com/narenaryan/gorestful`.

As we previously discussed, you should set the GOPATH first. Let us assume the GOPATH is `/home/naren/go`. Create a directory called `romanserver` in the following path. Replace *narenaryan* with your GitHub username (this is just a namespace for the code belonging to different users):

```
mkdir -p $GOPATH/src/github.com/narenaryan/romanserver
```

Our project is ready. We don't have any database configured yet. Create an empty file called `main.go`:

```
touch $GOPATH/src/github.com/narenaryan/romanserver/main.go
```

Our main logic for the API server goes into this file. For now, we can create a data file which works as a data service for our main program. Create one more directory for packaging the Roman numeral data:

```
mkdir $GOPATH/src/github.com/narenaryan/romanNumerals
```

Now, create an empty file called `data.go` in the `romanNumerals` directory. The `src` directory structure so far looks like this:

```
├── github.com
│     └── narenaryan
│           ├── romanNumerals
│           │     └── data.go
│           └── romanserver
│                 └── main.go
```

Now let us start adding code to the files. Create data for the Roman numerals:

```go
// data.go
package romanNumerals

var Numerals = map[int]string{
    10: "X",
    9: "IX",
    8: "VIII",
    7: "VII",
    6: "VI",
    5: "V",
    4: "IV",
    3: "III",
    2: "II",
    1: "I",
}
```

We are creating a map called **Numerals**. This map holds information for converting a given integer to its Roman equivalent. We are going to import this variable into our main program to serve the request from the client.

Open `main.go` and add the following code:

```go
// main.go
package main

import (
    "fmt"
```

```
    "github.com/narenaryan/romanNumerals"
    "html"
    "net/http"
    "strconv"
    "strings"
    "time"
)

func main() {
    // http package has methods for dealing with requests
    http.HandleFunc("/", func(w http.ResponseWriter, r *http.Request) {
        urlPathElements := strings.Split(r.URL.Path, "/")
        // If request is GET with correct syntax
        if urlPathElements[1] == "roman_number" {
            number, _ := strconv.Atoi(strings.TrimSpace(urlPathElements[2]))
            if number == 0 || number > 10 {
            // If resource is not in the list, send Not Found status
                w.WriteHeader(http.StatusNotFound)
                w.Write([]byte("404 - Not Found"))
            } else {
                fmt.Fprintf(w, "%q",
html.EscapeString(romanNumerals.Numerals[number]))
            }
        } else {
            // For all other requests, tell that Client sent a bad request
            w.WriteHeader(http.StatusBadRequest)
            w.Write([]byte("400 - Bad request"))
        }
    })
    // Create a server and run it on 8000 port
    s := &http.Server{
      Addr: ":8000",
      ReadTimeout: 10 * time.Second,
      WriteTimeout: 10 * time.Second,
      MaxHeaderBytes: 1 << 20,
    }
    s.ListenAndServe()
}
```

 Always use the Go fmt tool to format your Go code.

Usage example: `go fmt github.com/narenaryan/romanserver`

Now, install this project with the Go command `install`:

`go install github.com/narenaryan/romanserver`

This step does two things:

- Compiles the package `romanNumerals` and places a copy in the `$GOPATH/pkg` directory
- Places a binary in the `$GOPATH/bin`

We can run the preceding API server as this:

```
$GOPATH/bin/romanserver
```

The server is up and running on `http://localhost:8000`. Now we can make a `GET` request to the API using a client like `Browser` or the `CURL` command. Let us fire a `CURL` command with a proper API `GET` request.

Request one is as follows:

```
curl -X GET "http://localhost:8000/roman_number/5" # Valid request
```

The response is as follows:

```
HTTP/1.1 200 OK
Date: Sun, 07 May 2017 11:24:32 GMT
Content-Length: 3
Content-Type: text/plain; charset=utf-8

"V"
```

Let us try a few incorrectly formed requests.

Request two is as follows:

```
curl -X GET "http://localhost:8000/roman_number/12" # Resource out of range
```

The response is as follows:

```
HTTP/1.1 404 Not Found
Date: Sun, 07 May 2017 11:22:38 GMT
Content-Length: 15
Content-Type: text/plain; charset=utf-8

404 - Not Found
```

Request three is as follows:

```
curl -X GET "http://localhost:8000/random_resource/3" # Invalid resource
```

The response is as follows:

```
"HTTP/1.1 400 Bad request
Date: Sun, 07 May 2017 11:22:38 GMT
Content-Length: 15
Content-Type: text/plain; charset=utf-8
400 - Bad request
```

Our little Roman numerals API is doing the right thing. The right status codes are being returned. That is the point all API developers should keep in mind. The client should be informed why something went wrong.

Breaking down the code

We just updated the empty files in one single go and started running the server. Let me now explain each and every piece of the file `main.go`:

- Imported a few packages. `github.com/narenaryan/romanNumerals` is the data service we created before.
- `net/http` is the core package we used to handle an HTTP request through its `HandleFunc` function. That function's arguments are `http.Request` and `http.ResponseWriter`. Those two deal with the request and response of an HTTP request.
- `r.URL.Path` is the URL path of the HTTP request. For the CURL Request one, it is `/roman_number/5`. We are splitting this path and using the second argument as a resource and the third argument as a value to get the Roman numeral. The `Split` function is in a core package called `strings`.
- The `Atoi` function converts an alphanumeric string to an integer. For the numerals map to consume, we need to convert the integer string to an integer. The `Atoi` function comes from a core package called `strconv`.
- We use `http.StatusXXX` to set the status code of the response header. The `WriteHeader` and `Write` functions are available on the response object for writing the header and body, respectively.
- Next, we created an HTTP server using `&http` while initializing a few parameters like address, port, timeout, and so on.
- The `time` package is used to define seconds in the program. It says, after 10 seconds of inactivity, automatically return a 408 request timeout back to the client.

- `EscapeString` escapes special characters to become valid HTML characters. For example, Fran & Freddie's becomes `Fran &amp; Freddie's&#34`.
- Finally, start the server with the `ListenAndServe` function. It keeps your web server running until you kill it.

> One should write unit tests for their API. In the upcoming chapters, we will see how to test an API end to end.

Live reloading the application with supervisord and Gulp

Gulp is a nice tool for creating workflows. A workflow is a step-by-step process. It is nothing but a task streamlining application. You need NPM and Node installed on your machine. We use Gulp to watch the files and then update the binary and restart the API server. Sounds cool, right?

The supervisor is an application to reload your server whenever the application gets killed. A process ID will be assigned to your server. To restart the app properly, we need to kill the existing instances and restart the application. We can write one such program in Go. But in order to not reinvent the wheel, we are using a popular program called supervisord.

Monitoring your Go web server with supervisord

Sometimes your web application may stop due to operating system restarts or crashes. Whenever your web server gets killed, it is supervisor's job to bring it back to life. Even the system restart cannot take your web server away from the customers. So, strictly use supervisord for your app monitoring.

Installing supervisord

We can easily install supervisord on Ubuntu 16.04, with the `apt-get` command:

```
sudo apt-get install -y supervisor
```

This installs two tools, `supervisor` and `supervisorctl`. `supervisorctl` is intended to control the supervisord and add tasks, restart tasks, and so on.

On macOS X, we can install `supervisor` using the `brew` command:

```
brew install supervisor
```

Now, create a configuration file at:

```
/etc/supervisor/conf.d/goproject.conf
```

You can add any number of configuration files, and supervisord treats them as separate processes to run. Add the following content to the preceding file:

```
[supervisord]
logfile = /tmp/supervisord.log

[program:myserver]
command=$GOPATH/bin/romanserver
autostart=true
autorestart=true
redirect_stderr=true
```

By default, we have a file called `.supervisord.conf` at `/etc/supervisor/`. Look at it for more reference. In macOS X, the same file will be located at `/usr/local/etc/supervisord.ini`.

Coming to the preceding configuration:

- The `[supervisord]` section tells the location of the log file for supervisord
- `[program:myserver]` is the task block which traverses to the given directory and executes the command given

Now we can ask our `supervisorctl` to re-read the configuration and restart the tasks (process). For that, just say:

- `supervisorctl reread`
- `supervisorctl update`

Then, launch `supervisorctl` with the command:

```
supervisorctl
```

You will see something like this:

`supervisorctl` is a great tool for controlling supervisor programs.

```
root@SiteB-Host1:~# supervisorctl
myserver                        RUNNING    pid 11405, uptime 0:00:01
supervisor> help

default commands (type help <topic>):
=======================================
add     exit      open  reload  restart   start   tail
avail   fg        pid   remove  shutdown  status  update
clear   maintail  quit  reread  signal    stop    version

supervisor>
```

Since we named our romanserver `myserver` in the supervisor configuration file, we can start, stop, and restart that program from `supervisorctl`.

Using Gulp for creating auto code compiling and server reloading

With the little introduction we gave about Gulp in the preceding section, we are going to write a gulpfile for telling the computer to execute a few tasks.

I install Gulp and Gulp-shell using npm:

```
npm install gulp gulp-shell
```

After this, create a `gulpfile.js` in the root directory of the project. Here, it is `github.com/src/narenaryan/romanserver`. Now add this content to `gulpfile.js`. First, whenever a file changes, install binary task gets executed. Then, the supervisor will be restarted. The watch task looks for any file change and executes the preceding tasks. We are also ordering the tasks so that they occur one after the other synchronously. All of these tasks are Gulp tasks and can be defined by the `gulp.task` function. It takes two arguments with task name, task. `sell.task` allows Gulp to execute system commands:

```
var gulp = require("gulp");
var shell = require('gulp-shell');

// This compiles new binary with source change
gulp.task("install-binary", shell.task([
  'go install github.com/narenaryan/romanserver'
]));

// Second argument tells install-binary is a deapendency for restart-
supervisor
gulp.task("restart-supervisor", ["install-binary"], shell.task([
  'supervisorctl restart myserver'
]))

gulp.task('watch', function() {
  // Watch the source code for all changes
  gulp.watch("*", ['install-binary', 'restart-supervisor']);

});

gulp.task('default', ['watch']);
```

Now, if you run the `gulp` command in the `source` directory, it starts watching your source code changes:

```
gulp
```

Now, if we modify the code, then the code is compiled, installed, and the server restarted in a flash:

```
[20:50:38] Starting 'watch'...
[20:50:38] Finished 'watch' after 45 ms
[20:50:38] Starting 'default'...
[20:50:38] Finished 'default' after 11 µs
[20:50:46] Starting 'install-binary'...
[20:50:47] Finished 'install-binary' after 1.07 s
[20:50:47] Starting 'restart-supervisor'...
myserver: stopped
myserver: started
[20:50:48] Finished 'restart-supervisor' after 1.14 s
```

Understanding the gulpfile

In the gulpfile, we are performing the following instructions:

1. Import Gulp and Gulp-shell.
2. Create tasks with `shell.task` as the function to execute.
3. `shell.task` can execute a command-line instruction. Keep your shell commands inside that function.
4. Add a watch task for watching source files. The task list will be executed when files are modified.
5. Create a default task for running. Add a watch to it.

Gulp is a great tool for these kinds of use cases. So, please go through the official documentation of Gulp at http://gulpjs.com/.

Summary

In this chapter, we gave an introduction to the REST API. We saw that REST is not a protocol, but an architectural pattern. HTTP is the actual protocol on which we can implement our REST service. We jumped into the fundamentals of the REST API to be clear about what they actually are. Then we explored types of web services. Before REST, we have something called SOAP, which uses XML as the data format. REST operates on JSON as the primary format. REST has verbs and status codes. We saw what a given status code refers to. We built a simple service which serves the Roman numerals for given numbers. In this process, we also saw how to package a Go project. We understood the GOPATH environment variable. It is a workspace defining a variable in Go. All packages and projects reside in that path. We then saw how to reload a development project on the fly with the help of supervisord and Gulp. These are node tools but can help us to keep our Go project up and running.

In the next chapter, we dig deeper into URL routing. Starting from the built-in router, we explore Gorilla Mux, a powerful URL routing library.

2
Handling Routing for Our REST Services

In this chapter, we will discuss routing of the application. For creating an API, the first step is to define routes. So, to define routes, we need to figure out available constructs in Go. We begin with the basic internal routing mechanism in Go. Then, we see how to create a custom Multiplexer. Since ServeMux's capabilities are very limited, we will explore a few other frameworks built to serve this purpose. This chapter also includes creating routes using third-party libraries such as `httprouter` and `Gorilla Mux`. We are going to build a URL-shortening API throughout this book. In this chapter, we define routes for the API. Then, we discuss topics like SQL injection of an URL. A web framework allows the developer to create a route as the first step and then attach handlers to it. Those handlers hold the business logic of the application. The crux of this chapter is teaching you how to create HTTP routers in Go using `Gorilla Mux`. We also discuss how URL-shortening service functions and try to design a logical implementation.

We will cover the following topics:

- Building a basic web server in Go
- Understanding the net/http package
- ServeMux, a basic router in Go
- Understanding httprouter, a router package
- Introducing Gorilla Mux, a powerful HTTP router
- Introducing URL shortening service design

Getting the code

You can download the code for this chapter from `https://github.com/narenaryan/gorestful/tree/master/chapter2`. Feel free to add the comments and pull requests. Clone the code and use the code samples in the `chapter2` directory.

Understanding Go's net/http package

Go's `net/http` package deals with HTTP client and server implementations. Here, we are mainly interested in the server implementation. Let us create a small Go program called `basicHandler.go` that defines the route and a function handler:

```
package main
import (
    "io"
    "net/http"
    "log"
)
// hello world, the web server
func MyServer(w http.ResponseWriter, req *http.Request) {
    io.WriteString(w, "hello, world!\n")
}
func main() {
    http.HandleFunc("/hello", MyServer)
    log.Fatal(http.ListenAndServe(":8000", nil))
}
```

This code does the following things:

1. Create a route called `/hello`.
2. Create a handler called `MyServer`.
3. Whenever the request comes on the route (`/hello`), the handler function will be executed.
4. Write `hello, world` to the response.
5. Start the server on port `8000`. `ListenAndServe` returns `error` if something goes wrong. So log it using `log.Fatal`.
6. The `http` package has a function called `HandleFunc`, using which we can map an URL to a function.

7. Here, `w` is a response writer. A `ResponseWriter` interface is used by an HTTP handler to construct an HTTP response.

8. `req` is a request object, which deals with all the properties and methods of an HTTP request.

 Use the log function to debug potential errors. The `ListenAndServe` function returns an error if there are any.

Running the code

We can run the preceding code as a standalone program. Name the preceding program `basicHandler.go`. Store it anywhere you wish to, then run it using the following command:

```
go run basicHandler.go
```

Now fire up a shell or browser to see the server in action. Here, I use the CURL request:

```
curl -X GET http://localhost:8000/hello
```

The response is:

```
hello, world
```

Go has a different concept for handling request and response. We used the `io` library to write to the response. For web development, we can use a template to automatically fill in the details. Go's internal URL handlers use a ServeMux multiplexer.

ServeMux, a basic router in Go

ServeMux is an HTTP request multiplexer. The `HandleFunc` we used in the preceding section is actually a method of ServeMux. By creating a new ServeMux, we can handle multiple routes. Before that, we can also create our own multiplexer. A multiplexer just handles the logic of separating routes with a function called `ServeHTTP`. So if we create a new struct with the `ServeHTTP` method, it can do the job.

Consider a route as a key in a dictionary (map), then the handler as its value. The router finds the handler from the route and tries to execute the ServeHTTP function. Let us create a program called customMux.go and see this implementation in action:

```
package main
import (
    "fmt"
    "math/rand"
    "net/http"
)
// CustomServeMux is a struct which can be a multiplexer
type CustomServeMux struct {
}
// This is the function handler to be overridden
func (p *CustomServeMux) ServeHTTP(w http.ResponseWriter, r *http.Request)
{
    if r.URL.Path == "/" {
        giveRandom(w, r)
        return
    }
    http.NotFound(w, r)
    return
}
func giveRandom(w http.ResponseWriter, r *http.Request) {
    fmt.Fprintf(w, "Your random number is: %f", rand.Float64())
}
func main() {
    // Any struct that has serveHTTP function can be a multiplexer
    mux := &CustomServeMux{}
    http.ListenAndServe(":8000", mux)
}
```

In this code, we are creating a custom struct called CustomServeMux, which is going to take care of our routing. We implemented a function called ServeHTTP in order to capture the request and write a response back to it. The fmt package is usually used to create strings. Fprinf composes the string out of supplied parameters.

In the main function, we are creating an instance of our CustomServeMux and passing it to the ListenAndServe function on http. "math/rand" is the library that takes care of generating random numbers. This basic foundation is going to be helpful for us when we discuss adding authentication to our API server.

Running the code

Let us fire a CURL request and see what the response is for various routes:

```
go run customMux.go
```

Now, fire up a shell or browser to see the server in action. Here, I use the CURL request:

```
curl -X GET http://localhost:8000/
```

The response is:

```
Your random number is: 0.096970
```

 Use *Ctrl* + *C* or *Cmd* + *C* to stop your Go server. If you are running it as a background process, use `pgrep go` to find the `processID` and kill it using `kill pid`.

Adding multiple handlers using ServeMux

The preceding custom Mux that we created can be cumbersome when we have different endpoints with different functionalities. To add that logic, we need to add many `if/else` conditions to manually check the URL route. We can instantiate a new `ServeMux` and define many handlers like this:

```
newMux := http.NewServeMux()

newMux.HandleFunc("/randomFloat", func(w http.ResponseWriter, r
*http.Request) {
  fmt.Fprintln(w, rand.Float64())
})

newMux.HandleFunc("/randomInt", func(w http.ResponseWriter, r
*http.Request) {
  fmt.Fprintln(w, rand.Int(100))
})
```

This code snippet shows how to create a ServerMux and attach multiple handlers to it. `randomFloat` and `randomInt` are the two routes we created for returning a random `float` and random `int`, respectively. Now we can pass this to the `ListenAndServe` function. `Intn(100)` returns a random integer number from the range 0-100. For more details on random functions, visit the Go random package page at `http://golang.org`.

```
http.ListenAndServe(":8000", newMux)
```

The complete code looks like this:

```
package main
import (
    "fmt"
    "math/rand"
    "net/http"
)
func main() {
    newMux := http.NewServeMux()
    newMux.HandleFunc("/randomFloat", func(w http.ResponseWriter, r
*http.Request) {
        fmt.Fprintln(w, rand.Float64())
    })
    newMux.HandleFunc("/randomInt", func(w http.ResponseWriter, r
*http.Request) {
        fmt.Fprintln(w, rand.Intn(100))
    })
    http.ListenAndServe(":8000", newMux)
}
```

Running the code

We can run the program directly using the run command:

```
go run customMux.go
```

Now, let us fire two CURL commands and see the output:

```
curl -X GET http://localhost:8000/randomFloat
curl -X GET http://localhost:8000/randomInt
```

The responses will be:

```
0.6046602879796196
87
```

 Your response may change due to the random number generator.

We saw how we can create a URL router with basic Go constructs. Now we are going to look at a few popular URL routing frameworks that are widely used by the Go community for their API servers.

Introducing httprouter, a lightweight HTTP router

httprouter, as the name suggests, routes the HTTP requests to particular handlers. Compared to the basic router, it has the following features:

- Allows variables in the route paths
- It matches the REST methods (`GET`, `POST`, `PUT`, and so on)
- No compromising on performance

We are going to discuss these qualities in more detail in the following section. Before that, there are a few noteworthy points that make httprouter an even better URL router:

- httprouter plays well with the inbuilt `http.Handler`
- httprouter explicitly says that a request can only match to one route or none
- The router's design encourages building sensible, hierarchical RESTful APIs
- You can build efficient static file servers

Installation

To install httprouter, we just need to run the `get` command:

```
go get github.com/julienschmidt/httprouter
```

So, now we have `httprouter`. We can refer to the library in our source code as this:

```
import "github.com/julienschmidt/httprouter"
```

The basic usage of httprouter can be understood through an example. In this example, let us create a small API to get information about files and programs installed from the server. Before jumping straight into the program, you should know how to execute system commands on Go. There is a package called `os/exec`. It allows us to execute system commands and get the output back to the program.

```
import "os/exec"
```

Then it can be accessed in the code as this:

```
// arguments... means an array of strings unpacked as arguments in Go
cmd := exec.Command(command, arguments...)
```

`exec.Command` is the function that takes a command and an additional arguments array. Additional arguments are the options or input for the command. It can then be executed in two ways:

- Run the command instantly
- Start and wait for it to finish

We can collect the output of the command by attaching `Stdout` to a custom string. Get that string and send it back to the client. The code makes more sense here. Let us write a Go program to create a REST service that does two things:

- Gets the Go version
- Gets the file contents of a given file

This program uses `Hhttprouter` to create the service. Let us name it as `execService.go`:

```go
package main
import (
        "bytes"
        "fmt"
        "log"
        "net/http"
        "os/exec"
        "github.com/julienschmidt/httprouter"
)
// This is a function to execute a system command and return output
func getCommandOutput(command string, arguments ...string) string {
        // args... unpacks arguments array into elements
        cmd := exec.Command(command, arguments...)
        var out bytes.Buffer
        var stderr bytes.Buffer
        cmd.Stdout = &out
        cmd.Stderr = &stderr
        err := cmd.Start()
        if err != nil {
                log.Fatal(fmt.Sprint(err) + ": " + stderr.String())
        }
        err = cmd.Wait()
        if err != nil {
                log.Fatal(fmt.Sprint(err) + ": " + stderr.String())
        }
        return out.String()
}
func goVersion(w http.ResponseWriter, r *http.Request, params
httprouter.Params) {
```

```
        fmt.Fprintf(w, getCommandOutput("/usr/local/bin/go", "version"))
}
func getFileContent(w http.ResponseWriter, r *http.Request, params
httprouter.Params) {
        fmt.Fprintf(w, getCommandOutput("/bin/cat",
params.ByName("name")))
}
func main() {
        router := httprouter.New()
        // Mapping to methods is possible with HttpRouter
        router.GET("/api/v1/go-version", goVersion)
        // Path variable called name used here
        router.GET("/api/v1/show-file/:name", getFileContent)
        log.Fatal(http.ListenAndServe(":8000", router))
}
```

Program explanation

The preceding program is trying to implement a REST service using `httprouter`. We are defining two routes here:

- `/api/v1/go-version`
- `/api/v1/show-file/:name`

The `:name` here is the path parameter. It indicates the API that shows the file named xyz. The basic Go router cannot handle these parameters, by using `httprouter`, we can also match the REST methods. In the program, we matched `GET` requests.

In a step-by-step process, the preceding program:

- Imported the `httprouter` and other necessary Go packages
- Created a new router using the `New()` method of `httprouter`
- The router has methods like `GET`, `POST`, `DELETE`, and so on
- The `GET` method takes two arguments, `URL path expression` and `Handler function`
- This router can be passed to the `ListenAndServe` function of http
- Now, coming to the handlers, they look similar to the ones belonging to ServeMux, but a third argument called `httprouter.Params` holds information about all parameters that are supplied with a `GET` request
- We defined the path parameter (a variable in the URL path) called `name` and used it in our program

- The `getCommandOutput` function takes commands and arguments and returns output
- The first API calls the Go version and returns the output to the client
- The second API performs a `cat` command of the file and returns it to the client

 If you observe the code, I used `/usr/local/bin/go` as the Go executable location because it is the Go compiler location on my MacBook. While executing `exec.Command`, you should give the absolute path of the executable. So if you are working on an Ubuntu machine or Windows, use the path to your executable. On Linux machines, you can easily find that out by using the `$ which go` command.

Now create two new files in the same directory. These files will be served by our file server program. You can create any custom files in this directory for testing:

`Latin.txt`:

```
Lorem ipsum dolor sit amet, consectetuer adipiscing elit. Aenean commodo
ligula eget dolor. Aenean massa. Cum sociis natoque penatibus et magnis dis
parturient montes, nascetur ridiculus mus. Donec quam felis, ultricies nec,
pellentesque eu, pretium quis, sem. Nulla consequat massa quis enim. Donec
pede justo, fringilla vel, aliquet nec, vulputate eget, arcu.
```

`Greek.txt`:

Οἱ δὲ Φοίνικες οὗτοι οἱ σὺν Κάδμῳ ἀπικόμενοι.. ἐσήγαγον διδασκάλια ἐς τοὺς Ἕλληνας καὶ δὴ καὶ γράμματα, οὐκ ἐόντα πρὶν Ἕλλησι ὡς ἐμοὶ δοκέειν, πρῶτα μὲν τοῖσι καὶ ἅπαντες χρέωνται Φοίνικες· μετὰ δὲ χρόνου προβαίνοντος ἅμα τῇ φωνῇ μετέβαλον καὶ τὸν ῥυθμὸν τῶν γραμμάτων. Περιοίκεον δέ σφεας τὰ πολλὰ τῶν χώρων τοῦτον τὸν χρόνον Ἑλλήνων Ἴωνες· οἳ παραλαβόντες διδαχῇ παρὰ τῶν Φοινίκων τὰ γράμματα, μεταρρυθμίσαντές σφεων ὀλίγα ἐχρέωντο, χρεώμενοι δὲ ἐφάτισαν, ὥσπερ καὶ τὸ δίκαιον ἔφερε ἐσαγαγόντων Φοινίκων ἐς τὴν Ἑλλάδα, φοινικήια κεκλῆσθαι.

Now run the program with this command. This time, instead of firing a CURL command, let us use the browser as our output for GET. Windows users may not have CURL as the firsthand application. They can use API testing software like the postman client while developing the REST API. Take a look at the following command:

```
go run execService.go
```

The output for the first GET request looks like this:

curl -X GET http://localhost:8000/api/v1/go-version

The result will be this:

```
go version go1.8.3 darwin/amd64
```

The second GET request requesting Greek.txt is:

```
curl -X GET http://localhost:8000/api/v1/show-file/greek.txt
```

Now, we will see the file output in Greek as this:

Οἱ δὲ Φοίνικες οὗτοι οἱ σὺν Κάδμῳ ἀπικόμενοι.. ἐσήγαγον διδασκάλια ἐς τοὺς Ἕλληνας καὶ δὴ καὶ γράμματα, οὐκ ἐόντα πρὶν Ἕλλησι ὡς ἐμοὶ δοκέειν, πρῶτα μὲν τοῖσι καὶ ἅπαντες χρέωνται Φοίνικες· μετὰ δὲ χρόνου προβαίνοντος ἅμα τῇ φωνῇ μετέβαλον καὶ τὸν ῥυθμὸν τῶν γραμμάτων. Περιοίκεον δέ σφεας τὰ πολλὰ τῶν χώρων τοῦτον τὸν χρόνον Ἑλλήνων Ἴωνες· οἱ παραλαβόντες διδαχῇ παρὰ τῶν Φοινίκων τὰ γράμματα, μεταρρυθμίσαντές σφεων ὀλίγα ἐχρέωντο, χρεώμενοι δὲ ἐφάτισαν, ὥσπερ καὶ τὸ δίκαιον ἔφερε ἐσαγαγόντων Φοινίκων ἐς τὴν Ἑλλάδα, φοινικήια κεκλῆσθαι.

Building the simple static file server in minutes

Sometimes, as part of the API, we should serve static files. The other application of httprouter is building scalable file servers. It means that we can build a Content Delivery Platform of our own. Some of the clients need static files from the server. Traditionally, we use Apache2 or Nginx for that purpose. But, from within the Go server, in order to serve the static files, we need to route them through a universal route like this:

```
/static/*
```

See the following code snippet for our implementation. The idea is to use the http.Dir method to load the filesystem, and then use the ServeFiles function of the httprouter instance. It should serve all the files in the given public directory. Usually, static files are kept in the folder /var/public/www on a Linux machine. Since I am using OS X, I create a folder called static in my home directory:

```
mkdir /users/naren/static
```

Now, I copy the Latin.txt and Greek.txt files, which we created for the previous example, to the preceding static directory. After doing this, let us write the program for the file server. You will be amazed at the simplicity of httprouter. Create a program called fileserver.go:

```
package main
import (
    "github.com/julienschmidt/httprouter"
```

```
        "log"
        "net/http"
)
func main() {
        router := httprouter.New()
        // Mapping to methods is possible with HttpRouter
        router.ServeFiles("/static/*filepath",
http.Dir("/Users/naren/static"))
        log.Fatal(http.ListenAndServe(":8000", router))
}
```

Now run the server and see the output:

```
go run fileserver.go
```

Now, let us open another terminal and fire this CURL request:

```
http://localhost:8000/static/latin.txt
```

Now, the output will be a static file content server from our file server:

```
Lorem ipsum dolor sit amet, consectetuer adipiscing elit. Aenean commodo
ligula eget dolor. Aenean massa. Cum sociis natoque penatibus et magnis dis
parturient montes, nascetur ridiculus mus. Donec quam felis, ultricies nec,
pellentesque eu, pretium quis, sem. Nulla consequat massa quis enim. Donec
pede justo, fringilla vel, aliquet nec, vulputate eget, arcu.
```

Introducing Gorilla Mux, a powerful HTTP router

Mux stands for the multiplexer. Similarly, Gorilla Mux is a multiplexer designed to multiplex HTTP routes (URLs) to different handlers. Handlers are the functions which can handle the given requests. Gorilla Mux is a wonderful package for writing beautiful routes for our web applications and API servers.

Gorilla Mux provides tons of options to control how routing is done to your web application. It allows a lot of features. Some of them are:

- Path-based matching
- Query-based matching
- Domain-based matching

- Sub-domain based matching
- Reverse URL generation

Installation

Installing the Mux package is fairly simple. You need to run this command in the Terminal (Mac and Linux):

```
go get -u github.com/gorilla/mux
```

If you get any errors saying `package github.com/gorilla/mux: cannot download, $GOPATH not set. For more details see--go help gopath,` set the `$GOPATH` environment variable using the following command:

```
export GOPATH=~/go
```

As we discussed in the previous chapter, this says that all the packages and programs go into this directory. It has three folders: `bin`, `pkg`, and `src`. Now, add `GOPATH` to the `PATH` variable, to use the installed bin files as system utilities that have no `./executable` style. Refer to the following command:

```
PATH="$GOPATH/bin:$PATH"
```

These settings stay until you turn off your machine. So, to make it a permanent change, add the preceding lines to your bash profile:

```
vi ~/.profile
(or)
vi ~/.zshrc
```

Now, we are ready to go. Assuming Gorilla Mux is installed, proceed to the basics.

Fundamentals of Gorilla Mux

Gorilla Mux allows us to create a new router, similar to httprouter. But the attachment of the handler function to a given URL route is different in both. If we observe, Mux's way of attaching a handler is similar to that of basic ServeMux. Unlike httprouter, it modifies the request object instead of using an additional argument to pass the URL parameters to the handler function. We can access parameters using the `Vars` method.

I am going to take an example from the Gorilla Mux homepage to explain how useful it is. Create a file called `muxRouter.go` and add the following code:

```go
package main
import (
    "fmt"
    "log"
    "net/http"
    "time"
    "github.com/gorilla/mux"
)
// ArticleHandler is a function handler
func ArticleHandler(w http.ResponseWriter, r *http.Request) {
    // mux.Vars returns all path parameters as a map
    vars := mux.Vars(r)
    w.WriteHeader(http.StatusOK)
    fmt.Fprintf(w, "Category is: %v\n", vars["category"])
    fmt.Fprintf(w, "ID is: %v\n", vars["id"])
}
func main() {
    // Create a new router
    r := mux.NewRouter()
    // Attach a path with handler
    r.HandleFunc("/articles/{category}/{id:[0-9]+}", ArticleHandler)
    srv := &http.Server{
        Handler: r,
        Addr: "127.0.0.1:8000",
        // Good practice: enforce timeouts for servers you create!
        WriteTimeout: 15 * time.Second,
        ReadTimeout: 15 * time.Second,
    }
    log.Fatal(srv.ListenAndServe())
}
```

Now run the file using the following command:

```
go run muxRouter.go
```

By running the CURL command this way, we can get the output as follows:

```
curl http://localhost:8000/articles/books/123

Category is: books
ID is: 123
```

Mux parses the variables in the path. All the variables that are parsed are available calling the `Vars` function. Don't get caught up in the custom server details of the preceding program. Just observe the Mux code. We attached a handler to the URL. We have written the parsed variables back to the HTTP response. This line is crucial. Here, an `id` has a regular expression saying that `id` is a number (0–9) with one or more digits:

```
r.HandleFunc("/articles/{category}/{id:[0-9]+}", ArticleHandler)
```

Let us call it a route. With this flexibility of pattern matching, we can design the RESTful API very comfortably.

> Use `http.StatusOK` to write to the header of a response to announce that an API request is successful. Similarly, http has many status codes for various types of HTTP request. Use the appropriate one to convey the right message. For example, 404 - Not found, 500 - Server error, and so on.

Reverse mapping URL

In simple words, a reverse-mapping URL is just getting the URL for an API resource. Reverse-mapping is quite useful when we need to share links to our web application or API. But in order to create a URL from the data, we should associate a `Name` with the Mux route:

```
r.HandlerFunc("/articles/{category}/{id:[0-9]+}", ArticleHandler).
   Name("articleRoute")
```

Now, if we have data, we can form an URL:

```
url, err := r.Get("articleRoute").URL("category", "books", "id", "123")
fmt.Printf(url.URL) // prints /articles/books/123
```

Gorilla Mux provides a lot of flexibility in creating custom routes. It also allows method chaining to add properties to a created route.

Custom paths

We can define the preceding route in two steps:

- First, define the path on the router:

```
r := mux.NewRouter()
```

- Next, define the handler on the router:

```
    r.Path("/articles/{category}/{id:[0-
9]+}").HandlerFunc(ArticleHandler) //chaining is possible
```

Be aware that the method chained here is `HandlerFunc` and not `HandleFunc`, as shown in the preceding code. We can create a top-level path and add subpaths to different handlers easily in Mux using `Subrouter`:

```
r := mux.NewRouter()
s := r.PathPrefix("/articles").Subrouter()
s.HandleFunc("{id}/settings", settingsHandler)
s.HandleFunc("{id}/details", detailsHandler)
```

So all the URLs of the form `http://localhost:8000/articles/123/settings` redirect to `settingsHandler` and URLs of the form `http://localhost:8000/articles/123/details` redirect to the `detailsHandler`. This might be useful when we create a namespace for grouping particular URL paths.

Path Prefix

Path Prefix is a wildcard for matching after a defined path. The general use case is when we serve files from our static folder and all URLs should be served as-is. From the official Mux documentation, we can use this for serving static files. This is the Mux version of the static file server that we created in the preceding program using `httprouter`:

```
r.PathPrefix("/static/").Handler(http.StripPrefix("/static/",
http.FileServer(http.Dir("/tmp/static"))))
```

This can serve all kinds of files in the directory:

`http://localhost:8000/static/js/jquery.min.js`

Strict Slash

Strict Slash is a parameter on the Mux router by which we can order the router to redirect URL routes with trailing slashes to those without them. For example, `/articles/` can be the original path, but routes coming with `/path` will be redirected to the original path:

```
r := mux.NewRouter()
r.StrictSlash(true)
r.Path("/articles/").Handler(ArticleHandler)
```

This URL redirects to the preceding `ArticleHandler` if the `StrictSlash` parameter is set to `true`:

```
http://localhost:8000/articles
```

Encoded paths

We can have encoded paths from a few clients. To handle these encoded paths, Mux provides a method called `UseEncodedPath`. If we call this method on the router variable, we can even match the encoded URL route and forward it to the given handler:

```
r := NewRouter()
r.UseEncodedPath()
r.NewRoute().Path("/category/id")
```

This can match the URL:

```
http://localhost:8000/books/1%2F2
```

`%2F` stands for / in the un-encoded form. If the method `UseEncodedPath` is not used, the router might understand it as `/v1/1/2`.

Query-based matching

Query parameters are those that get passed along with the URL. This is what we commonly see in a REST `GET` request. Gorilla Mux can create a route for matching a URL with the given query parameters:

```
http://localhost:8000/articles/?id=123&category=books
```

Let us add functionality to our program:

```
// Add this in your main program
r := mux.NewRouter()
r.HandleFunc("/articles", QueryHandler)
r.Queries("id", "category")
```

It limits the query with the preceding URL. The `id` and `category` match with the `Queries` list. Empty values are allowed for parameters. `QueryHandler` looks like this. You can use `request.URL.Query()` to obtain query parameters in your handler function:

```
func QueryHandler(w http.ResponseWriter, r *http.Request){
  queryParams := r.URL.Query()
  w.WriteHeader(http.StatusOK)
  fmt.Fprintf(w, "Got parameter id:%s!\n", queryParams["id"])
  fmt.Fprintf(w, "Got parameter category:%s!", queryParams["category"])
}
```

Host-based matching

Sometimes we need to allow requests from specific hosts. If the host is matched, then the request proceeds to the route handlers. This could be very helpful if we have multiple domains and subdomains and match them with the custom routes.

Using the `Host` method on the router variable, we can regulate from which hosts routes can be directed:

```
r := mux.NewRouter()
r.Host("aaa.bbb.ccc")
r.HandleFunc("/id1/id2/id3", MyHandler)
```

If we set this, all requests coming from the host `aaa.bbb.ccc` of the form `http://aaa.bbb.ccc/111/222/333` will be matched. Similarly, we can regulate HTTP schemes (http, https) using `Schemes` and REST methods like (`GET`, `POST`) using `Methods` Mux functions. The program `queryParameters.go` explains how to use query parameters in the handler:

```
package main
import (
    "fmt"
    "log"
    "net/http"
    "time"
    "github.com/gorilla/mux"
)
func QueryHandler(w http.ResponseWriter, r *http.Request) {
    // Fetch query parameters as a map
    queryParams := r.URL.Query()
    w.WriteHeader(http.StatusOK)
    fmt.Fprintf(w, "Got parameter id:%s!\n", queryParams["id"][0])
    fmt.Fprintf(w, "Got parameter category:%s!",
queryParams["category"][0])
```

```
}
func main() {
    // Create a new router
    r := mux.NewRouter()
    // Attach a path with handler
    r.HandleFunc("/articles", QueryHandler)
    r.Queries("id", "category")
    srv := &http.Server{
        Handler: r,
        Addr: "127.0.0.1:8000",
        // Good practice: enforce timeouts for servers you create!
        WriteTimeout: 15 * time.Second,
        ReadTimeout: 15 * time.Second,
    }
    log.Fatal(srv.ListenAndServe())
}
```

The output looks like this:

```
go run queryParameters.go
```

Let us fire a CURL request in this format in a terminal:

```
curl -X GET http://localhost:8000/articles\?id\=1345\&category\=birds
```

We need to escape special characters in the shell. If it is in the browser, there is no problem escaping. The output is like this:

```
Got parameter id:1345!
Got parameter category:birds!
```

The r.URL.Query() function returns a map with all the parameter and value pairs. They are basically strings, and in order to use them in our program logic we need to convert the number strings to integers. We can use Go's strconv package to convert a string to an integer, and vice versa.

 Its pattern matching features and simplicity push Gorilla Mux as a popular choice for an HTTP router in projects. Many successful projects worldwide are already using Mux for their routing needs.

SQL injections in URLs and ways to avoid them

SQL injection is the process of attacking a database with malicious scripts. If we are not careful while writing secure URL routes, there may be an opportunity for SQL injection. These attacks usually happen for the POST, PUT, and DELETE HTTP verbs. For example, if we are allowing the client to pass variables to the server, then there is a chance for an attacker to append a string to those variables. If we are inserting those users sending parameters directly into an SQL query, then it could be injectable. The right way to talk to DB is to allow driver functions to check the parameters before inserting the string and executing it in the database:

```
username := r.Form.Get("id")
password := r.Form.Get("category")
sql := "SELECT * FROM article WHERE id='" + username + "' AND category='" +
password + "'"
Db.Exec(sql)
```

In this snippet, we are trying to get information about an article by id and category. We are executing an SQL query. But since we are appending the values directly, we may include malicious SQL statements like (--) comments and (ORDER BY n) range clauses in the query:

```
?category=books&id=10 ORDER BY 10--
```

This will leak information about columns the table has. We can change the number and see the breaking point where we get an error message from the database saying:

```
Unknown column '10' in 'order clause'
```

We will see more about this in our upcoming chapters, where we build full-fledged REST services with other methods, like POST, PUT, and so on:

Now, how to avoid these injections. There are a few ways:

- Set the user level permissions to various tables
- While using URL parameters, carefully observe the pattern
- Use the HTMLEscapeString function from Go's text/template package to escape special characters in the API parameters, like body and path
- Use a driver program instead of executing raw SQL queries
- Stop database debug messages getting relayed back to the client
- Use security tools like sqlmap to find out vulnerabilities

Creating a basic API layout for URL shortening services

Have you ever wondered how URL shortening services work? They take a very long URL and give a shortened, crisp, and memorable URL back to the user. At first sight, it looks like magic, but it is a simple math trick.

In a single statement, URL shortening services are built upon two things:

- A string mapping algorithm to map long strings to short strings (Base 62)
- A simple web server that redirects a short URL to the original URL

There are a few obvious advantages of URL shortening:

- Users can remember the URL; easy to maintain
- Users can use the links where there are restrictions on text length; for example, Twitter
- Predictable shortened URL length

Take a look at the following diagram:

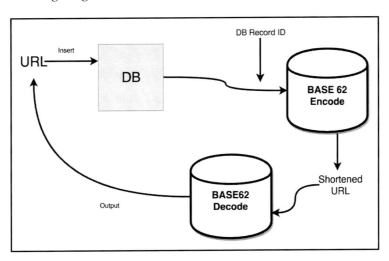

Under the hood, these things happen silently in a URL shortening service:

- Take the original URL.
- Apply Base62 encoding on it. It generates a shortened URL.

- Store that URL in the database. Map it to the original URl (`[shortened_url: orignial_url]`).
- Whenever a request comes to the shortened URL, just do an HTTP redirect to the original URL.

We will implement the complete logic in upcoming chapters when we integrate databases to our API server, but before that, though, we should specify the API design documentation. Let us do that. Take a look at the following table:

URL	REST Verb	Action	Success	Failure
/api/v1/new	POST	Create a shortened URL	200	500, 404
/api/v1/:url	GET	Redirect to original URL	301	404

As an exercise, the reader is allowed to implement this from the fundamentals we have built thus far. You can use a dummy JSON file instead of a database like we did in the first chapter. We will implement this in upcoming chapters, anyway.

Summary

In this chapter, we first introduced the HTTP router. We tried to build a basic application using Go's http package. Then we briefly discussed ServeMux, with an example. We saw how to add multiple handlers to multiple routes. Then we introduced a lightweight router package called `httprouter`. `httprouter` allows developers to create scalable routes, with the option of parsing parameters passed in the URL path. We can also serve files over the HTTP using `httprouter`. We built a small service to get the Go version and file contents (read-only). That example can be extended to any system information.

Next, we introduced the popular Go routing library: `Gorilla Mux`. We discussed how it is different from `httprouter` and explored its functionality by implementing solid examples. We explained how `Vars` can be used to get path parameters and `r.URL.Query` to parse query parameters. Then we discussed SQL injection and how it can happen in our applications. We gave a few pointers on how to avoid it. We will see some of these measures in upcoming chapters when we build a complete REST service, which includes a database. Finally, we laid down the logic for URL shortening and created an API design document.

In the next chapter, we look at `Middleware` functions, which act as tamperers for HTTP requests and responses. That phenomenon will help us modify the API response on-the-fly. The next chapter also features `RPC` (Remote Procedure Call).

3
Working with Middleware and RPC

In this chapter, we are going to look at middleware functionality. What is middleware, and how can we build it from scratch? Next, we will move to a better middleware solution written for us, called Gorilla Handlers. We will then try to understand a few use cases where middleware can be helpful. After that, we will start building our RPC services with Go's internal RPC and JSON RPC. Then we will move to an advanced RPC framework, such Gorilla HTTP RPC.

The topics we cover in this chapter are:

- What is middleware?
- What is an RPC (Remote Procedure Call)?
- How can we implement RPC and JSON RPC in Go?

Getting the code

All the code for this chapter is available at `https://github.com/narenaryan/gorestful/tree/master/chapter3`. Please refer to `Chapter 1`, *Getting Started with the REST API Development*, for setting up Go projects and running the programs. It is better to clone the entire `gorestful` repository from GitHub.

What is middleware?

Middleware is an entity that hooks into a server's request/response processing. The middleware can be defined in many components. Each component has a specific function to perform. Whenever we define the handlers for our URL patterns (as in the last chapter), the request hits the handler and executes the business logic. So virtually all middleware should perform these functions in order:

1. Process the request before hitting the handler (function)
2. Process the handler function
3. Process the response before giving it to the client

We can see the previous points in the form of a visual illustration:

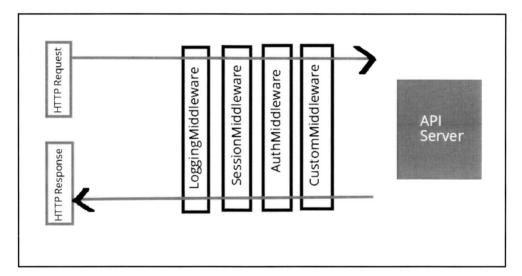

If we observe the diagram carefully, the journey of the request starts with the client. In an application with no middleware, a request reaches the API server and will get handled by some function handler. The response is immediately sent back from the server and the client receives it. But in applications with middleware, it passes through a set of stages, like logging, authentication, session validation, and so on, and then proceeds to the business logic. This is to filter the wrong requests from interacting with the business logic. The most common use cases are:

- Use a logger to log each and every request hitting the REST API
- Validate the session of the user and keep the communication alive

- Authenticate the user, if not identified
- Write custom logic to scrap the request data
- Attach properties to responses while serving the client

With the help of middleware, we can keep the housekeeping work, like authentication, in its proper place. Let us create a basic middleware and tamper an HTTP request in Go.

Middleware functions should be defined when a piece of code needs to be executed for every request or subset of HTTP requests. Without them, we need to duplicate the logic in each and every handler.

Creating a basic middleware

Building middleware is simple and straightforward. Let us build a program based on the knowledge gained from the second chapter. If you are not familiar with closure functions, a closure function returns another function. This principle helps us write middleware. The first thing we should do is implement a function that satisfies the http.Handler interface.

A sample closure called `closure.go` looks like this:

```
package main
import (
    "fmt"
)
func main() {
    numGenerator := generator()
    for i := 0; i < 5; i++ {
        fmt.Print(numGenerator(), "\t")
    }
}
// This function returns another function
func generator() func() int {
    var i = 0
    return func() int {
        i++
        return i
    }
}
```

If we run this code:

```
go run closure.go
```

Numbers will be generated and printed using tab spaces:

1 2 3 4 5

We are creating a closure function called generator and calling it to get a new number. A generator pattern generates a new item each time, based on given conditions. The inner function getting returned is an anonymous function with no arguments and one return type of integer. The variable `i` that is defined inside the outer function is available to the anonymous function, making it useful to compute logic in the future. The other good example application of closure is creating a counter. You can implement it by following the same logic applied in the preceding code.

In Go, the function signature of the outer function should exactly match the anonymous function's signature. In the previous example, `func() int` is the signature for both the outer and inner functions.

This example is given to understand how closure works in Go. Now, let us use this concept to compose our first middleware:

```
package main
import (
    "fmt"
    "net/http"
)
func middleware(handler http.Handler) http.Handler {
    return http.HandlerFunc(func(w http.ResponseWriter, r *http.Request) {
        fmt.Println("Executing middleware before request phase!")
        // Pass control back to the handler
        handler.ServeHTTP(w, r)
        fmt.Println("Executing middleware after response phase!")
    })
}
func mainLogic(w http.ResponseWriter, r *http.Request) {
    // Business logic goes here
    fmt.Println("Executing mainHandler...")
    w.Write([]byte("OK"))
}
func main() {
    // HandlerFunc returns a HTTP Handler
    mainLogicHandler := http.HandlerFunc(mainLogic)
    http.Handle("/", middleware(mainLogicHandler))
    http.ListenAndServe(":8000", nil)
}
```

Let us run the code:

```
go run customMiddleware.go
```

If you do a CURL request or see `http://localhost:8000` in your browser, the console will receive this message:

```
Executing middleware before request phase!
Executing mainHandler...
Executing middleware after response phase!
```

If you observe the middleware illustration diagram provided before, the request phase is pointed to by the right arrow, and the response is the left one. This program is actually the one in the rightmost rectangle, that is, `CustomMiddleware`.

In simple steps, the preceding program breaks down into this:

- Create a handler function by passing the main handler function (`mainLogic`) to `http.HandlerFunc()`.
- Create a middleware function that accepts a handler and returns a handler.
- The method `ServeHTTP` allows a handler to execute the handler logic that is mainLogic.
- The `http.Handle` function expects an HTTP handler. By taking that into consideration, we wrapped up our logic in such a way that, finally, a handler gets returned, but the execution is modified.
- We are passing the main handler into the middleware. Then middleware takes it and returns a function while embedding this main handler logic in it. This makes all the requests coming to the handler pass through the middleware logic.
- The order of the print statement explains the request's journey.
- Finally, we are serving the server on the `8000` port.

Go web frameworks like Martini, Gin provide middleware by default. We will see more about them in upcoming chapters. It is good for a developer to understand the low-level details of middleware.

The following diagram can help you understand how the logic flow happens in the middleware:

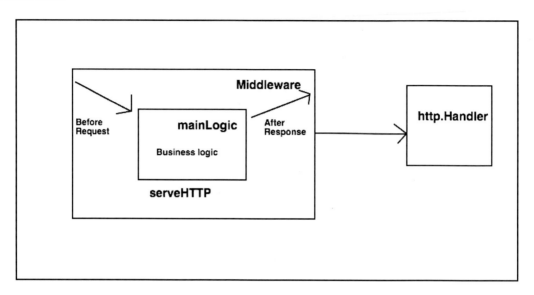

Multiple middleware and chaining

In the previous section, we built a single middleware to perform an action before or after the request hits the handler. It is also possible to chain a group of middleware. In order to do that, we should follow the same closure logic as the preceding section. Let us create a city API for saving city details. For simplicity's sake, the API will have one POST method, and the body consists of two fields: city name and city area.

Let us think about a scenario where an API developer only allows the JSON media type from clients and also needs to send the server time in UTC back to the client for every request. Using middleware, we can do that.

The functions of two middleware are:

- In the first middleware, check whether the content type is JSON. If not, don't allow the request to proceed
- In the second middleware, add a timestamp called Server-Time (UTC) to the response cookie

First, let us create the POST API:

```go
package main

import (
    "encoding/json"
    "fmt"
    "net/http"
)

type city struct {
    Name string
    Area uint64
}

func mainLogic(w http.ResponseWriter, r *http.Request) {
    // Check if method is POST
    if r.Method == "POST" {
        var tempCity city
        decoder := json.NewDecoder(r.Body)
        err := decoder.Decode(&tempCity)
        if err != nil {
            panic(err)
        }
        defer r.Body.Close()
        // Your resource creation logic goes here. For now it is plain
print to console
        fmt.Printf("Got %s city with area of %d sq miles!\n",
tempCity.Name, tempCity.Area)
        // Tell everything is fine
        w.WriteHeader(http.StatusOK)
        w.Write([]byte("201 - Created"))
    } else {
        // Say method not allowed
        w.WriteHeader(http.StatusMethodNotAllowed)
        w.Write([]byte("405 - Method Not Allowed"))
    }
}

func main() {
    http.HandleFunc("/city", mainLogic)
    http.ListenAndServe(":8000", nil)
}
```

If we run this:

```
go run cityAPI.go
```

Then give a CURL request:

```
curl -H "Content-Type: application/json" -X POST http://localhost:8000/city
-d '{"name":"New York", "area":304}'
```

```
curl -H "Content-Type: application/json" -X POST http://localhost:8000/city
-d '{"name":"Boston", "area":89}'
```

Go gives us the following:

```
Got New York city with area of 304 sq miles!
Got Boston city with area of 89 sq miles!
```

CURL responses will be:

```
201 - Created
201 - Created
```

In order to chain, we need to pass the handler between multiple middlewares.

Here is the program in simple steps:

- We created a REST API with a POST as the allowed method. It is not complete because we are not storing data to a database or file.
- We imported the json package and used it to decode the POST body given by the client. Next, we created a structure that maps the JSON body.
- Then, JSON got decoded and printed the information to the console.

Only one handler is involved in the preceding example. But now, for the upcoming task, the idea is to pass the main handler to multiple middleware handlers. The complete code looks like this:

```
package main
import (
    "encoding/json"
    "log"
    "net/http"
    "strconv"
    "time"
)
type city struct {
    Name string
    Area uint64
```

```
}
// Middleware to check content type as JSON
func filterContentType(handler http.Handler) http.Handler {
    return http.HandlerFunc(func(w http.ResponseWriter, r *http.Request) {
        log.Println("Currently in the check content type middleware")
        // Filtering requests by MIME type
        if r.Header.Get("Content-type") != "application/json" {
            w.WriteHeader(http.StatusUnsupportedMediaType)
            w.Write([]byte("415 - Unsupported Media Type. Please send
JSON"))
            return
        }
        handler.ServeHTTP(w, r)
    })
}
// Middleware to add server timestamp for response cookie
func setServerTimeCookie(handler http.Handler) http.Handler {
    return http.HandlerFunc(func(w http.ResponseWriter, r *http.Request) {
        handler.ServeHTTP(w, r)
        // Setting cookie to each and every response
        cookie := http.Cookie{Name: "Server-Time(UTC)", Value:
strconv.FormatInt(time.Now().Unix(), 10)}
        http.SetCookie(w, &cookie)
        log.Println("Currently in the set server time middleware")
    })
}
func mainLogic(w http.ResponseWriter, r *http.Request) {
    // Check if method is POST
    if r.Method == "POST" {
        var tempCity city
        decoder := json.NewDecoder(r.Body)
        err := decoder.Decode(&tempCity)
        if err != nil {
            panic(err)
        }
        defer r.Body.Close()
        // Your resource creation logic goes here. For now it is plain
print to console
        log.Printf("Got %s city with area of %d sq miles!\n",
tempCity.Name, tempCity.Area)
        // Tell everything is fine
        w.WriteHeader(http.StatusOK)
        w.Write([]byte("201 - Created"))
    } else {
        // Say method not allowed
        w.WriteHeader(http.StatusMethodNotAllowed)
        w.Write([]byte("405 - Method Not Allowed"))
    }
```

```
    }
func main() {
    mainLogicHandler := http.HandlerFunc(mainLogic)
    http.Handle("/city",
filterContentType(setServerTimeCookie(mainLogicHandler)))
    http.ListenAndServe(":8000", nil)
    }
```

Now, if we run this:

```
go run multipleMiddleware.go
```

And run this for the CURL command:

```
curl -i -H "Content-Type: application/json" -X POST
http://localhost:8000/city -d '{"name":"Boston", "area":89}'
```

The output is:

```
HTTP/1.1 200 OK
Date: Sat, 27 May 2017 14:35:46 GMT
Content-Length: 13
Content-Type: text/plain; charset=utf-8

201 - Created
```

But if we try to remove `Content-Type:application/json` from the CURL command, the middleware blocks us from executing the main handler:

```
curl -i -X POST http://localhost:8000/city -d '{"name":"New York",
"area":304}'

HTTP/1.1 415 Unsupported Media Type
Date: Sat, 27 May 2017 15:36:58 GMT
Content-Length: 46
Content-Type: text/plain; charset=utf-8

415 - Unsupported Media Type. Please send JSON
```

And the cookie will be set from the other middleware.

In the preceding program, we used log instead of the fmt package. Even though both do the same thing, log formats the output by attaching a timestamp of the log. It can also be easily directed to a file.

There are a few interesting things in this program. The middleware functions we defined have quite common use cases. We can extend them to perform any action. The program is composed of many elements. If you read it function by function, the logic can be easily unwound. Take a look at the following points:

- A struct called city was created to store city details, as in the last example.
- filterContentType is the first middleware we added. It actually checks the content type of the request and allows or blocks the request from proceeding further. For checking, we are using r.Header.GET (content type). If it is application/json, we are allowing the request to call the handler.ServeHTTP function, which executes the mainLogicHandler code.
- setServerTimeCookie is the second middleware that we designed to add a cookie to the response with a value of the server time. We are using Go's time package to find the current UTC time in the Unix epoch.
- For the cookie, we are setting Name and Value. The cookie also accepts another parameter called Expire, which tells the expiry time of the cookie.
- If the content type is not application/json, our application returns the 415-Media type not supported status code.
- In the mainhandler, we are using json.NewDecoder to parse the JSON and fill them into the city struct.
- strconv.FormatInt allows us to convert an int64 number to a string. If it is a normal int, then we use strconv.Itoa.
- 201 is the correct status code to be returned when the operation is successful. For all other methods, we are returning 405, that is, a method not allowed.

The form of chaining we did here is readable for two to three middleware:

```
http.Handle("/city",
filterContentType(setServerTimeCookie(mainLogicHandler)))
```

If an API server wishes a request to go through many middlewares, then how can we make that chaining simple and readable? There is a very good library called Alice to solve this problem. It allows you to semantically order and attach your middleware to the main handler. We will see it briefly in the next chapter.

Painless middleware chaining with Alice

The Alice library reduces the complexity of chaining the middleware when the list of middleware is big. It provides us with a clean API to pass the handler to the middleware. In order to install it, use the go get command, like this:

```
go get github.com/justinas/alice
```

Now we can import the Alice package in our program and use it straight away. We can modify the sections of the preceding program to bring the same functionality with improved chaining. In the import section, add github.com/justinas/alice, like the following code snippet:

```
import (
    "encoding/json"
    "github.com/justinas/alice"
    "log"
    "net/http"
    "strconv"
    "time"
)
```

Now, in the main function, we can modify the handler part like this:

```
func main() {
    mainLogicHandler := http.HandlerFunc(mainLogic)
    chain := alice.New(filterContentType,
setServerTimeCookie).Then(mainLogicHandler)
    http.Handle("/city", chain)
    http.ListenAndServe(":8000", nil)
}
```

The complete code with these added changes is available as a file called `multipleMiddlewareWithAlice.go` in the `chapter 3` folder from the book's GitHub repository. With the knowledge of the preceding concepts, let us build a logging middleware with a library from the Gorilla toolkit called Handlers.

Using Gorilla's Handlers middleware for Logging

The Gorilla Handlers package provides various kinds of middleware for common tasks. The most important ones in the list are:

- `LoggingHandler`: For logging in Apache Common Log Format
- `CompressionHandler`: For zipping the responses
- `RecoveryHandler`: For recovering from unexpected panics

Here, we use the `LoggingHandler` to perform API-wide logging. First, install this library using go get:

```
go get "github.com/gorilla/handlers"
```

This logging server enables us to create a server like a log with time and option. For example, when you see `apache.log`, you find something like this:

```
192.168.2.20 - - [28/Jul/2006:10:27:10 -0300] "GET /cgi-bin/try/ HTTP/1.0"
200 3395
127.0.0.1 - - [28/Jul/2006:10:22:04 -0300] "GET / HTTP/1.0" 200 2216
```

The format is `IP-Date-Method:Endpoint-ResponseStatus`. Writing our own such middleware will take some effort. But Gorilla Handlers already implements it for us. Take a look at the following code snippet:

```
package main
import (
    "github.com/gorilla/handlers"
    "github.com/gorilla/mux"
    "log"
    "os"
    "net/http"
)
func mainLogic(w http.ResponseWriter, r *http.Request) {
    log.Println("Processing request!")
    w.Write([]byte("OK"))
```

```
        log.Println("Finished processing request")
    }
    func main() {
        r := mux.NewRouter()
        r.HandleFunc("/", mainLogic)
        loggedRouter := handlers.LoggingHandler(os.Stdout, r)
        http.ListenAndServe(":8000", loggedRouter)
    }
```

Now run the server:

go run loggingMiddleware.go

Now, let us open http://127.0.0.1:8000 in the browser, or do a CURL, and you will
see the following output:

```
2017/05/28 10:51:44 Processing request!
2017/05/28 10:51:44 Finished processing request
127.0.0.1 - - [28/May/2017:10:51:44 +0530] "GET / HTTP/1.1" 200 2
127.0.0.1 - - [28/May/2017:10:51:44 +0530] "GET /favicon.ico HTTP/1.1" 404
19
```

If you observe, the last two logs are generated by the middleware. Gorilla
LoggingMiddleware writes them at response time.

In the previous example, we always checked the API on localhost. In this example, we
explicitly specified replacing localhost with 127.0.0.1 because the former will show as an
empty IP in the logs.

Coming to the program, we are importing the Gorilla Mux router and Gorilla handlers.
Then we are attaching a handler called mainLogic to the router. Next, we are wrapping the
router in the handlers.LoggingHandler middleware. It returns one more handler, which
we can pass safely to http.ListenAndServe.

You can try other middleware from handlers, too. This section's motto is to introduce you to
Gorilla Handlers. There are many other external packages available for Go. There is one
library worth mentioning for writing middleware directly on net/http. It is Negroni
(github.com/urfave/negroni). It also provides the functionality of Alice, the Gorilla
LoggingHandler. So please have a look at it.

We can easily build cookie-based authentication middleware using a library called go.uuid
(github.com/satori/go.uuid) and cookies.

What is RPC?

Remote Procedure Call (RPC) is an interprocess communication that exchanges information between various distributed systems. A computer called Alice can call functions (procedures) in another computer called Bob in protocol format and can get the computed result back. Without implementing the functionality locally, we can request things from a network that lies in another place or geographical region.

The entire process can be broken down into the following steps:

- Clients prepare function name and arguments to send
- Clients send them to an RPC server by dialing the connection
- The server receives the function name and arguments
- The server executes the remote process
- The message will be sent back to the client
- The client collects the data from the request and uses it appropriately

The server needs to expose its service for the client to connect and request a remote procedure. Take a look at the following diagram:

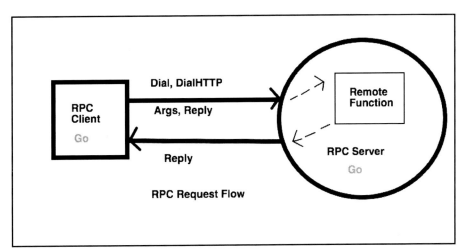

Go provides a library to implement both the RPC server and RPC client. In the preceding diagram, the RPC client dials the connection with the details like the host and port. It sends two things along with the request. One is arguments and the reply pointer. Since it is a pointer, the server can modify it and send it back. Then the client can use the data filled into the pointer. Go has two libraries, net/rpc, and net/rpc/jsonrpc, for working with RPC. Let us write an RPC server that talks to the client and serves the server time.

Creating an RPC server

Let us create a simple RPC server that sends the UTC server time back to the RPC client. First, we start with the server.

The RPC server and RPC client should agree upon two things:

1. Arguments passed
2. Value returned

The types for the preceding two parameters should exactly match for both server and client:

```
package main
import (
    "log"
    "net"
    "net/http"
    "net/rpc"
    "time"
)
type Args struct{}
type TimeServer int64
func (t *TimeServer) GiveServerTime(args *Args, reply *int64) error {
    // Fill reply pointer to send the data back
    *reply = time.Now().Unix()
    return nil
}
func main() {
    // Create a new RPC server
    timeserver := new(TimeServer)
    // Register RPC server
    rpc.Register(timeserver)
    rpc.HandleHTTP()
    // Listen for requests on port 1234
    l, e := net.Listen("tcp", ":1234")
    if e != nil {
        log.Fatal("listen error:", e)
```

```
        }
    http.Serve(l, nil)
}
```

We first create the Args struct. This holds information about arguments passed from the client (RPC) to the server. Then, we created a `TimeServer` number to register with the `rpc.Register`. Here, the server wishes to export an object of type `TimeServer (int64)`. `HandleHTTP` registers an HTTP handler for RPC messages to `DefaultServer`. Then we started a TCP server that listens on port 1234. The `http.Serve` function is used to serve it as a running program. `GiveServerTime` is the function that will be called by the client, and the current server time is returned.

There are a few points to note from the preceding example:

- `GiveServerTime` takes the `Args` object as the first argument and a reply pointer object
- It sets the reply pointer object but does not return anything except an error
- The `Args` struct here has no fields because this server is not expecting the client to send any arguments

Before running this program, let us write the RPC client, too. Both can be run simultaneously.

Creating an RPC client

Now, the client also uses the same net/rpc package but uses different methods to dial to the server and get the remote function executed. The only way to get data back is to pass the reply pointer object along with the request, as shown in the following code snippet:

```
package main
import (
    "log"
    "net/rpc"
)
type Args struct {
}
func main() {
    var reply int64
    args := Args{}
    client, err := rpc.DialHTTP("tcp", "localhost"+":1234")
    if err != nil {
        log.Fatal("dialing:", err)
    }
```

```
err = client.Call("TimeServer.GiveServerTime", args, &reply)
if err != nil {
    log.Fatal("arith error:", err)
}
log.Printf("%d", reply)}
```

The client is performing the following things here:

1. Do a `DialHTTP` to connect to the RPC server, which is running on the localhost on port `1234`.
2. Call the `Remote` function with the `Name:Function` format with `args` and reply with the pointer object.
3. Get the data collected into the `reply` object.
4. The `Call` function is sequential in nature.

Now we can run both the server and client to see them in action:

go run RPCServer.go

This runs the server. Now open another shell tab and run this:

go run RPCClient.go

Now the server console will output the following UNIX time string:

2017/05/28 19:26:31 1495979791

See the magic? The client is running as an independent program. Here, both the programs can be on different machines and the computing can still be shared. This is the core concept of distributed systems. The tasks are divided and given to various RPC servers. Finally, the client collects the results and uses them for further actions.

Custom RPC code is only useful when the client and server are both written in Go. So in order to have the RPC server consumed by multiple services, we need to define the JSON RPC over HTTP. Then, any other programming language can send a JSON string and get JSON as a result.

RPC should be secured because it is executing the remote functions. Authorization is needed while collecting requests from the client.

JSON RPC using Gorilla RPC

We saw that the Gorilla toolkit helps us by providing many useful libraries. Then we explored Mux, Handlers, and now, the Gorilla RPC library. Using this, we can create RPC servers and clients that talk using a JSON instead of a custom reply pointer. Let us convert the preceding example into a much more useful one.

Consider this scenario. We have a JSON file on the server that has details of books (name, ID, author). The client requests book information by making an HTTP request. When the RPC server receives the request, it reads the file from the filesystem and parses it. If the given ID matches any book, then the server sends the information back to the client in the JSON format. We can install Gorilla RPC with the following command:

```
go get github.com/gorilla/rpc
```

This package derives from the standard `net/rpc` package but uses a single HTTP request per call instead of persistent connections. Other differences compared to `net/rpc`: are explained in the following sections.

Multiple codecs can be registered in the same server. A codec is chosen based on the `Content-Type` header from the request. Service methods also receive the `http.Request` as a parameter. This package can be used on Google App Engine. Now, let us write an RPC JSON server. Here we are implementing the JSON1.0 specification. For 2.0, you should use Gorilla JSON2:

```
package main
import (
    jsonparse "encoding/json"
    "io/ioutil"
    "log"
    "net/http"
    "os"
    "github.com/gorilla/mux"
    "github.com/gorilla/rpc"
    "github.com/gorilla/rpc/json"
)
// Args holds arguments passed to JSON RPC service
type Args struct {
    Id string
}
// Book struct holds Book JSON structure
type Book struct {
    Id string `"json:string,omitempty"`
    Name string `"json:name,omitempty"`
    Author string `"json:author,omitempty"`
```

```go
}
type JSONServer struct{}
// GiveBookDetail
func (t *JSONServer) GiveBookDetail(r *http.Request, args *Args, reply
*Book) error {
    var books []Book
    // Read JSON file and load data
    raw, readerr := ioutil.ReadFile("./books.json")
    if readerr != nil {
        log.Println("error:", readerr)
        os.Exit(1)
    }
    // Unmarshal JSON raw data into books array
    marshalerr := jsonparse.Unmarshal(raw, &books)
    if marshalerr != nil {
        log.Println("error:", marshalerr)
        os.Exit(1)
    }
    // Iterate over each book to find the given book
    for _, book := range books {
        if book.Id == args.Id {
            // If book found, fill reply with it
            *reply = book
            break
        }
    }
    return nil
}
func main() {
    // Create a new RPC server
    s := rpc.NewServer()    // Register the type of data requested as JSON
    s.RegisterCodec(json.NewCodec(), "application/json")
    // Register the service by creating a new JSON server
    s.RegisterService(new(JSONServer), "")
    r := mux.NewRouter()
    r.Handle("/rpc", s)
    http.ListenAndServe(":1234", r)
}
```

This program might look different from the preceding RPC server implementation. It is because of the inclusion of the Gorilla Mux, Gorilla rpc, and jsonrpc packages. Let us run the preceding program before explaining what is happening. Run the server with the following command:

go run jsonRPCServer.go

Now where it the client? Here the client can be a CURL command since the RPC server is serving requests over HTTP. We need to post JSON with a book ID to get the details. So fire up another shell and execute this CURL request:

```
curl -X POST \
    http://localhost:1234/rpc \
    -H 'cache-control: no-cache' \
    -H 'content-type: application/json' \
    -d '{
    "method": "JSONServer.GiveBookDetail",
    "params": [{
    "Id": "1234"
    }],
    "id": "1"
}'
```

The output will be nice JSON, that served directly from the JSON RPC server:

```
{"result":{"Id":"1234","Name":"In the sunburned country","Author":"Bill
Bryson"},"error":null,"id":"1"}
```

Now, coming to the program, we have a lot to understand. The documentation for creating RPC services is very limited. So the technique we used in the program can be applied to a wide variety of use cases. First, we are creating the `Args` and `Book` structs to hold the information about the JSON arguments passed and the book structure, respectively. We are defining a remote function called `GiveBookDetail` on a resource called `JSONServer`. This struct is a service created to register with the `RegisterService` function of the RPC server. If you notice, we are also registering the codec as JSON.

Whenever we get a request from the client, we load the JSON file called `books.json` into memory and then into the `Book` struct using JSON's `Unmarshal` method. `jsonparse` is the alias given for the Go package `encoding/json` because the JSON package from the Gorilla import has the same name. In order to remove conflict, we used an alias.

The `reply` reference is passed to the remote function. In the remote function, we are setting the value of the reply with the matched book. If the ID sent by the client matches with any of the books in JSON, then the data is filled. If there is no match, then empty data will be sent back by the RPC server. In this way, one can create a JSON RPC to allow clients to be universal. Here, we didn't write a Go client. Any client can access data from the service.

Prefer JSON RPC when multiple client technologies need to connect to your RPC service.

Summary

In this chapter, we first looked into what middleware is, exactly, including how middleware processes a request and response. We then explored middleware code with a few practical examples. After that, we saw how to chain our middleware by passing one middleware to another. Then, we used a package called `Alice` for intuitive chaining. We also took a look at the Gorilla handlers middleware for logging. Next, we learned what an RPC is and how an RPC server and client can be built. After that, we explained what a JSON RPC is, and we saw how one can create a JSON RPC using Gorilla toolkit. We introduced many third-party packages for middleware and RPC, with examples.

In the next chapter, we are going to explore few famous web frameworks those further simplify the REST API creation. They have batteries included by possessing inbuilt middleware and HTTP routers.

4
Simplifying RESTful Services with Popular Go Frameworks

In this chapter, we are going to cover topics related to using a framework for simplifying building REST services. First, we will take a quick look at go-restful, a REST API creation framework, and then move on to a framework called `Gin`. We will try to build a Metro Rail API in this chapter. The frameworks we are about to discuss are fully-fledged web frameworks which can also be used to create REST APIs in a short time. We will talk a lot about resources and REST verbs in this chapter. We will try to integrate a small database called `Sqlite3` with our API. Finally, we will inspect `Revel.go` and see how to prototype our REST API with it.

Overall, the topics we will cover in this chapter are as follows:

- How to use SQLite3 in Go
- Creating a REST API with the go-restful package
- Introducing the Gin framework for creating a REST API
- Introducing Revel.go for creating a REST API
- Basics for building CRUD operations

Getting the code

You can get the code samples for this chapter from `https://github.com/narenaryan/gorestful/tree/master/chapter4`. This chapter's examples are in the form of a project instead of single programs. So, copy the respective directory to your `GOPATH` to run the code samples properly.

go-restful, a framework for REST API creation

go-restful is a package for building REST-style web services in Go. REST, as we discussed in the preceding section, asks developers to follow a set of design protocols. We have already discussed how the REST verbs should be defined and what they do to the resources.

Using go-restful, we can separate the logic for API handlers and attach REST verbs. The benefit of this is that it clearly tells us by looking at the code what API we are creating. Before jumping into an example, we need to install a database called SQLite3 for our REST API with go-restful. The installation steps are as follows:

- On Ubuntu, run this command:

   apt-get install sqlite3 libsqlite3-dev

- On OS X, you can use the brew command to install SQLite3:

   brew install sqlite3

- Now, install the go-restful package with the following get command:

   go get github.com/emicklei/go-restful

We are ready to go. First, let us write a simple program showing what go-restful can do in a few lines of code. Let us create a simple ping server that echoes the server time back to the client:

```
package main
import (
    "fmt"
    "github.com/emicklei/go-restful"
    "io"
    "net/http"
    "time"
)
func main() {
    // Create a web service
    webservice := new(restful.WebService)
    // Create a route and attach it to handler in the service
    webservice.Route(webservice.GET("/ping").To(pingTime))
    // Add the service to application
    restful.Add(webservice)
```

```
       http.ListenAndServe(":8000", nil)
   }
   func pingTime(req *restful.Request, resp *restful.Response) {
       // Write to the response
       io.WriteString(resp, fmt.Sprintf("%s", time.Now()))
   }
```

If we run this program:

```
go run basicExample.go
```

The server will be running on port 8000 of localhost. So, we can either make a curl request or use a browser to see the GET request output:

```
curl -X GET "http://localhost:8000/ping"
2017-06-06 07:37:26.238146296 +0530 IST
```

In the preceding program, we imported the go-restful library and we created a new service using a new instance of the restful.WebService struct. Next, we can create a REST verb using the following statement:

```
webservice.GET("/ping")
```

We can attach a function handler to execute this verb; pingTime is one such function. These chained functions are passed to a Route function to create a router. Then comes the following important statement:

```
restful.Add(webservice)
```

This registers the newly created webservice with the go-restful. If you observe, we are not passing any ServeMux objects to the http.ListenServe function; go-restful will take care of it. The main concept here is to use the resource-based REST API creation in go-restful. Going from the basic example, let us build something practical.

Take a scenario where your city is getting a new Metro Rail and you need to develop a REST API for other developers to consume and create an app accordingly. We will create one such API in this chapter and use various frameworks to show the implementation. Before that, for **Create, Read, Update, Delete (CRUD)** operations, we should know how to query or insert them into the SQLite DB with Go code.

CRUD operations and SQLite3 basics

All SQLite3 operations are going to be done using a library called `go-sqlite3`. We can install that package using the following command:

```
go get github.com/mattn/go-sqlite3
```

The special thing about this library is that it uses the internal `sql` package of Go. We usually import `database/sql` and use `sql` to execute database queries on the database (here, SQLite3):

```
import "database/sql"
```

Now, we can create a database driver and then execute the SQL commands on it using a method called `Query`:

sqliteFundamentals.go:

```go
package main
import (
    "database/sql"
    "log"
    _ "github.com/mattn/go-sqlite3"
)
// Book is a placeholder for book
type Book struct {
    id int
    name string
    author string
}
func main() {
    db, err := sql.Open("sqlite3", "./books.db")
    log.Println(db)
    if err != nil {
        log.Println(err)
    }
    // Create table
    statement, err := db.Prepare("CREATE TABLE IF NOT EXISTS books (id
INTEGER PRIMARY KEY, isbn INTEGER, author VARCHAR(64), name VARCHAR(64)
NULL)")
    if err != nil {
        log.Println("Error in creating table")
    } else {
        log.Println("Successfully created table books!")
    }
    statement.Exec()
```

```
    // Create
    statement, _ = db.Prepare("INSERT INTO books (name, author, isbn)
VALUES (?, ?, ?)")
    statement.Exec("A Tale of Two Cities", "Charles Dickens", 140430547)
    log.Println("Inserted the book into database!")
    // Read
    rows, _ := db.Query("SELECT id, name, author FROM books")
    var tempBook Book
    for rows.Next() {
        rows.Scan(&tempBook.id, &tempBook.name, &tempBook.author)
        log.Printf("ID:%d, Book:%s, Author:%s\n", tempBook.id,
tempBook.name, tempBook.author)
    }
    // Update
    statement, _ = db.Prepare("update books set name=? where id=?")
    statement.Exec("The Tale of Two Cities", 1)
    log.Println("Successfully updated the book in database!")
    //Delete
    statement, _ = db.Prepare("delete from books where id=?")
    statement.Exec(1)
    log.Println("Successfully deleted the book in database!")
}
```

This program explains how we can perform CRUD operations on a SQL database. Currently, the database is SQLite3. Let us run this using the following command:

```
go run sqliteFundamentals.go
```

And the output looks like the following, printing all the log statements:

```
2017/06/10 08:04:31 Successfully created table books!
2017/06/10 08:04:31 Inserted the book into database!
2017/06/10 08:04:31 ID:1, Book:A Tale of Two Cities, Author:Charles Dickens
2017/06/10 08:04:31 Successfully updated the book in database!
2017/06/10 08:04:31 Successfully deleted the book in database!
```

 This program runs on Windows and Linux without any problem. In Go versions less than 1.8.1, you may see problems on macOS X such as *Signal Killed*. This is because of the Xcode version; please keep this in mind.

Coming to the program, we are first importing `database/sql` and `go-sqlite3`. Then, we are opening a db file on the filesystem using the `sql.Open()` function. It takes two arguments, type of database and filename. It returns an error if something goes wrong, or else, a database driver. In the `sql` library, in order to escape the SQL injection vulnerability, the package provides a function called `Prepare` on the database driver:

```
statement, err := db.Prepare("CREATE TABLE IF NOT EXISTS books (id INTEGER
PRIMARY KEY, isbn INTEGER, author VARCHAR(64), name VARCHAR(64) NULL)")
```

The preceding statement just creates a statement without filling in any details. Actual data passed to the SQL query uses an `Exec` function in the statement. For example, in the preceding code snippet we used:

```
statement, _ = db.Prepare("INSERT INTO books (name, author, isbn) VALUES
(?, ?, ?)")
statement.Exec("A Tale of Two Cities", "Charles Dickens", 140430547)
```

If you pass incorrect values, such as strings that cause SQL injection, the driver rejects the SQL operation instantly. For getting data back from the database, use the `Query` method. It returns an iterator that returns all the rows for the matched query using the `Next` method. We should use that iterator in a loop to process, as shown in the following code:

```
rows, _ := db.Query("SELECT id, name, author FROM books")
var tempBook Book
for rows.Next() {
    rows.Scan(&tempBook.id, &tempBook.name, &tempBook.author)
    log.Printf("ID:%d, Book:%s, Author:%s\n", tempBook.id, tempBook.name,
tempBook.author)
}
```

What if we need to pass criteria to the `SELECT` statement? Then, you should prepare a statement and then pass wildcard(?) data to it.

Building a Metro Rail API with go-restful

Let us use the knowledge we gained in the previous section and create an API for the City Metro Rail project we talked about in the preceding section. The roadmap is as follows:

1. Design a REST API document.
2. Create models for a database.
3. Implement the API logic.

Design specification

Before creating any API, we should know what the specifications of APIs are in the form of a document. We showed a few examples in the previous chapters, including the URL shortener API design document. Let us try to create one for this Metro Rail project. Take a look at the following table:

HTTP verb	Path	Action	Resource
POST	/v1/train (details as JSON body)	Create	Train
POST	/v1/station (details as JSON body)	Create	Station
GET	/v1/train/id	Read	Train
GET	/v1/station/id	Read	Station
POST	/v1/schedule (source and destination)	Create	Route

We can also include the UPDATE and DELETE methods. By implementing the preceding design, it will be obvious for users to implement them on their own.

Creating database models

Let us write a few SQL strings for creating the tables for the preceding train, station, and route resources. We are going to create a project layout for this API. The project layout will look like the following screenshot:

```
/home/naren/workspace/src/github.com/narenaryan

├── dbutils
│   ├── init-tables.go
│   └── models.go
├── railAPI
│   └── main.go
└── railapi.db

2 directories, 4 files
```

We create our projects in `$GOPATH/src/github.com/user/`. Here, the user is `narenaryan`, `railAPI` is our project source, and `dbutils` is our own package for handling database initialization utility functions. Let us start with the `dbutils/models.go` file. I will add three models each for train, station, and schedule in the `models.go` file:

```
package dbutils

const train = `
      CREATE TABLE IF NOT EXISTS train (
            ID INTEGER PRIMARY KEY AUTOINCREMENT,
            DRIVER_NAME VARCHAR(64) NULL,
            OPERATING_STATUS BOOLEAN
      )
`

const station = `
      CREATE TABLE IF NOT EXISTS station (
          ID INTEGER PRIMARY KEY AUTOINCREMENT,
          NAME VARCHAR(64) NULL,
          OPENING_TIME TIME NULL,
          CLOSING_TIME TIME NULL
      )
`
const schedule = `
      CREATE TABLE IF NOT EXISTS schedule (
          ID INTEGER PRIMARY KEY AUTOINCREMENT,
          TRAIN_ID INT,
          STATION_ID INT,
          ARRIVAL_TIME TIME,
          FOREIGN KEY (TRAIN_ID) REFERENCES train(ID),
          FOREIGN KEY (STATION_ID) REFERENCES station(ID)
      )
`
```

These are plain multi-line strings that are delimited by the backtick (`` ` ``) character. The schedule holds the information of a train arriving at a particular station at a given time. Here, train and station are foreign keys to the schedule table. For train, the details related to it are columns. The package name is `dbutils`. When we mention the package names, all the Go programs in that package can share variables and functions exported without any need of actual importing.

Now, let us add code to initialize the (create tables) database in the `init-tables.go` file:

```
package dbutils
import "log"
import "database/sql"
```

```
func Initialize(dbDriver *sql.DB) {
    statement, driverError := dbDriver.Prepare(train)
    if driverError != nil {
        log.Println(driverError)
    }
    // Create train table
    _, statementError := statement.Exec()
    if statementError != nil {
        log.Println("Table already exists!")
    }
    statement, _ = dbDriver.Prepare(station)
    statement.Exec()
    statement, _ = dbDriver.Prepare(schedule)
    statement.Exec()
    log.Println("All tables created/initialized successfully!")
}
```

We are importing `database/sql` to pass the type of argument in the function. All other statements in the function are similar to the SQLite3 example we gave in the preceding code. It is just creating three tables in the SQLite3 database. Our main program should pass the database driver to this function. If you observe here, we are not importing train, station, and schedule. But, since this file is in the `db utils` package, variables in `models.go` are accessible here.

Now our initial package is finished. You can build the object code for this package using the following command:

go build github.com/narenaryan/dbutils

It is not useful until we create and run our main program. So, let us write a simple main program that imports the `Initialize` function from the `dbutils` package. Let us call the file `main.go`:

```
package main

import (
    "database/sql"
    "log"

    _ "github.com/mattn/go-sqlite3"
    "github.com/narenaryan/dbutils"
)

func main() {
    // Connect to Database
    db, err := sql.Open("sqlite3", "./railapi.db")
```

```
    if err != nil {
        log.Println("Driver creation failed!")
    }
    // Create tables
    dbutils.Initialize(db)
}
```

And run the program from the `railAPI` directory using the following command:

```
go run main.go
```

The output you see should be something like the following:

```
2017/06/10 14:05:36 All tables created/initialized successfully!
```

In the preceding program, we added the code for creating a database driver and passed the table creation task to the `Initialize` function from the `dbutils` package. We can do that straight away in our main program, but it is good to decompose the logic into multiple packages and components. Now, we will extend this simple layout to create an API using the `go-restful` package. The API should implement all the functions of our API design document.

 The `railapi.db` file from the preceding directory tree picture gets created once we run our main program. SQLite3 will take care of creating the database file if it doesn't exist. SQLite3 databases are simple files. You can enter into the SQLite shell using the `$ sqlite3 file_name` command.

Let us modify the main program into a new one. We will go step by step and understand how to build REST services using `go-restful` in this example. First, add the necessary imports to the program:

```
package main
import (
    "database/sql"
    "encoding/json"
    "log"
    "net/http"
    "time"
    "github.com/emicklei/go-restful"
    _ "github.com/mattn/go-sqlite3"
    "github.com/narenaryan/dbutils"
)
```

We need two external packages, `go-restful` and `go-sqlite3`, for building the API logic. The first one is for handlers and the second package is for adding persistence features. `dbutils` is the one we previously created. The `time` and `net/http` packages are for general purpose tasks.

Even though concrete names are given to the columns in the SQLite database's tables, in GO programming we need a few structs to handle data coming in and out of the database. There should be data holders for all the models, so we will define them next. Take a look at the following code snippet:

```go
// DB Driver visible to whole program
var DB *sql.DB
// TrainResource is the model for holding rail information
type TrainResource struct {
    ID int
    DriverName string
    OperatingStatus bool
}
// StationResource holds information about locations
type StationResource struct {
    ID int
    Name string
    OpeningTime time.Time
    ClosingTime time.Time
}
// ScheduleResource links both trains and stations
type ScheduleResource struct {
    ID int
    TrainID int
    StationID int
    ArrivalTime time.Time
}
```

The `DB` variable is allocated to hold the global database driver. All the above structs are exact representations of the database models in the SQL. Go's `time.Time` struct type can actually hold the `TIME` field from the database.

Now comes the actual `go-restful` implementation. We need to create a container for our API in `go-restful`. Then, we should register the web services to that container. Let us write the `Register` function, as shown in the following code snippet:

```
// Register adds paths and routes to container
func (t *TrainResource) Register(container *restful.Container) {
    ws := new(restful.WebService)
    ws.
        Path("/v1/trains").
        Consumes(restful.MIME_JSON).
        Produces(restful.MIME_JSON) // you can specify this per route as
well
    ws.Route(ws.GET("/{train-id}").To(t.getTrain))
    ws.Route(ws.POST("").To(t.createTrain))
    ws.Route(ws.DELETE("/{train-id}").To(t.removeTrain))
    container.Add(ws)
}
```

Web services in `go-restful` mainly work based on resources. So here, we are defining a function called `Register` on `TrainResource`, taking containers as arguments. We create a new `WebService` and add paths to it. A path is the URL endpoint and routes are the path parameters or query parameters attached to the function handlers. `ws` is the web service created to serve the `Train` resource. We attached three REST methods, namely GET, POST, and DELETE to three function handlers, `getTrain`, `createTrain`, and `removeTrain` respectively:

```
Path("/v1/trains").
Consumes(restful.MIME_JSON).
Produces(restful.MIME_JSON)
```

These statements say that API will only entertain `Content-Type` as application/JSON in the request. For all other types, it automatically returns a 415--Media Not Supported error. The returned response is automatically converted to a pretty JSON. We can also have a list of formats such as XML, JSON, and so on. `go-restful` provides this feature out of the box.

Now, let us define the function handlers:

```
// GET http://localhost:8000/v1/trains/1
func (t TrainResource) getTrain(request *restful.Request, response
*restful.Response) {
    id := request.PathParameter("train-id")
    err := DB.QueryRow("select ID, DRIVER_NAME, OPERATING_STATUS FROM train
where id=?", id).Scan(&t.ID, &t.DriverName, &t.OperatingStatus)
    if err != nil {
        log.Println(err)
        response.AddHeader("Content-Type", "text/plain")
        response.WriteErrorString(http.StatusNotFound, "Train could not be
found.")
    } else {
        response.WriteEntity(t)
    }
}
// POST http://localhost:8000/v1/trains
func (t TrainResource) createTrain(request *restful.Request, response
*restful.Response) {
    log.Println(request.Request.Body)
    decoder := json.NewDecoder(request.Request.Body)
    var b TrainResource
    err := decoder.Decode(&b)
    log.Println(b.DriverName, b.OperatingStatus)
    // Error handling is obvious here. So omitting...
    statement, _ := DB.Prepare("insert into train (DRIVER_NAME,
OPERATING_STATUS) values (?, ?)")
    result, err := statement.Exec(b.DriverName, b.OperatingStatus)
    if err == nil {
        newID, _ := result.LastInsertId()
        b.ID = int(newID)
        response.WriteHeaderAndEntity(http.StatusCreated, b)
    } else {
        response.AddHeader("Content-Type", "text/plain")
        response.WriteErrorString(http.StatusInternalServerError,
err.Error())
    }
}
// DELETE http://localhost:8000/v1/trains/1
func (t TrainResource) removeTrain(request *restful.Request, response
*restful.Response) {
    id := request.PathParameter("train-id")
    statement, _ := DB.Prepare("delete from train where id=?")
    _, err := statement.Exec(id)
    if err == nil {
        response.WriteHeader(http.StatusOK)
    } else {
```

```
        response.AddHeader("Content-Type", "text/plain")
        response.WriteErrorString(http.StatusInternalServerError,
    err.Error())
        }
    }
```

All these REST methods are defined on the instance of the `TimeResource` struct. Coming to the `GET` handler, it is passing `Request` and `Response` as its arguments. The `path` parameters can be fetched using the `request.PathParameter` function. The argument passed to it will be in agreement with the route we added in the preceding code snippet. That is, `train-id` will be returned into the handler so that we can strip it and use it as criteria to fetch a record from our SQLite database.

In the `POST` handler function, we are parsing the request body with the JSON package's `NewDecoder` function. `go-restful` doesn't have a function to parse raw data posted from the client. There are functions available to strip query parameters and form parameters, but this one is missing. So, we wrote our own logic to strip and parsed the JSON body, and used those results to insert data into our SQLite database. That handler is creating a `db` record for the train with the supplied details in the request.

The `DELETE` function is quite obvious if you understand the previous two handlers. We are making a `DELETE` SQL command using `DB.Prepare` and returning a 201 Status OK back, telling us the delete operation was successful. Otherwise, we are sending back the actual error as a server error. Now, let us write the main function handler, which is an entry point for our program:

```
func main() {
    var err error
    DB, err = sql.Open("sqlite3", "./railapi.db")
    if err != nil {
        log.Println("Driver creation failed!")
    }
    dbutils.Initialize(DB)
    wsContainer := restful.NewContainer()
    wsContainer.Router(restful.CurlyRouter{})
    t := TrainResource{}
    t.Register(wsContainer)
    log.Printf("start listening on localhost:8000")
    server := &http.Server{Addr: ":8000", Handler: wsContainer}
    log.Fatal(server.ListenAndServe())
}
```

The first four lines here are performing the database-related housekeeping. Then, we are creating a new container using `restful.NewContainer`. Then, we are using a router called `CurlyRouter` (which allows us to use `{train_id}` syntax in paths while setting routes) for our container. Then, we created an instance of the `TimeResource` struct and passed this container to the `Register` method. That container can indeed act as an HTTP handler; so, we can pass it to the `http.Server` easily.

> Use `request.QueryParameter` to fetch the query parameters from an HTTP request in the `go-restful` handler.

This code is available in the GitHub repo. Now, when we run the `main.go` file within the `$GOPATH/src/github.com/narenaryan` directory, we see this:

```
go run railAPI/main.go
```

And make a curl `POST` request to create a train:

```
curl -X POST \
     http://localhost:8000/v1/trains \
     -H 'cache-control: no-cache' \
     -H 'content-type: application/json' \
     -d '{"driverName": "Menaka", "operatingStatus": true}'
```

This creates a new train with the driver and operation status details. The response is the newly created resource with the train ID allocated:

```
{
 "ID": 1,
 "DriverName": "Menaka",
 "OperatingStatus": true
}
```

Now, let us make a curl request to check the `GET`:

```
CURL -X GET "http://localhost:8000/v1/trains/1"
```

You will see the JSON output, as follows:

```
{
  "ID": 1,
  "DriverName": "Menaka",
  "OperatingStatus": true
  }
```

We can use the same names for both posting data and JSON returned, but in order to show the difference between two operations, different variable names are used. Now, delete the resource we created in the preceding code snippet with the DELETE API call:

```
CURL -X DELETE "http://localhost:8000/v1/trains/1"
```

It won't return any response body; it returns Status 200 ok if the operation was successful. Now, if we try to do a GET on the ID 1 train, then it returns us this response:

```
Train could not be found.
```

These implementations can be extended to PUT and PATCH. We need to add two more routes to the web service in the Register method and define respective handlers. Here, we created a web service for the Train resource. In a similar way, web services can be created for doing CRUD operations on the Station and Schedule tables. That task is left for the readers to explore.

 go-restful is a lightweight library that is powerful in creating RESTful services in an elegant way. The main theme is to convert resources (models) into consumable APIs. Using other heavy frameworks may speed up the development, but the API can end up slower because of the wrapping of code. go-restful is a lean and low-level package for API creation.

go-restful also provides built-in support for documenting the REST API with **swagger**. It is a tool that runs and generates templates for documenting the REST API we build. By integrating it with our go-restful-based web services, we can generate documentation on the fly. For more information, visit https://github.com/emicklei/go-restful-swagger12.

Building RESTful APIs with the Gin framework

Gin-gonic is a framework based on the `httprouter`. We learned about the `httprouter` in Chapter 2, *Handling Routing for Our REST Services*. It is an HTTP multiplexer like Gorilla Mux, but it is faster. `Gin` allows a high-level API to create REST services in a clean way. `Gin` compares itself with another web framework called `martini`. All web frameworks allow us to do a lot more things such as templating and web server design, additional to service creation. Install the `Gin` package using the following command:

```
go get gopkg.in/gin-gonic/gin.v1
```

Let us write a simple hello world program in `Gin` to get familiarized with the `Gin` constructs. The file is `ginBasic.go`:

```go
package main
import (
    "time"
    "github.com/gin-gonic/gin"
)
func main() {
    r := gin.Default()
    /* GET takes a route and a handler function
       Handler takes the gin context object
    */
    r.GET("/pingTime", func(c *gin.Context) {
        // JSON serializer is available on gin context
        c.JSON(200, gin.H{
            "serverTime": time.Now().UTC(),
        })
    })
    r.Run(":8000") // Listen and serve on 0.0.0.0:8080
}
```

This simple server tries to implement a service that provides the UTC server time to the clients. We implemented one such service in Chapter 3, *Working with Middleware and RPC*. But here, if you look, `Gin` allows you to do a lot of stuff with just a few lines of code; all the boilerplate details are taken away. Coming to the preceding program, we are creating a router with the `gin.Default` function. Then, we are attaching routes with REST verbs as we did in `go-restful`; a route to the function handler. Then, we are calling the `Run` function by passing the port to run. The default port will be `8080`.

`c` is the `gin.Context` that holds the information of the individual request. We can serialize data into JSON before sending it back to the client using the `context.JSON` function. Now, if we run and see the preceding program:

```
go run ginExamples/ginBasic.go
```

Make a curl request:

```
CURL -X GET "http://localhost:8000/pingTime"

Output
=======
{"serverTime":"2017-06-11T03:59:44.135062688Z"}
```

At the same time, the console where we are running the `Gin` server is beautifully presented with debug messages:

```
[9:29:34] naren:ginExamples git:(master*) $ go run ginBasic.go
[GIN-debug] [WARNING] Running in "debug" mode. Switch to "release" mode in production.
 - using env:   export GIN_MODE=release
 - using code:  gin.SetMode(gin.ReleaseMode)

[GIN-debug] GET    /pingTime                 --> main.main.func1 (3 handlers)
[GIN-debug] Listening and serving HTTP on :8000
[GIN] 2017/06/11 - 09:29:44 | 200 |     184.984µs | ::1 |   GET    /pingTime
```

It is Apache-style debug logging showing the endpoint, the latency of the request, and the REST method.

In order to run `Gin` in production mode, set the `GIN_MODE = release` environment variable. Then the console output will be muted and log files can be used for monitoring the logs.

Now, let us write our Rail API in `Gin` to show how to implement exactly the same thing using the `Gin` framework. I will use the same project layout, name my new project `railAPIGin`, and use the `dbutils` as it is. First, let us prepare the imports for our program:

```
package main
import (
    "database/sql"
    "log"
    "net/http"
    "github.com/gin-gonic/gin"
    _ "github.com/mattn/go-sqlite3"
    "github.com/narenaryan/dbutils"
)
```

We imported `sqlite3` and `dbutils` for database-related actions. We imported `gin` for creating our API server. `net/http` is useful in providing the intuitive status codes to be sent along with the response. Take a look at the following code snippet:

```
// DB Driver visible to whole program
var DB *sql.DB
// StationResource holds information about locations
type StationResource struct {
    ID int `json:"id"`
    Name string `json:"name"`
    OpeningTime string `json:"opening_time"`
    ClosingTime string `json:"closing_time"`
}
```

We created a database driver that is available to all handler functions. `StationResource` is the placeholder for our JSON that decoded from both request body and data coming from the database. In case you noticed, it is slightly modified from the example of `go-restful`. Now, let us write the handlers implementing GET, POST, and DELETE methods for the `station` resource:

```
// GetStation returns the station detail
func GetStation(c *gin.Context) {
    var station StationResource
    id := c.Param("station_id")
    err := DB.QueryRow("select ID, NAME, CAST(OPENING_TIME as CHAR),
CAST(CLOSING_TIME as CHAR) from station where id=?", id).Scan(&station.ID,
&station.Name, &station.OpeningTime, &station.ClosingTime)
    if err != nil {
        log.Println(err)
        c.JSON(500, gin.H{
            "error": err.Error(),
```

```
        })
    } else {
        c.JSON(200, gin.H{
            "result": station,
        })
    }
}
// CreateStation handles the POST
func CreateStation(c *gin.Context) {
    var station StationResource
    // Parse the body into our resrource
    if err := c.BindJSON(&station); err == nil {
        // Format Time to Go time format
        statement, _ := DB.Prepare("insert into station (NAME,
OPENING_TIME, CLOSING_TIME) values (?, ?, ?)")
        result, _ := statement.</span>Exec(station.Name,
station.OpeningTime, station.ClosingTime)
        if err == nil {
            newID, _ := result.LastInsertId()
            station.ID = int(newID)
            c.JSON(http.StatusOK, gin.H{
                "result": station,
            })
        } else {
            c.String(http.StatusInternalServerError, err.Error())
        }
    } else {
        c.String(http.StatusInternalServerError, err.Error())
    }
}
// RemoveStation handles the removing of resource
func RemoveStation(c *gin.Context) {
    id := c.Param("station-id")
    statement, _ := DB.Prepare("delete from station where id=?")
    _, err := statement.Exec(id)
    if err != nil {
        log.Println(err)
        c.JSON(500, gin.H{
            "error": err.Error(),
        })
    } else {
        c.String(http.StatusOK, "")
    }
}
```

In `GetStation`, we are using the `c.Param` to strip the `station_id` path parameter. After that, we are using that ID to fetch a database record from the SQLite3 station table. If you observed carefully, the SQL query is bit different. We are using the `CAST` method to retrieve the SQL `TIME` field as a string for Go to consume properly. If you remove the casting, a panic error will be raised because we are trying to load a `TIME` field into the Go string at runtime. To give you an idea, the `TIME` field looks like *8:00:00, 17:31:12*, and so on. Next, we are returning back the result using the `gin.H` method if there is no error.

In `CreateStation`, we are trying to perform an insert query. But before that, in order to get data from the body of the `POST` request, we are using a function called `c.BindJSON`. This function loads the data into the struct that is passed as the argument. It means the station struct will be loaded with the data supplied from the body. That is why `StationResource` has the JSON inference strings to tell what key values are expected. For example, this is such field of `StationResource` struct with inference string.

```
ID int `json:"id"`
```

After collecting the data, we are preparing a database insert statement and executing it. The result is the ID of the inserted record. We are using that ID to send station details back to the client. In `RemoveStation`, we are performing a `DELETE` SQL query. If the operation was successful, we return a 200 OK status back. Otherwise, we are sending the appropriate reason for a 500 Internal Server Error.

Now comes the main program, which runs the database logic first to make sure tables are created. Then, it tries to create a `Gin` router and adds routes to it:

```
func main() {
    var err error
    DB, err = sql.Open("sqlite3", "./railapi.db")
    if err != nil {
        log.Println("Driver creation failed!")
    }
    dbutils.Initialize(DB)
    r := gin.Default()
    // Add routes to REST verbs
    r.GET("/v1/stations/:station_id", GetStation)
    r.POST("/v1/stations", CreateStation)
    r.DELETE("/v1/stations/:station_id", RemoveStation)
    r.Run(":8000") // Default listen and serve on 0.0.0.0:8080
}
```

We are registering the `GET`, `POST`, and `DELETE` routes with the `Gin` router. Then, we are passing routes and handlers to them. Finally, we are starting the server using the `Run` function of Gin with `8000` as the port. Run the preceding program, as follows:

```
go run railAPIGin/main.go
```

Now, we can insert a new record by performing a `POST` request:

```
curl -X POST \
  http://localhost:8000/v1/stations \
  -H 'cache-control: no-cache' \
  -H 'content-type: application/json' \
  -d '{"name":"Brooklyn", "opening_time":"8:12:00",
"closing_time":"18:23:00"}'
```

It returns:

```
{"result":{"id":1,"name":"Brooklyn","opening_time":"8:12:00","closing_time"
:"18:23:00"}}
```

And now try to fetch the details using `GET`:

```
CURL -X GET "http://10.102.78.140:8000/v1/stations/1"

Output
======
{"result":{"id":1,"name":"Brooklyn","opening_time":"8:12:00","closing_time"
:"18:23:00"}}
```

We can also delete the station record using the following command:

```
CURL -X DELETE "http://10.102.78.140:8000/v1/stations/1"
```

It returns a 200 OK status, confirming the resource was successfully deleted. As we already discussed, `Gin` provides intuitive debugging on the console, showing the attached handler and highlighting the latency and REST verbs with colors:

```
[GIN-debug] GET    /v1/stations/:station_id  --> main.GetStation (3 handlers)
[GIN-debug] POST   /v1/stations              --> main.CreateStation (3 handlers)
[GIN-debug] DELETE /v1/stations/:station_id  --> main.RemoveStation (3 handlers)
[GIN-debug] Listening and serving HTTP on :8000
[GIN] 2017/06/11 - 16:07:35 | 200 |    384.756µs | 10.101.254.223 |   GET    /v1/stations/1
[GIN] 2017/06/11 - 16:09:11 | 200 |    222.511µs | 10.101.254.223 |   GET    /v1/stations/2
[GIN] 2017/06/11 - 16:09:59 | 404 |      1.162µs | 10.101.254.223 |   GET    /v1/station/1
[GIN] 2017/06/11 - 16:10:03 | 200 |    232.36µs  | 10.101.254.223 |   GET    /v1/stations/1
[GIN] 2017/06/11 - 16:55:15 | 200 |    290.281µs | 10.101.254.223 |   GET    /v1/stations/1
[GIN] 2017/06/11 - 16:56:10 | 200 |    282.856µs | 10.101.254.223 |   DELETE /v1/stations/1
```

For example, a `200` is green, a `404` is yellow, `DELETE` is red, and so on. `Gin` provides many other features such as the categorization of routes, redirects, and middleware functions.

> Use the `Gin` framework if you are quickly prototyping a REST web service. You can also use it for many other things such as static file serving and so on. Remember that it is a fully-fledged web framework. For fetching the query parameters in Gin, use the following method on the `Gin` context object: `c.Query("param")`.

Building a RESTful API with Revel.go

Revel.go is also a fully-fledged web framework like Python's Django. It is older than Gin, and is termed as a high productivity web framework. It is an asynchronous, modular, and stateless framework. Unlike the `go-restful` and `Gin` frameworks where we created the project ourselves, Revel generates a scaffold for working directly.

Install `Revel.go` using the following command:

```
go get github.com/revel/revel
```

In order to run the scaffold tool, we should install one more supplementary package:

```
go get github.com/revel/cmd/revel
```

Make sure that `$GOPATH/bin` is in your `PATH` variable. Some external packages install the binary in the `$GOPATH/bin` directory. If it is in the path, we can access executables system-wide. Here, Revel installs a binary called `revel`. On Ubuntu or macOS X, you can do it using the following command:

```
export PATH=$PATH:$GOPATH/bin
```

Add the preceding line to `~/.bashrc` to save the setting. On Windows, you need to directly call the executable by its location. Now we are ready to start with Revel. Let us create a new project called `railAPIRevel` in `github.com/narenaryan`:

```
revel new railAPIRevel
```

This creates a project scaffold without writing a single line of code. This is how web frameworks abstract things for quick prototyping. A Revel project layout tree looks like this:

```
conf/                Configuration directory
    app.conf         Main app configuration file
    routes           Routes definition file

app/                 App sources
    init.go          Interceptor registration
    controllers/     App controllers go here
    views/           Templates directory

messages/            Message files

public/              Public static assets
    css/             CSS files
    js/              Javascript files
    images/          Image files

tests/               Test suites
```

Out of all those boilerplate directories, three things are important for creating an API. Those are:

- app/controllers
- conf/app.conf
- conf/routes

Controllers are the logic containers that execute the API logic. app.conf allows us to set the host, port, and dev mode/production mode and so on. routes defines the triple of the endpoint, REST verb, and function handler (here, controller's function). This means to define a function in the controller and attach it to a route in the routes file.

Let us use the same example we have seen for go-restful, creating an API for trains. But here, due to the redundancy, we will drop the database logic. We will see shortly how to build GET, POST, and DELETE actions for the API using Revel. Now, modify the routes file to this:

```
# Routes Config
#
# This file defines all application routes (Higher priority routes first)
#

module:testrunner
```

```
# module:jobs


GET       /v1/trains/:train-id                    App.GetTrain
POST      /v1/trains                              App.CreateTrain
DELETE    /v1/trains/:train-id                    App.RemoveTrain
```

The syntax may look a bit new. It is a configuration file where we simply define a route in this format:

```
VERB        END_POINT          HANDLER
```

We haven't defined handlers yet. In the endpoint, the path parameters are accessed using the `:param` notation. This means for the GET request in the file, `train-id` will be passed as the `path` parameter. Now, move to the `controllers` folder and modify the existing controller in `app.go` file to this:

```go
package controllers
import (
    "log"
    "net/http"
    "strconv"
    "github.com/revel/revel"
)
type App struct {
    *revel.Controller
}
// TrainResource is the model for holding rail information
type TrainResource struct {
    ID int `json:"id"`
    DriverName string `json:"driver_name"`
    OperatingStatus bool `json:"operating_status"`
}
// GetTrain handles GET on train resource
func (c App) GetTrain() revel.Result {
    var train TrainResource
    // Getting the values from path parameters.
    id := c.Params.Route.Get("train-id")
    // use this ID to query from database and fill train table....
    train.ID, _ = strconv.Atoi(id)
    train.DriverName = "Logan" // Comes from DB
    train.OperatingStatus = true // Comes from DB
    c.Response.Status = http.StatusOK
    return c.RenderJSON(train)
}
// CreateTrain handles POST on train resource
func (c App) CreateTrain() revel.Result {
```

```
    var train TrainResource
    c.Params.BindJSON(&train)
    // Use train.DriverName and train.OperatingStatus to insert into train
table....
    train.ID = 2
    c.Response.Status = http.StatusCreated
    return c.RenderJSON(train)
}
// RemoveTrain implements DELETE on train resource
func (c App) RemoveTrain() revel.Result {
    id := c.Params.Route.Get("train-id")
    // Use ID to delete record from train table....
    log.Println("Successfully deleted the resource:", id)
    c.Response.Status = http.StatusOK
    return c.RenderText("")
}
```

We created API handlers in the file `app.go`. Those handler names should match the ones we mentioned in the routes file. We can create a Revel controller using a struct with `*revel.Controller` as its member. Then, we can attach any number of handlers to it. The controller holds the information of incoming HTTP requests so that we can use the information such as query parameters, path parameters, JSON body, form data, and so on in our handler.

We are defining `TrainResource` to work as a data holder. In `GetTrain`, we are fetching the path parameters using the `c.Params.Route.Get` function. The argument to that function is the path parameter we specified in the route file (here, `train-id`). The value will be a string. We need to convert it to `Int` type to map it with `train.ID`. Then, we are setting the response status as `200 OK` using the `c.Response.Status` variable (not function). `c.RenderJSON` takes a struct and transforms it into the JSON body.

In `CreateTrain,` we are adding the `POST` request logic. We are creating a new `TrainResource` struct and passing it to a function called `c.Params.BindJSON`. What `BindJSON` does is it plucks the parameters from the JSON `POST` body and tries to find matching fields in the struct and fill them. When we marshal a Go struct to JSON, field names will be translated to keys as it is. But, if we attach the `` `jason:"id"` `` string format to any struct field, it explicitly says that the JSON that is marshaled from this struct should have the key `id`, not **ID**. This is a good practice in Go while working with JSON. Then, we are adding a status of 201 created to the HTTP response. We are returning the train struct, which will be converted into JSON internally.

The `RemoveTrain` handler logic is similar to that of `GET`. A subtle difference is that nothing is sent in the body. As we previously mentioned, database CRUD logic is omitted from the preceding example. It is an exercise for readers to try adding SQLite3 logic by observing what we have done in the `go-restful` and `Gin` sections.

Finally, the default port on which the Revel server runs is `9000`. The configuration to change the port number is in the `conf/app.conf` file. Let us follow the tradition of running our app on `8000`. So, modify the `http` port section of the file to the following. This tells the Revel server to run on a different port:

```
......
# The IP address on which to listen.
http.addr =

# The port on which to listen.
http.port = 8000 # Change from 9000 to 8000 or any port

# Whether to use SSL or not.
http.ssl = false
......
```

Now, we can run our Revel API server using this command:

```
revel run github.com/narenaryan/railAPIRevel
```

Our app server starts at `http://localhost:8000`. Now, let us make a few API requests:

```
CURL -X GET "http://10.102.78.140:8000/v1/trains/1"

Output
=======
{
  "id": 1,
  "driver_name": "Logan",
  "operating_status": true
}
```

`POST` request:

```
curl -X POST \
   http://10.102.78.140:8000/v1/trains \
   -H 'cache-control: no-cache' \
   -H 'content-type: application/json' \
   -d '{"driver_name":"Magneto", "operating_status": true}'

Output
======
```

```
{
  "id": 2,
  "driver_name": "Magneto",
  "operating_status": true
}
```

`DELETE` is the same as `GET` but no body is returned. Here, the code is illustrated to show how to handle the request and response. Remember, Revel is more than a simple API framework. It is a fully-fledged web framework similar to Django (Python) or Ruby on Rails. We have got templating, tests, and many more inbuilt in Revel.

 Make sure that you create a new Revel project for `GOPATH/user`. Otherwise, your Revel command-line tool may not find the project while running the project.

There is middleware support in all the web frameworks we saw in this chapter. `go-restful` names its middleware `Filters`, whereas `Gin` names it custom middleware. Revel calls its middleware interceptors. A middleware reads or writes the request and response before and after a function handler respectively. In `Chapter 3`, *Working with Middleware and RPC*, we discuss more about middleware.

Summary

In this chapter, we tried to build a Metro Rail API with the help of a few web frameworks available in Go. The most popular ones are `go-restful`, `Gin Gonic`, and `Revel.go`. We started by learning our first database integration in our Go applications. We chose SQLite3 and tried to write a sample application using the `go-sqlite3` library.

Next, we explored `go-restful` and looked in detail at how to create routes and handlers. `go-restful` has the concept of building APIs on top of resources. It provides an intuitive way of creating APIs that can consume and produce various formats such as XML and JSON. We used the train as a resource and built an API that performs CRUD operations on the database. We explained why `go-restful` is lightweight and can be used to create low latency APIs. Next, we saw the `Gin` framework and tried to repeat the same API, but created an API around the station resource. We saw how to store time in the SQL database time field. We suggested `Gin` for quickly prototyping your API.

Finally, we tried to create another API on the train resource, but this time with the `Revel.go` web framework. We started creating a project, inspected the directory structure, then moved on to write a few services (without `db` integration). We also saw how to run the application and change the port using a configuration file.

The main theme of this chapter was to give you a push towards a few wonderful frameworks for creating RESTful APIs. Each framework may do things differently, choose the one you are comfortable with. Use `Revel.go` when you need an end-to-end web application (templates and UI), use `Gin` to quickly create REST services, and use `go-rest` when the performance of the API is critical.

5
Working with MongoDB and Go to Create REST APIs

In this chapter, we are going to introduce the NoSQL database called `MongoDB`. We will learn how well MongoDB suits modern web services. We will begin by learning about `MongoDB` collections and documents. We will try to create an example API with `MongoDB` as the database. In this process, we will use a driver package called `mgo`. We will then try to design a document model for the e-commerce REST services.

Basically, we are going to discuss the following topics:

- Installing and using MongoDB
- Working with the Mongo shell
- Building REST APIs with MongoDB as the database
- Basics of database indexing
- Designing an e-commerce document model

Getting the code

You can get the code samples for this chapter from `https://github.com/narenaryan/gorestful/tree/master/chapter5`. This chapter's examples are a combination of single programs and projects. So, copy the respective directory to your `GOPATH` to run the code samples properly.

Introduction to MongoDB

MongoDB is a popular NoSQL database that is attracting a lot of developers worldwide. It is different from traditional relational databases such as MySQL, PostgreSQL, and SQLite3. The main big difference of MongoDB compared to other databases is the ease of scalability at the time of internet traffic. It also has JSON as its data model, which allows us to store JSON directly into the database.

Many huge companies such as Expedia, Comcast, and Metlife built their applications on MongoDB. It is already proven as a vital element in modern internet businesses. MongoDB stores data in a document; think of this as a row in SQL databases. All MongoDB documents are stored in a collection, and the collection is a table (in SQL analogy). A sample document for an IMDB movie looks like this:

```
{
  _id: 5,
  name: 'Star Trek',
  year: 2009,
  directors: ['J.J. Abrams'],
  writers: ['Roberto Orci', 'Alex Kurtzman'],
  boxOffice: {
      budget:150000000,
      gross:257704099
  }
}
```

The main advantages of MongoDB over relational databases are:

- Easy to model (schema free)
- Can leverage querying power
- Document structure suits modern-day web applications (JSON)
- More scalable than relational databases

Installing MongoDB and using the shell

MongoDB can be easily installed on any platform. On Ubuntu 16.04, we need to perform some processes before running the `apt-get` command:

```
sudo apt-key adv --keyserver hkp://keyserver.ubuntu.com:80 --recv
0C49F3730359A14518585931BC711F9BA15703C6

echo "deb [ arch=amd64,arm64 ] http://repo.mongodb.org/apt/ubuntu
```

```
xenial/mongodb-org/3.4 multiverse" | sudo tee
/etc/apt/sources.list.d/mongodb-org-3.4.list

sudo apt-get update && sudo apt-get install mongodb-org
```

It will ask for confirmation of installation in the last step; press *Y*. Once the installation is done, we need to start the MongoDB daemon using the following command:

```
systemctl start mongod
```

All the preceding commands are to be run by the root. If the user is not root, use the prepend `sudo` keyword before each command.

> We can also download MongoDB manually from the website and run the server with the `~/mongodb/bin/mongod/` command. For this, we need to create an init script because the server will be killed if we close the terminal. We can also use `nohup` for running the server in the background. Usually, it is better to install it using `apt-get`.

For installing MongoDB on macOS X, use the Homebrew software. We can easily install it using the following command:

```
brew install mongodb
```

After that, we need to create the db directory where MongoDB stores its database:

```
mkdir -p /data/db
```

Then, change the permissions of that file using `chown`:

```
chown -R `id -un` /data/db
```

Now we have MongoDB ready. We can run it in a terminal window with the following command, which starts the MongoDB daemon:

```
mongod
```

Take a look at the following screenshot:

```
[10:03:52] naren:~ $ mongod
2017-07-01T10:03:58.130+0530 I CONTROL  [initandlisten] MongoDB starting : pid=86550 port=27017 dbpath=/data/db 64-bit host=Narens
-MacBook-Air.local
2017-07-01T10:03:58.131+0530 I CONTROL  [initandlisten] db version v3.4.5
2017-07-01T10:03:58.131+0530 I CONTROL  [initandlisten] git version: 520b8f3092c48d934f0cd78ab5f40fe594f96863
2017-07-01T10:03:58.131+0530 I CONTROL  [initandlisten] OpenSSL version: OpenSSL 1.0.2l  25 May 2017
2017-07-01T10:03:58.131+0530 I CONTROL  [initandlisten] allocator: system
2017-07-01T10:03:58.131+0530 I CONTROL  [initandlisten] modules: none
2017-07-01T10:03:58.131+0530 I CONTROL  [initandlisten] build environment:
2017-07-01T10:03:58.131+0530 I CONTROL  [initandlisten]     distarch: x86_64
2017-07-01T10:03:58.131+0530 I CONTROL  [initandlisten]     target_arch: x86_64
```

On Windows, we can manually download the installer binary and launch it by adding the installation `bin` directory to the `PATH` variable. Then, we can run it using the `mongod` command.

Working with the Mongo shell

Whenever we start using MongoDB, the first thing we should do is play with it for a while. Looking for available databases, collections, documents, and so on can be done with a simple tool called Mongo shell. This shell is packaged along with the installation steps we mentioned in the preceding section. We need to launch it using the following command:

```
mongo
```

Refer to the following screenshot:

```
[10:04:05] naren:~ $ mongo
MongoDB shell version v3.4.5
connecting to: mongodb://127.0.0.1:27017
MongoDB server version: 3.4.5
Welcome to the MongoDB shell.
For interactive help, type "help".
For more comprehensive documentation, see
        http://docs.mongodb.org/
Questions? Try the support group
        http://groups.google.com/group/mongodb-user
Server has startup warnings:
2017-07-01T10:03:58.675+0530 I CONTROL  [initandlisten]
2017-07-01T10:03:58.675+0530 I CONTROL  [initandlisten] ** WARNING: Access control is not enabled for the database.
2017-07-01T10:03:58.675+0530 I CONTROL  [initandlisten] **          Read and write access to data and configuration is unrestricte
d.
2017-07-01T10:03:58.675+0530 I CONTROL  [initandlisten]
>
```

If you see this screen, everything worked fine. If you are getting any errors, the server is not running or there is some other issue. For troubleshooting, you can look at the official MongoDB troubleshooting guide at `https://docs.mongodb.com/manual/faq/diagnostics`. The client gives the information about MongoDB versions and other warnings. To see all available shell commands, use the `help` command.

Now we are ready with our setup. Let us create a new collection called `movies` and insert the preceding example document into it. By default, the database will be a test database. You can switch to a new database using the `use` command:

```
> show databases
```

It shows all available databases. By default, `admin`, `test`, and `local` are the three databases available. In order to create a new database, just use `use db_name`:

```
> use appdb
```

This switches the current database to the `appdb` database. If you try to see this in the available databases, it won't show up because MongoDB creates a database only when data is inserted into it (first collection or document). So, now we can create a new collection by inserting a document from the shell. Then, we can insert the preceding Star Trek movie record into a collection called `movies`, using this command:

```
> db.movies.insertOne({ _id: 5, name: 'Star Trek', year: 2009, directors:
['J.J. Abrams'], writers: ['Roberto Orci', 'Alex Kurtzman'], boxOffice: {
budget:150000000, gross:257704099 } } )
{
      "acknowledged" : true,
      "insertedId" : 5
}
```

The JSON you inserted has an ID called `_id`. We can either provide it while inserting a document or MongoDB can insert one for you itself. In SQL databases, we use *auto-increment* along with an `ID` schema to increment the `ID` field. Here, MongoDB generates a unique hash `ID` rather than a sequence. Let us insert one more document about `The Dark Knight`, but this time let us not pass the `_id` field:

```
> db.movies.insertOne({ name: 'The Dark Knight ', year: 2008, directors:
['Christopher Nolan'], writers: ['Jonathan Nolan', 'Christopher Nolan'],
boxOffice: { budget:185000000, gross:533316061 } } )> db.movies.insertOne({
name: 'The Dark Knight ', year: 2008, directors: ['Christopher Nolan'],
writers: ['Jonathan Nolan', 'Christopher Nolan'], boxOffice: {
budget:185000000, gross:533316061 } } )
{
      "acknowledged" : true,
      "insertedId" : ObjectId("59574125bf7a73d140d5ba4a")
}
```

If you observe the acknowledgement JSON response, `insertId` has now changed to a very lengthy `59574125bf7a73d140d5ba4a`. This is the unique hash generated by MongoDB. Now, let us see all the documents in our collection. We can also insert a batch of documents at a given time using an `insertMany` function:

```
> db.movies.find()

{ "_id" : 5, "name" : "Star Trek", "year" : 2009, "directors" : [ "J.J.
Abrams" ], "writers" : [ "Roberto Orci", "Alex Kurtzman" ], "boxOffice" : {
```

```
"budget" : 150000000, "gross" : 257704099 } }
{ "_id" : ObjectId("59574125bf7a73d140d5ba4a"), "name" : "The Dark Knight
", "year" : 2008, "directors" : [ "Christopher Nolan" ], "writers" : [
"Jonathan Nolan", "Christopher Nolan" ], "boxOffice" : { "budget" :
185000000, "gross" : 533316061 } }
```

Using the `find` function on the movies collection returns all matched documents in the collection. In order to return a single; document, use the `findOne` function. It returns the latest document from multiple results:

```
> db.movies.findOne()
```

```
{ "_id" : 5, "name" : "Star Trek", "year" : 2009, "directors" : [ "J.J.
Abrams" ], "writers" : [ "Roberto Orci", "Alex Kurtzman" ], "boxOffice" : {
"budget" : 150000000, "gross" : 257704099 }}
```

How do we fetch a document with some criteria? This means querying. Querying in MongoDB is known as filtering data and returning a result. If we need to filter for movies that were released in 2008, then we can do this:

```
> db.movies.find({year: {$eq: 2008}})
```

```
{ "_id" : ObjectId("59574125bf7a73d140d5ba4a"), "name" : "The Dark Knight
", "year" : 2008, "directors" : [ "Christopher Nolan" ], "writers" : [
"Jonathan Nolan", "Christopher Nolan" ], "boxOffice" : { "budget" :
185000000, "gross" : 533316061 } }
```

The filter query from the preceding mongo statement is:

```
{year: {$eq: 2008}}
```

This states that the searching criteria is the *year* and the value should be *2008*. $eq is called a filtering operator, which helps to relate the condition between the field and data. It is equivalent to the = operator in SQL. In SQL, the equivalent query can be written as:

```
SELECT * FROM movies WHERE year=2008;
```

We can simplify the last written mongo query statement to this:

```
> db.movies.find({year: 2008})
```

This find query and above mongo query were the same, returning the same set of documents. The former syntax is using the `$eq` which is a query operator. From now on, let us call a *query operator* simply an *operator*. Other operators are:

Operator	Function
$lt	Less than
$gt	Greater than
$in	In the
$lte	Less than or equal to
$ne	Not equal to

Now, let us pose a question to ourselves. We want to fetch all the documents whose budget is more than $150,000,000. How can we filter it with the knowledge we gained previously? Take a look at the following code snippet:

```
> db.movies.find({'boxOffice.budget': {$gt: 150000000}})

{ "_id" : ObjectId("59574125bf7a73d140d5ba4a"), "name" : "The Dark Knight
", "year" : 2008, "directors" : [ "Christopher Nolan" ], "writers" : [
"Jonathan Nolan", "Christopher Nolan" ], "boxOffice" : { "budget" :
185000000, "gross" : 533316061 } }
```

If you observe, we accessed the budget key within the JSON using `boxOffice.budget`. The beauty of MongoDB is that it allows us to query the JSON with a lot of freedom. Can't we add two or more operators to the criteria while fetching documents? Yes, we can! Let us find all movies in the database that were released in 2009 with a budget of more than $150,000,000:

```
> db.movies.find({'boxOffice.budget': {$gt: 150000000}, year: 2009})
```

This returns nothing because we don't have any documents that match the given criteria. Comma-separated fields actually combine with the AND operation. Now, let us relax our condition and find movies that were either released in 2009 or had a budget of more than $150,000,000:

```
> db.movies.find({$or: [{'boxOffice.budget': {$gt: 150000000}}, {year:
2009}]})

{ "_id" : 5, "name" : "Star Trek", "year" : 2009, "directors" : [ "J.J.
Abrams" ], "writers" : [ "Roberto Orci", "Alex Kurtzman" ], "boxOffice" : {
"budget" : 150000000, "gross" : 257704099 } }
```

```
{ "_id" : ObjectId("59574125bf7a73d140d5ba4a"), "name" : "The Dark Knight
", "year" : 2008, "directors" : [ "Christopher Nolan" ], "writers" : [
"Jonathan Nolan", "Christopher Nolan" ], "boxOffice" : { "budget" :
185000000, "gross" : 533316061 } }
```

Here, the query is bit different. We used an operator called $or for finding the predicate of two conditions. The result will be the criteria for fetching the documents. $or needs to be assigned to a list that has a list of JSON condition objects. Since JSON can be nested, conditions can also be nested. This style of querying might look new to people coming from an SQL background. The MongoDB team designed it for the intuitive filtering of data. We can also write advanced queries such as inner joins, outer joins, nested queries, and so on easily in MongoDB with the clever use of operators.

Unknowingly, we have finished three operations in CRUD. We saw how to create a database and a collection. Then, we inserted documents and read them using filters. Now it is time for the delete operation. We can delete a document from a given collection using the `deleteOne` and `deleteMany` functions:

```
> db.movies.deleteOne({"_id": ObjectId("59574125bf7a73d140d5ba4a")})
{ "acknowledged" : true, "deletedCount" : 1 }
```

The argument passed to the `deleteOne` function is the filtering criteria, which is similar to the read operation. All the documents that match the given criteria will be removed from the collection. The response has a nice acknowledgment message with a count of documents that got deleted.

All the preceding sections discuss the basics of MongoDB, but with the shell, which executes JavaScript statements. It is not quite useful executing `db` statements from the shell manually. We need to call the API of Mongo DB in Go using a driver program. In the upcoming section, we will see such a driver package called `mgo`. The official MongoDB drivers include languages such as Python, Java, and Ruby. Go's `mgo` driver is a third-party package.

Introducing mgo, a MongoDB driver for Go

mgo is a rich MongoDB driver that facilitates developers to write applications that talk to MongoDB without the need for the Mongo shell. The Go application can talk easily with MongoDB for all its CRUD operations using the mgo driver. It is an open-source implementation that can be used and modified freely. It is maintained by Labix. We can think it of as a wrapper around the MongoDB API. Installing the package is very simple, refer to the following command:

```
go get gopkg.in/mgo.v2
```

This installs the package in $GOPATH. Now, we can refer the package to our Go programs, as follows:

```
import "gopkg.in/mgo.v2"
```

Let us write a simple program that talks to MongoDB and inserts The Dark Knight movie record:

```
package main

import (
        "fmt"
        "log"

        mgo "gopkg.in/mgo.v2"
        "gopkg.in/mgo.v2/bson"
)

// Movie holds a movie data
type Movie struct {
        Name        string    `bson:"name"`
        Year        string    `bson:"year"`
        Directors []string `bson:"directors"`
        Writers   []string `bson:"writers"`
        BoxOffice `bson:"boxOffice"`
}

// BoxOffice is nested in Movie
type BoxOffice struct {
        Budget uint64 `bson:"budget"`
        Gross  uint64 `bson:"gross"`
}

func main() {
        session, err := mgo.Dial("127.0.0.1")
```

```go
    if err != nil {
            panic(err)
    }
    defer session.Close()

    c := session.DB("appdb").C("movies")

    // Create a movie
    darkNight := &Movie{
            Name:      "The Dark Knight",
            Year:      "2008",
            Directors: []string{"Christopher Nolan"},
            Writers:   []string{"Jonathan Nolan", "Christopher Nolan"},
            BoxOffice: BoxOffice{
                    Budget: 185000000,
                    Gross:  533316061,
            },
    }

    // Insert into MongoDB
    err = c.Insert(darkNight)
    if err != nil {
            log.Fatal(err)
    }

    // Now query the movie back
    result := Movie{}
    // bson.M is used for nested fields
    err = c.Find(bson.M{"boxOffice.budget": bson.M{"$gt":
150000000}}).One(&result)
    if err != nil {
            log.Fatal(err)
    }

    fmt.Println("Movie:", result.Name)
}
```

If you observe the code, we imported the mgo package as well as the bson package. Next, we created the structs that model our JSON to be inserted into the DB. In the main function, we created a session using the mgo.Dial function. After that, we fetched a collection using the DB and C functions in a chained manner:

```go
c := session.DB("appdb").C("movies")
```

Here, c stands for collection. We are fetching the movies collection from appdb. Then, we are creating a struct object by filling in data. Next, we used the Insert function on the c collection to insert darkNight data into the collection. This function can also take a list of struct objects to insert a batch of movies. Then, we used the Find function on the collection to read a movie with a given criteria. Here, the criteria (querying) is formed differently compared to the one we used in the shell. Since Go is not the JavaScript shell, we need a translator that can convert a normal filter query to the MongoDB understandable query. The bson.M function is designed for that in mgo package:

```
bson.M{"year": "2008"}
```

But, what if we need to perform advanced queries with operators? We can do this by just replacing the plain JSON syntax with the bson.M function. We can find a movie from the database whose budget is more than $150,000,000 with this query:

```
bson.M{"boxOffice.budget": bson.M{"$gt": 150000000}}
```

If you contrast this with the shell command, we just added bson.M in front of the JSON query and wrote the remaining query as it is. The operator symbol should be a string here ("$gt").

One more notable thing in the struct definition is that we added a bson:identifier tag to each field. Without this, Go stores the BoxOffice as boxoffice. So, in order for Go to maintain the CamelCase, we add these tags. Now, let us run this program and see the output:

```
go run mgoIntro.go
```

The output looks like the following:

```
Movie: The Dark Knight
```

The result from a query can be stored in a new struct and can be serialized to JSON for the client to use.

RESTful API with Gorilla Mux and MongoDB

In the previous chapters, we explored all the possible ways of building a RESTful API. We first looked into HTTP routers, then web frameworks. But as a personal choice, in order to make our API lightweight, one prefers Gorilla Mux as the default choice and mgo for the MongoDB driver. In this section, we are going to build a proper movies API with an end-to-end integration of the database and HTTP router. We saw how to create a new resource and retrieve it back using Go and MongoDB. Using that knowledge, let us write this program:

```go
package main

import (
        "encoding/json"
        "io/ioutil"
        "log"
        "net/http"
        "time"

        "github.com/gorilla/mux"
        mgo "gopkg.in/mgo.v2"
        "gopkg.in/mgo.v2/bson"
)

// DB stores the database session imformation. Needs to be initialized once
type DB struct {
        session    *mgo.Session
        collection *mgo.Collection
}

type Movie struct {
        ID        bson.ObjectId `json:"id" bson:"_id,omitempty"`
        Name      string        `json:"name" bson:"name"`
        Year      string        `json:"year" bson:"year"`
        Directors []string      `json:"directors" bson:"directors"`
        Writers   []string      `json:"writers" bson:"writers"`
        BoxOffice BoxOffice     `json:"boxOffice" bson:"boxOffice"`
}

type BoxOffice struct {
        Budget uint64 `json:"budget" bson:"budget"`
        Gross  uint64 `json:"gross" bson:"gross"`
}

// GetMovie fetches a movie with a given ID
func (db *DB) GetMovie(w http.ResponseWriter, r *http.Request) {
        vars := mux.Vars(r)
```

```
            w.WriteHeader(http.StatusOK)
            var movie Movie
            err := db.collection.Find(bson.M{"_id":
bson.ObjectIdHex(vars["id"])}).One(&movie)
            if err != nil {
                    w.Write([]byte(err.Error()))
            } else {
                    w.Header().Set("Content-Type", "application/json")
                    response, _ := json.Marshal(movie)
                    w.Write(response)
            }

}

// PostMovie adds a new movie to our MongoDB collection
func (db *DB) PostMovie(w http.ResponseWriter, r *http.Request) {
        var movie Movie
        postBody, _ := ioutil.ReadAll(r.Body)
        json.Unmarshal(postBody, &movie)
        // Create a Hash ID to insert
        movie.ID = bson.NewObjectId()
        err := db.collection.Insert(movie)
        if err != nil {
                w.Write([]byte(err.Error()))
        } else {
                w.Header().Set("Content-Type", "application/json")
                response, _ := json.Marshal(movie)
                w.Write(response)
        }
}

func main() {
        session, err := mgo.Dial("127.0.0.1")
        c := session.DB("appdb").C("movies")
        db := &DB{session: session, collection: c}
        if err != nil {
                panic(err)
        }
        defer session.Close()
        // Create a new router
        r := mux.NewRouter()
        // Attach an elegant path with handler
        r.HandleFunc("/v1/movies/{id:[a-zA-Z0-9]*}",
db.GetMovie).Methods("GET")
        r.HandleFunc("/v1/movies", db.PostMovie).Methods("POST")
        srv := &http.Server{
                Handler: r,
                Addr:    "127.0.0.1:8000",
```

```
                    // Good practice: enforce timeouts for servers you create!
                    WriteTimeout: 15 * time.Second,
                    ReadTimeout:  15 * time.Second,
        }
        log.Fatal(srv.ListenAndServe())
}
```

Let us name this program `movieAPI.go` and run it:

```
go run movieAPI.go
```

Next, we can make a POST API request using curl or Postman to create a new movie:

```
curl -X POST \
  http://localhost:8000/v1/movies \
  -H 'cache-control: no-cache' \
  -H 'content-type: application/json' \
  -H 'postman-token: 6ef9507e-65b3-c3dd-4748-3a2a3e055c9c' \
  -d '{ "name" : "The Dark Knight", "year" : "2008", "directors" : [
"Christopher Nolan" ], "writers" : [ "Jonathan Nolan", "Christopher Nolan"
], "boxOffice" : { "budget" : 185000000, "gross" : 533316061 }
}'
```

This returns the following response:

```
{"id":"5958be2a057d926f089a9700","name":"The Dark
Knight","year":"2008","directors":["Christopher
Nolan"],"writers":["Jonathan Nolan","Christopher
Nolan"],"boxOffice":{"budget":185000000,"gross":533316061}}
```

Our movie is successfully created. Here, the ID that is returned is generated by the mgo package. MongoDB expects the driver to provide the unique ID. If it's not provided, then Db creates one itself. Now, let us make a GET API request using curl:

```
curl -X GET \
  http://localhost:8000/v1/movies/5958be2a057d926f089a9700 \
  -H 'cache-control: no-cache' \
  -H 'postman-token: 00282916-e7f8-5977-ea34-d8f89aeb43e2'
```

It returns the same data that we got while creating the resource:

```
{"id":"5958be2a057d926f089a9700","name":"The Dark
Knight","year":"2008","directors":["Christopher
Nolan"],"writers":["Jonathan Nolan","Christopher
Nolan"],"boxOffice":{"budget":185000000,"gross":533316061}}
```

A lot of things are happening in the preceding program. We will explain it in detail in the upcoming sections.

 In the preceding program, the trivial logic for assigning the correct status codes is skipped in `PostMovie` for the sake of simplicity. The reader can feel free to modify the program to add the correct status codes for operations (200 OK, 201 Created, and so on).

At first, we are importing the necessary packages for our program. We imported mgo and bson for MongoDB-related implementation, Gorilla Mux for the HTTP router encoding/JSON, and ioutil for reading and writing JSON in the life cycle of an HTTP request.

Then, we created a struct called DB that stores the session and collection information of MongoDB. We need to have this in order to have a global session and use it for multiple things instead of creating a new session (client connection). Take a look at the following code snippet:

```
// DB stores the database session imformation. Needs to be initialized once
type DB struct {
    session *mgo.Session
    collection *mgo.Collection
}
```

We need this because multiple HTTP handlers of Mux need this information. This is a simple trick of attaching common data to different functions. In Go, we can create a struct and add functions to it so that data in the struct is accessible in the functions. Then, we declared the structs that hold the information of the nested JSON for a movie. In Go, in order to create a nested JSON structure, we should nest the structures too.

Next, we defined two functions on the DB struct. We will use these functions as handlers for the Gorilla Mux router later. These two functions can access session and collection information without creating a new one. The GetMovie handler function reads the data from MongoDB and returns JSON back to the client. PostMovie creates a new resource (movie here) in the database in a collection called moviex.

Now, coming to the main function, we are creating the session and collection here. The session will be constant throughout the program's lifetime. But if needed, handler functions can override the collection by using a session variable. This allows us to write reusable database parameters. Then, we created a new router and attached handler functions and routes using HandleFunc. Then, we created a server that runs on the 8000 port of localhost.

In `PostMovie`, we are creating a new hash ID using `bson.NewObjectId()` of the `mgo` function. This function returns the new hash each and every time we call it. We then pass this to the struct that we insert into the DB. We insert a document in the collection using the `collection.Insert` movie function. This returns an error if something goes wrong. For sending a message back, we are marshaling a struct using `json.Marshal`. If you carefully observe the structure of the `Movie` struct, it is like this:

```
type Movie struct {
    ID         bson.ObjectId `json:"id" bson:"_id,omitempty"`
    Name       string        `json:"name" bson:"name"`
    Year       string        `json:"year" bson:"year"`
    Directors  []string      `json:"directors" bson:"directors"`
    Writers    []string      `json:"writers" bson:"writers"`
    BoxOffice  BoxOffice     `json:"boxOffice" bson:"boxOffice"`
}
```

The identifier on the right side, `` `json:"id" bson:"_id,omitempty"` ``, is a helper to show how to serialize when marshaling or unmarshaling is performed on the struct. The `bson` tag shows how to insert the fields into MongoDB. `json` shows what format our HTTP handler should receive and send data from and to the client respectively.

In `GetMovie`, we are fetching the ID passed as the path parameter using the `Mux.vars` map. We cannot directly pass the ID to MongoDB because it expects a BSON object instead of a plain string. In order to achieve that, we use the `bson.ObjectIdHex` function. Once we get the movie of the given ID, that will be loaded into the struct object. Next, we serialize it to JSON using the `json.Marshal` function and will send it back to the client. We can easily add PUT (update) and DELETE methods to the preceding code. We just need to define two more handlers, as shown in the following code:

```
// UpdateMovie modifies the data of given resource
func (db *DB) UpdateMovie(w http.ResponseWriter, r *http.Request) {
    vars := mux.Vars(r)
    var movie Movie
    putBody, _ := ioutil.ReadAll(r.Body)
    json.Unmarshal(putBody, &movie)
    // Create an Hash ID to insert
    err := db.collection.Update(bson.M{"_id":
bson.ObjectIdHex(vars["id"])}, bson.M{"$set": &movie})
    if err != nil {
        w.WriteHeader(http.StatusOK)
        w.Write([]byte(err.Error()))
    } else {
        w.Header().Set("Content-Type", "text")
        w.Write([]byte("Updated succesfully!"))
```

```
        }
    }

// DeleteMovie removes the data from the db
func (db *DB) DeleteMovie(w http.ResponseWriter, r *http.Request) {
    vars := mux.Vars(r)
    // Create an Hash ID to insert
    err := db.collection.Remove(bson.M{"_id":
bson.ObjectIdHex(vars["id"])})
    if err != nil {
        w.WriteHeader(http.StatusOK)
        w.Write([]byte(err.Error()))
    } else {
        w.Header().Set("Content-Type", "text")
        w.Write([]byte("Deleted succesfully!"))
    }
}
```

The approach is exactly the same, except the DB methods of `mgo` are different. Here, we used the `Update` and `Remove` functions. Since these are not important ones, we can just send the status back to the client with no body. For those handlers to be active, we need to add these two lines in the main block of the preceding program:

```
r.HandleFunc("/v1/movies/{id:[a-zA-Z0-9]*}", db.UpdateMovie).Methods("PUT")
r.HandleFunc("/v1/movies/{id:[a-zA-Z0-9]*}",
db.DeleteMovie).Methods("DELETE")
```

The complete code for these additions is available in the `chapter5/movieAPI_updated.go` file.

Boosting the querying performance with indexing

We all know that while reading a book, indexes are very important. When we try to search for a topic in the book, we first roll our eyes through the index page. If the index is found, then we go to the specific page number for that topic. But there is a drawback here. We are using additional pages for the sake of this indexing. Similarly, MongoDB needs to go through all the documents whenever we query for something. If the document stores indexes for important fields, it can give back data to us quickly. At the same time, we are wasting extra space for indexing.

In the computing field, the B-tree is an important data structure to implement indexing because it can categorize nodes. By traversing that tree, we can find the data we need in fewer steps. We can create an index using the `createIndex` function provided by MongoDB. Let us take an example of students and their scores in an examination. We will be doing `GET` operations more frequently with the sorting of scores. The indexing for this scenario can be visualized in this form. Take a look at the following diagram:

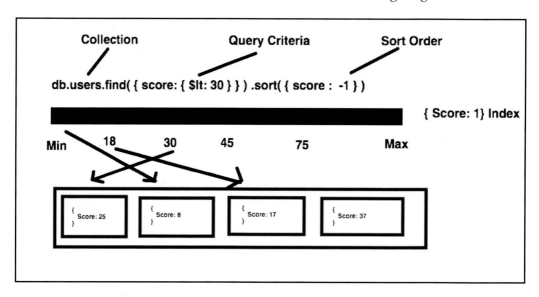

This is the official example given by the MongoDB website. The score is the field to be indexed because of frequent use. Once it is indexed, the database stores the address for each document in a binary tree. Whenever someone queries this field, it checks for the range operator (in this case, it's `$lt`), traverses the binary tree, and gets the addresses of documents in shorter steps. Since the score is indexed, the sort operations are less costly. So, the time that it takes for the database to return the sorted (ascending or descending) result is shorter.

Coming to our previous examples of the movies API, we can create indexes for data. By default, all `_id` fields are indexed, here using mongo shell to show that. Previously, we treated the year field as a string. Let us modify that to an integer and index it. Launch mongo shell using `mongo` command. Use a new mongo database and insert one document into it:

```
> db.movies.insertOne({ name: 'Star Trek',   year: 2009,   directors:
['J.J. Abrams'],   writers: ['Roberto Orci', 'Alex Kurtzman'],   boxOffice:
{        budget:150000000,        gross:257704099    } } )
{
```

```
    "acknowledged" : true,
    "insertedId" : ObjectId("595a6cc01226e5fdf52026a1")
}
```

Insert one more similar document with the different data:

```
> db.movies.insertOne({ name: 'The Dark Knight ', year: 2008, directors:
['Christopher Nolan'], writers: ['Jonathan Nolan', 'Christopher Nolan'],
boxOffice: { budget:185000000, gross:533316061 } } )
{
    "acknowledged" : true,
    "insertedId" : ObjectId("59603d3b0f41ead96110cf4f")
}
```

Now, let us add indexing to the year with the `createIndex` function:

```
db.movies.createIndex({year: 1})
```

This single line adds the magic for retrieving the database records faster. Now, all the queries related to year leverage the indexing:

```
> db.movies.find({year: {$lt: 2010}})
{ "_id" : ObjectId("5957397f4e5c31eb7a9ed48f"), "name" : "Star Trek",
"year" : 2009, "directors" : [ "J.J. Abrams" ], "writers" : [ "Roberto
Orci", "Alex Kurtzman" ], "boxOffice" : { "budget" : 150000000, "gross" :
257704099 } }
{ "_id" : ObjectId("59603d3b0f41ead96110cf4f"), "name" : "The Dark Knight
", "year" : 2008, "directors" : [ "Christopher Nolan" ], "writers" : [
"Jonathan Nolan", "Christopher Nolan" ], "boxOffice" : { "budget" :
185000000, "gross" : 533316061 } }
```

There is no difference in the query result. But the lookup mechanism for documents by MongoDB has changed by indexing. For a larger number of documents, that could reduce the lookup time drastically.

Indexing comes with a cost. Some queries run very slowly on different fields if indexing is not done properly. We can also have compound indexes in MongoDB that can index multiple fields.

 In order to see the time of execution of a query, use the `explain` function after a `query` function. For example, `db.movies.find({year: {$lt: 2010}}).explain("executionStats")`. This explains the winning plan for a query, the time taken in milliseconds, indexes used, and so on.

See the performance of indexed and non-indexed data using the `explain` function.

Designing an e-commerce data document model

Up until now, we have seen how to interact with MongoDB and perform CRUD operations for our REST API. Here, we are going to define a real-world JSON document that can be implemented by MongoDB. Let us lay down the design of JSON for an e-commerce problem. These five components are a must for any e-commerce design:

- Product
- Customer/user
- Category
- Order
- Review

Let us see a schema of each and every component:

Product:

```
{
    _id: ObjectId("59603d3b0f41ead96110cf4f"),
    sku: 1022,
    slug: "highlander-shirt-223",
    name: "Highlander casual shirt",
    description: "A nice looking casual shirt for men",
    details: {
        model_number: 235476,
        manufacturer: "HighLander",
        color: "light blue",
        mfg_date: new Date(2017, 4, 8),
        size: 40
    },
    reviews: 3,
    pricing: {
        cost: 23,
        retail: 29
    },
    categories: {
        ObjectId("3d3b10f41efad96g110vcf4f"),
        ObjectId("603d3eb0ft41ead96110cf4f")
    },
    tags: ["shirts", "men", "clothing"],
    reviews: {
        ObjectId("3bd310f41efad96g110vcf4f"),
        ObjectId("f4e603d3eb0ft41ead96110c"),
```

```
        ObjectId("96g3bd310f41efad110vcf4g")
      }
  }
```

Category:

```
{
    _id: ObjectId("6d3b56900f41ead96110cf4f"),
    name: "Casual Shirts",
    description: "All casual shirts for men",
    slug: "casual-shirts",
    parent_categories: [{
      slug: "home"
      name: "Home",
      _id: ObjectId("3d3b10f41efad96g110vcf4f"),
    },
    {
      slug: "shirts"
      name: "Shirts",
      _id: ObjectId("603d3eb0ft41ead96110cf4f"),
    }]
}
```

User:

```
{
  _id: ObjectId("4fcf3eb0ft41ead96110"),
  username: "John",
  email_address: "john.p@gmail.com",
  password: "5kj64k56hdfjkhdfkgdf98g79df7g9dfg",
  first_name: "John",
  last_name: "Pauling",
  address_multiple: [{
    type: "home"
    street: "601 Sherwood Ave",
    city: "San Bernardino",
    state: "California",
    pincode: 94565
  },
  {
    type: "work"
    street: "241 Indian Spring St",
    city: "Pittsburg",
    state: "California",
    pincode: 94565
  }] ,
  payments: {
    name: "Paypal",
```

```
    auth: {
      token: "dfghjvbsclka76asdadn89"
    }
  }
}
```

Order:

```
{
  _id: ObjectId(),
  user: ObjectId("4fcf3eb0ft41ead96110"),
  state: "cart",
  item_queue: [{
    item: ObjectId("59603d3b0f41ead96110cf4f"),
    quantity: 1,
    cost: 23
  }],
  shipping_address: {
    type: "work"
    street: "241 Indian Spring St",
    city: "Pittsburg",
    state: "California",
    pincode: 94565
  },
  total: 23,
}
```

Review:

```
{
  _id: ObjectId("5tcf3eb0ft41ead96110"),
  product: ObjectId("4fcf3eb0ft41ead96110"),
  posted_date: new Date(2017, 2, 6),
  title: "Overall satisfied with product",
  body: "The product is good and durable. After dry wash, the color hasn't
changed much",
  user: ObjectId(),
  rating: 4,
  upvotes: 3,
  downvotes: 0,
  upvoters: [ObjectId("41ea5tcf3eb0ftd9233476hg"),
             ObjectId("507f1f77bcf86cd799439011"),
             ObjectId("54f113fffba522406c9cc20f")
            ],
  downvoters: []
}
```

All the preceding schemas are to give an idea of how an e-commerce REST service can be designed. All the necessary fields should be included in the final data.

 Note that the preceding JSON is not true JSON, but the form used in the Mongo shell. Please observe that difference while creating the service. The schema is given so that the reader can see how e-commerce relational data is designed.

Since we defined the schema, there is a coding exercise for the reader. Can you create a REST service with the preceding schema by leveraging the knowledge we gained in the beginning sections of this chapter? Anyway, we will implement this model in other databases in upcoming chapters.

Summary

First, we started the chapter with an introduction to MongoDB and how it solves the problems of the modern web. MongoDB is a NoSQL database that is different from traditional relational databases. Then, we learned how to install MongoDB on all platforms and how to start the Mongo server. We then explored the features of the Mongo shell. The Mongo shell is a tool for quick checking or performing CRUD operations and many other operations in MongoDB. We looked at operator symbols for querying. We next introduced Go's MongoDB driver called `mgo` and learned its usages. We created a persistent movies API with the help of `mgo` and MongoDB. We saw how to map a Go struct to a JSON document.

Not all the queries are efficient in MongoDB. So, for boosting the query performance, we saw the indexing mechanism that reduces the document fetching time by arranging the documents in the order of a B-tree. We saw how to measure the execution time of a query using the `explain` command. Finally, we laid out an e-commerce document design by providing the BSON (Mongo shell's JSON).

6
Working with Protocol Buffers and GRPC

In this chapter, we are going to enter the world of protocol buffers. We are going to discover the benefits of using protocol buffers instead of JSON, and where to use both. We will use Google's `proto` library to compile protocol buffers. We will try to write a few web services with protocol buffers that can talk to either Go, or other applications such as Python, NodeJS, and so on. Then, we will explain GRPC, an advanced simplified form of RPC. We will learn how GRPC and protocol buffers can help us build services that can be consumed by any client. We will also discuss HTTP/2 and its benefits over plain HTTP/1.1 JSON-based services.

In short, we will cover the following topics:

- Protocol buffers introduction
- Format of the protocol buffers
- Compilation process of a protobuf
- GRPC, a modern RPC library
- Bidirectional streaming with GRPC

Getting the code

You can get the code samples for this chapter from `https://github.com/narenaryan/gorestful/tree/master/chapter6`. This chapter's examples are a combination of single programs and projects. So, copy the respective directory to your `GOPATH` to run the code samples properly.

Introduction to protocol buffers

HTTP/1.1 is the standard that is adopted by the web community. In recent times, HTTP/2 is becoming more popular because of its advantages. Some of the benefits of using HTTP/2 are:

- Encryption of data via TLS (HTTPS)
- Compression of headers
- Single TCP connection
- Fallback to HTTP/1.1
- Support from all major browsers

The technical definition from Google about protocol buffers is:

> *Protocol buffers are a flexible, efficient, automated mechanism for serializing structured data – think XML, but smaller, faster, and simpler. You define how you want your data to be structured once, then you can use special generated source code to easily write and read your structured data to and from a variety of data streams and using a variety of languages. You can even update your data structure without breaking deployed programs that are compiled against the "old" format.*

In Go, protocol buffers are coupled with HTTP/2. They are a format like JSON but strictly typed, understandable only from the client to the server. First, we will understand why protobufs (short form of protocol buffers) exist and how to use them.

Protocol buffers have many advantages over JSON/XML for serializing structured data, such as:

- They are simpler
- They are 3 to 10 times smaller
- They are 20 to 100 times faster
- They are less ambiguous
- They generate data access classes that are easier to use programmatically

Protocol buffer language

A protocol buffer is a file with a minimalistic language syntax. We compile a protocol buffer and the target file is generated for a programming language. For example, in Go, the compiled file will be a .go file with structs mapping the protobuf file. In Java, a class file will be created. Think protocol buffer as the skeleton for data with a particular order. We need to know the types before jumping into the actual code. In order to make things easier, I am going to first show JSON and its equivalent in protocol buffers. Then, we will implement a solid example.

 Here, we are going to use **proto3** as our protocol buffer version. There are slight variations in versions, but the latest one was released with improvements.

There are many types of protocol buffer elements. Some of them are:

- Scalar values
- Enumerations
- Default values
- Nested values
- Unknown types

First, let us see how to define a message type in a protobuf. Here, we try to define a simple network interface message:

```
syntax 'proto3';

message NetworkInterface {
  int index = 1;
  int mtu = 2;
  string name = 3;
  string hardwareaddr = 4;
}
```

The syntax may look new. In the preceding code, we were defining a message type called `NetworkInterface`. It has four fields: *index, maximum transmission unit (MTU), name,* and *hardware address (MAC).* If we wish to write the same in JSON, it would look like this:

```
{
    "networkInterface": {
        "index" : 0,
        "mtu" : 68,
        "name": "eth0",
        "hardwareAddr": "00:A0:C9:14:C8:29"
    }
}
```

The field names are changed to comply with the JSON style guide, but the essence and structure are the same. But, what are the sequential numbers (1,2,3,4) given to fields in the protobuf file? They are the ordering tags given to serialize and deserialize protocol buffer data between two systems. It is like hinting the protocol buffer encoding/decoding systems to write/read the data in that particular order, respectively. When the preceding protobuf file is compiled and the programming language target is generated, the protocol buffer message will be converted to a Go struct and fields are filled with empty default values.

Scalar values

The types we assigned to the fields in the `networkInterface` message are scalar types. These types are similar to Go types and exactly match with them. For other programming languages, they will be converted to the respective types. A protobuf is designed keeping Go in mind, so the majority of types such as `int`, `int32`, `int64`, `string`, and `bool` are exactly the same, but a few vary. They are:

Go type	Protobuf type
`float32`	`float`
`float64`	`double`
`uint32`	`fixed32`
`uint64`	`fixed64`
`[]byte`	`bytes`

These things should be kept in mind while defining messages in protbuf files. Apart from that, we are free to use other Go types as normal scalar types. **Default values** are the values that will be filled with those types if the user doesn't assign a value to those scalar values. We all know that in any given programming language, variables are defined and assigned. Defining allocates memory for the variable and assigning fills the variable with a value. In analogy, the scalar fields we defined in the preceding message will be assigned with default values. Let us see the default values for the given types:

Protobuf type	Default value
string	" "
bytes	empty bytes[]
bool	false
int, int32, int64, float, double	0
enum	0

Since protocol buffers make an agreement between end systems using a data structure, they don't take additional space for keys in JSON.

Enumerations and repeated fields

Enumerations provide the ordering of numbers for a given set of elements. The default order of values is from zero to *n*. So, in protocol buffer messages, we can have an enumeration type. Let us see an example of the enum:

```
syntax 'proto3';

message Schedule{
   enum Days{
       SUNDAY = 0;
       MONDAY = 1;
       TUESDAY = 2;
       WEDNESDAY = 3;
       THURSDAY = 4;
       FRIDAY = 5;
       SATURDAY = 6;
   }
}
```

What if we need to assign the same values for the multiple enumeration members. Protobuf3 allows an option called **allow aliases** to assign two different members the same value. For example:

```
enum EnumAllowingAlias {
   option allow_alias = true;
   UNKNOWN = 0;
   STARTED = 1;
   RUNNING = 1;
}
```

Here, STARTED and RUNNING both have a 1 tag. This means that both can have the same value in the data. If we try to remove duplicated values, we should also remove the allow_alias option. Otherwise, the proto compiler throws an error (we will see shortly what a proto compiler is).

Repeated fields are the fields in the message of a protocol buffer that represent a list of items. In JSON, we have a list of elements for a given key. Similarly, repeated fields allow us to define an array/list of elements of a particular type:

```
message Site{
    string url = 1;
    int latency = 2;
    repeated string proxies = 3;
}
```

In the preceding code, the third field is a repeated field, which means it is an array/list of proxies. The value could be something such as ["100.104.112.10", "100.104.112.12"], and so on. Apart from repeated fields, we can also use other messages as types. It is analogous to nested JSON. For example, take a look at the following code:

```
{
  outerJSON: {
      outerKey1: val1,
      innerJSON: {
          innerKey1: val2
      }
  }
}
```

We see we have a nested `innerJSON` as one of the members of `outerJSON`. How can we model the same thing in protobufs? We can do it using the nested messages, as shown in the following code:

```
message Site {
    string url = 1;
    int latency = 2;
    repeated Proxy proxies = 3;
}

message Proxy {
    string url = 1;
    int latency = 2;
}
```

Here, we are nesting the `Proxy` type into the `Site`. We will soon see a real example with all these types of fields.

Compiling a protocol buffer with protoc

Until now, we have discussed how to write a protocol buffer file that is previously written in JSON or another data format. But, how do we actually integrate it into our programs? Remember that protocol buffers are data formats, no more than that. They are a format of communication between various systems, similar to JSON. These are the practical steps we follow for using protobufs in our Go programs:

1. Install the `protoc` command-line tool and the `proto` library.
2. Write a protobuf file with the `.proto` extension.
3. Compile it to target a programming language (here, it is Go).
4. Import structs from the generated target file and serialize the data.
5. On a remote machine, receive the serialized data and decode it into a struct or class.

Take a look at the following diagram:

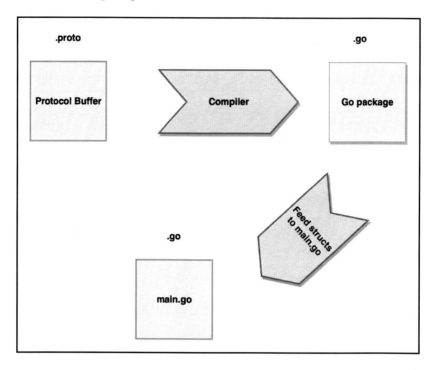

The first step is to install the protobuf compiler on our machine. For this, download the protobuf package from https://github.com/google/protobuf/releases. On macOS X, we can install protobuf using this command:

```
brew install protobuf
```

On Ubuntu or Linux, we can copy protoc to the /usr/bin folder:

```
# Make sure you grab the latest version
curl -OL
https://github.com/google/protobuf/releases/download/v3.3.0/protoc-3.3.0-li
nux-x86_64.zip
# Unzip
unzip protoc-3.3.0-linux-x86_64.zip -d protoc3
# Move only protoc* to /usr/bin/
sudo mv protoc3/bin/protoc /usr/bin/protoc
```

On Windows, we can just copy the executable (`.exe`) from `https://github.com/google/protobuf/releases/download/v3.3.0/protoc-3.3.0-win32.zip` to the `PATH` environment variable. Let us write a simple protocol buffer to illustrate how to compile and use structs from the target file. Create a folder called `protofiles` in `$GOPATH/src/github.com/narenaryan` (this is the place for our Go projects) using the following command:

```
mkdir $GOPATH/src/github.com/narenaryan/protofiles
```

Here, create a file called `person.proto`, which models a person's information. Add a few messages to it, as shown in the following code snippet:

```
syntax = "proto3";
package protofiles;

message Person {
  string name = 1;
  int32 id = 2;   // Unique ID number for this person.
  string email = 3;

  enum PhoneType {
    MOBILE = 0;
    HOME = 1;
    WORK = 2;
  }

  message PhoneNumber {
    string number = 1;
    PhoneType type = 2;
  }

  repeated PhoneNumber phones = 4;
}

// Our address book file is just one of these.
message AddressBook {
  repeated Person people = 1;
}
```

We created two main messages called `AddressBook` and `Person`. `AddressBook` has a list of persons. A `Person` has a `name`, `id`, `email`, and `phone Number`. In the second line, we declared the package as `protofiles` like this:

```
package protofiles;
```

This tells the compiler to add the generating file in relation to the given package name. Go cannot consume this `.proto` file directly. We need to compile it to a valid Go file. When compiled, this package name `protofiles` will be used to set the package of the output file (Go in this case). To compile this protocol buffer file, traverse to the `protofiles` directory and run this command:

```
protoc --go_out=. *.proto
```

This command converts the given protocol buffer file(s) to the Go file(s) with the same name. You will see that, after running this command, there is a new file created in the same directory:

```
[16:20:27] naren:protofiles git:(master*) $ ls -l
total 24
-rw-r--r-- 1 naren staff 5657 Jul 15 16:20 person.pb.go
-rw-r--r--@ 1 naren staff 433 Jul 15 15:58 person.proto
```

The new file name is `person.pb.go`. If we open and inspect this file, it contains the following important block:

```
. . . . . . . .
type Person_PhoneType int32

const (
  Person_MOBILE Person_PhoneType = 0
  Person_HOME   Person_PhoneType = 1
  Person_WORK   Person_PhoneType = 2
)

var Person_PhoneType_name = map[int32]string{
  0: "MOBILE",
  1: "HOME",
  2: "WORK",
}
var Person_PhoneType_value = map[string]int32{
  "MOBILE": 0,
  "HOME":   1,
  "WORK":   2,
}
. . . . . . .
```

This is just a part of that file. There will be many getter and setter methods created for the given structs such as `Person` and `AddressBook` in the output file. This code is automatically generated. We need to consume this code in the main program to create protocol buffer strings. Now, let us create a new directory called `protobufs`. This holds the `main.go` file that uses the `Person` struct from the `person.pb.go` file:

```
mkdir $GOPATH/src/github.com/narenaryan/protobufs
```

Now, for Go to serialize a struct to the protobinary format, we need to install the Go proto driver. Install it using the `go get` command:

```
go get github.com/golang/protobuf/proto
```

After this, let us compose `main.go`:

```go
package main

import (
  "fmt"

  "github.com/golang/protobuf/proto"
  pb "github.com/narenaryan/protofiles"
)

func main() {
  p := &pb.Person{
    Id:    1234,
    Name:  "Roger F",
    Email: "rf@example.com",
    Phones: []*pb.Person_PhoneNumber{
      {Number: "555-4321", Type: pb.Person_HOME},
    },
  }

  p1 := &pb.Person{}
  body, _ := proto.Marshal(p)
  _ = proto.Unmarshal(body, p1)
  fmt.Println("Original struct loaded from proto file:", p, "\n")
  fmt.Println("Marshaled proto data: ", body, "\n")
  fmt.Println("Unmarshaled struct: ", p1)
}
```

We are importing the **protocol buffer (pb)** from the `protofiles` package. There are structs that are mapped to the given protobuf in the `proto files`. We used the `Person` struct and initialized it. Then, we serialized the struct using the `proto.Marshal` function. If we run this program, the output looks like this:

```
go run main.go
Original struct loaded from proto file: name:"Roger F" id:1234
email:"rf@example.com" phones:<number:"555-4321" type:HOME >

Marshaled proto data: [10 7 82 111 103 101 114 32 70 16 210 9 26 14 114 102
64 101 120 97 109 112 108 101 46 99 111 109 34 12 10 8 53 53 53 45 52 51 50
49 16 1]

Unmarshaled struct: name:"Roger F" id:1234 email:"rf@example.com"
phones:<number:"555-4321" type:HOME >
```

The second output of marshaled data is not intuitive because the `proto` library serializes data into binary bytes. Another good thing about protocol buffers in Go is that the structs generated by compiling the proto files can be used to generate JSON on the fly. Let us modify the preceding example to this. Call it `main_json.go`:

```go
package main

import (
  "fmt"

  "encoding/json"
  pb "github.com/narenaryan/protofiles"
)

func main() {
  p := &pb.Person{
    Id:    1234,
    Name:  "Roger F",
    Email: "rf@example.com",
    Phones: []*pb.Person_PhoneNumber{
      {Number: "555-4321", Type: pb.Person_HOME},
    },
  }
  body, _ := json.Marshal(p)
  fmt.Println(string(body))
}
```

If we run this, it prints a JSON string that can be sent to any client that can understand JSON:

```
go run main_json.go

{"name":"Roger
F","id":1234,"email":"rf@example.com","phones":[{"number":"555-4321","type"
:1}]}
```

Any other language or platform can easily load this JSON string and use the data instantly. So, what is the benefit of using protocol buffers instead of JSON? First of all, protocol buffers are intended for two backend systems to communicate with each other with less overhead. Since the size of the binary is less than text, protocol marshaled data is of less size than JSON.

 By using protocol buffers we map both JSON and protocol buffer formats to the Go struct. This gives the best of both worlds by converting one format to another on the fly.

But, protocol buffers are just a data format. They don't have any importance if we don't communicate. So here, protocol buffers are used to pass messages between two end systems in the form of RPC. We saw how RPC works and also created an RPC client and server in the previous chapters. Now, we are going to extend that knowledge to use **Google Remote Procedure Call** (**GRPC**) with protocol buffers to scale our microservice communications. A server and client, in this case, can talk with each other in protocol buffer format.

Introduction to GRPC

GRPC is a transport mechanism that sends and receives messages between two systems. These two systems are traditionally a server and a client. As we described in the previous chapters, RPC can be implemented in Go for transferring JSON. We called it a JSON RPC service. Similarly, Google RPC is specially designed to transfer data in the form of protocol buffers.

GRPC makes the service creation easy and elegant. It provides a nice set of APIs to define services and start running them. In this section, we will mainly focus on how to create a GRPC service and use it. The main advantage of GRPC is that it can be understood by multiple programming languages. Protocol buffers provide a common data structure. So, the combination enables the seamless communication between various tech stacks and systems. This is the integral concept of distributed computing.

Square, Netflix, and so on leverage this GRPC to scale their huge traffic-prone services. Google's former product manager, Andrew Jessup, said in a conference that at Google, billions of GRPC calls are processed every single day. If any business organization needs to embrace what Google does, it too can handle the traffic demand with these tweaks in the services.

We need to install the `grpc` Go library and a `protoc-gen` plugin before writing the services. Install them using the following commands:

```
go get google.golang.org/grpc
go get -u github.com/golang/protobuf/protoc-gen-go
```

GRPC has the following benefits over traditional HTTP/REST/JSON architecture:

- GRPC uses HTTP/2, which is a binary protocol
- Header compression is possible in HTTP/2, which means less overhead
- We can multiplex many requests on one connection
- Usage of protobufs for strict typing of data
- Streaming of requests or responses is possible instead of request/response transactions

Take a look at the following diagram:

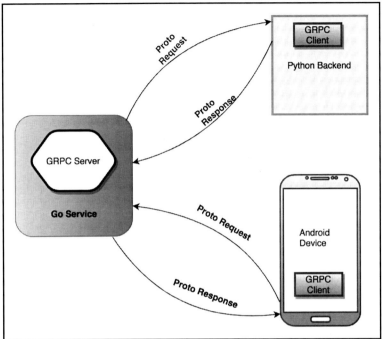

The diagram clearly shows that any backend system or mobile app can directly communicate to a GRPC server by firing a protocol buffer request. Let us write a money transaction service in Go using GRPC and protocol buffers. Here, we are going to show how the client and server can be implemented. The steps are:

1. Create the protocol buffer file for the service and messages.
2. Compile the protocol buffer file.
3. Use the generated Go package for creating a GRPC server.
4. Create a GRPC client that talks to the server.

For this project, create a folder called `datafiles` in your Go workspace (here, it is `$GOPATH/src/github.com/narenaryan/`):

```
mkdir grpc_example
cd grpc_example
mkdir datafiles
```

Create a file called `transaction.proto` in it with messages and a service defined. We will shortly see what a service is:

```
syntax = "proto3";
package datafiles;

message TransactionRequest {
    string from = 1;
    string to = 2;
    float amount = 3;
}

message TransactionResponse {
  bool confirmation = 1;
}

service MoneyTransaction {
    rpc MakeTransaction(TransactionRequest) returns (TransactionResponse)
{}
}
```

This is a minimalistic protocol buffer for a money transaction on the server. We already saw about message keywords in the proto file. The last keyword, `service`, is new to us. `service` tells GRPC to treat it as a service, and all the RPC methods will act as an interface for a server that implements this. A struct that implements a Go interface should implement all its functions. Now, let us compile this file:

```
protoc -I datafiles/ datafiles/transaction.proto --
go_out=plugins=grpc:datafiles
```

This command is slightly bigger than the one we used previously. This is because here we are using the `protoc-gen-go` plugin. The command simply says to use data files as the input directory for proto files and use the same directory for outputting the target Go files. Now, if we see the filesystem, there will be two files:

```
-rw-r--r-- 1 naren staff 6215 Jul 16 17:28 transaction.pb.go
-rw-r--r-- 1 naren staff 294 Jul 16 17:28 transaction.proto
```

Now, create two more directories for server and client logic in `$GOPATH/src/github.com/narenaryan/grpc_example`. The server implements the interface that is generated from the proto file:

```
mkdir grpcServer grpcClient
```

Now, add a file called `server.go` to the `grpcServer` directory, which implements the transaction service:

```go
package main

import (
  "log"
  "net"

  pb "github.com/narenaryan/grpc_example/datafiles"
  "golang.org/x/net/context"
  "google.golang.org/grpc"
  "google.golang.org/grpc/reflection"
)

const (
  port = ":50051"
)

// server is used to create MoneyTransactionServer.
type server struct{}

// MakeTransaction implements MoneyTransactionServer.MakeTransaction
func (s *server) MakeTransaction(ctx context.Context, in
*pb.TransactionRequest) (*pb.TransactionResponse, error) {
  log.Printf("Got request for money Transfer....")
  log.Printf("Amount: %f, From A/c:%s, To A/c:%s", in.Amount, in.From,
in.To)
  // Do database logic here....
  return &pb.TransactionResponse{Confirmation: true}, nil
}

func main() {
  lis, err := net.Listen("tcp", port)
  if err != nil {
    log.Fatalf("Failed to listen: %v", err)
  }
  s := grpc.NewServer()
  pb.RegisterMoneyTransactionServer(s, &server{})
  // Register reflection service on gRPC server.
  reflection.Register(s)
  if err := s.Serve(lis); err != nil {
    log.Fatalf("Failed to serve: %v", err)
  }
}
```

There are a lot of things happening in the preceding file. First, we imported all the necessary imports. The new ones here are `context` and `reflection`. Context is used to create a `context` variable, which lives throughout an RPC request's lifetime. Both of these libraries are used by GRPC for its internal functions.

Before explaining the next sections, if we open the generated `transaction.pb.go` file, we can clearly see that there are two important things:

- The `RegisterMoneyTransactionServer` function
- The `MakeTransaction` function as part of the `MoneyTransactionServer` interface

In order to implement a service, we need both of these things; `MakeTransaction` for the actual service functionality, and `RegisterMoneyTransactionServer` for registering the service (that is, create an RPC server to run on a port).

The `in` variable of `MakeTransaction` has the RPC request details. It is basically a struct that maps to the `TransactionRequest` message we defined in the protocol buffer file. What returns from `MakeTransaction` is `TransactionResponse`. This function signature matches with the one we defined in the protocol buffer file initially:

```
rpc MakeTransaction(TransactionRequest) returns (TransactionResponse) {}
```

Now, let us write a client. We can write a client (or) server in any programming language, but here we are writing both a client and server in Go for understanding the Go GRPC API. Add a file called `client.go` in the `grpcClient` directory:

```go
package main

import (
  "log"

  pb "github.com/narenaryan/grpc_example/datafiles"
  "golang.org/x/net/context"
  "google.golang.org/grpc"
)

const (
  address = "localhost:50051"
)

func main() {
  // Set up a connection to the server.
  conn, err := grpc.Dial(address, grpc.WithInsecure())
```

```
  if err != nil {
    log.Fatalf("Did not connect: %v", err)
  }
  defer conn.Close()
  c := pb.NewMoneyTransactionClient(conn)

  // Prepare data. Get this from clients like Frontend or App
  from := "1234"
  to := "5678"
  amount := float32(1250.75)

  // Contact the server and print out its response.
  r, err := c.MakeTransaction(context.Background(),
&pb.TransactionRequest{From: from,
    To: to, Amount: amount})
  if err != nil {
    log.Fatalf("Could not transact: %v", err)
  }
  log.Printf("Transaction confirmed: %t", r.Confirmation)
}
```

This client is also using the `grpc` package. It uses an empty context called `context.Background()` to pass to the `MakeTransaction` function. The second argument of the function is the `TransactionRequest` struct:

```
&pb.TransactionRequest{From: from, To: to, Amount: amount}
```

It clearly maps with the theory we discussed in the previous section. Now, let us run it and see the output. Open a new console and run the GRPC server by using the following command:

```
go run $GOPATH/src/github.com/narenaryan/grpc_example/grpcServer/server.go
```

The TCP server starts listening on port `50051`. Now, open one more terminal/shell and start the client program that talks to this server:

```
go run $GOPATH/src/github.com/narenaryan/grpc_example/grpcClient/client.go
```

It prints the output of the successful transaction:

```
2017/07/16 19:13:16 Transaction confirmed: true
```

At the same time, the server logs this message to the console:

```
2017/07/16 19:13:16 Amount: 1250.750000, From A/c:1234, To A/c:5678
```

Here, the client made a single request to the GRPC server and passed details of `From A/c` number, `To A/c` number, and `Amount`. The server picks those details, processes them, and sends a response back saying everything is fine.

 Since I am running code samples on my machine, I have `narenaryan` as the project directory under `github.com`. You can replace it with any other name.

Bidirectional streaming with GRPC

The main advantage of GRPC over traditional HTTP/1.1 is that it uses a single TCP connection for sending and receiving multiple messages between the server and the client. We saw the example of a money transaction before. Another real-world use case is a GPS installed in a taxi. Here, the taxi is the client that sends its geographical points to the server along its route. Finally, the server can calculate the total fare amount depending on the time spent between points and the total distance.

Another such use case is when a server needs to notify the client whenever some processing is performed. This is called a server push model. The server can send a stream of results back when a client asked for them only once. This is different to polling, where the client requests something each and every time. This can be useful when there are a series of time-taking steps that need to be done. The GRPC client can escalate that job to the GRPC server. Then, the server takes its time and relays the message back to the client, which reads them and does something useful. Let us implement this.

This concept is similar to WebSockets, but between any type of platform. Create a project called `serverPush`:

```
mkdir $GOPATH/src/github.com/narenaryan/serverPush
mkdir $GOPATH/src/github.com/narenaryan/serverPush/datafiles
```

Now, write in `datafiles` a protocol buffer that is similar to the previous one:

```
syntax = "proto3";
package datafiles;

message TransactionRequest {
    string from = 1;
    string to = 2;
    float amount = 3;
}
```

```
message TransactionResponse {
  string status = 1;
  int32 step = 2;
  string description = 3;
}

service MoneyTransaction {
    rpc MakeTransaction(TransactionRequest) returns (stream
TransactionResponse) {}
}
```

We have two messages and one service defined in the protocol buffer file. The exciting part is in the service; we are returning a stream instead of a plain response:

```
rpc MakeTransaction(TransactionRequest) returns (stream
TransactionResponse) {}
```

The use case of this project is: *the client sends a money transfer request to the server, the server does a few tasks and sends those step details as a stream of responses back to the server*. Now, let us compile that proto file:

```
protoc -I datafiles/ datafiles/transaction.proto --
go_out=plugins=grpc:datafiles
```

This creates a new file called `transaction.pb.go` in the `datafiles` directory. We use the definitions in this file in our server and client programs, which we will create shortly. Now, let us write the GRPC server code. This code is a bit different compared to the previous example because of the introduction of streams:

```
mkdir $GOPATH/src/github.com/narenaryan/serverPush/grpcServer
vi $GOPATH/src/github.com/narenaryan/serverPush/grpcServer/server.go
```

Now, add this program to the file:

```
package main

import (
  "fmt"
  "log"
  "net"
  "time"

  pb "github.com/narenaryan/serverPush/datafiles"
  "google.golang.org/grpc"
  "google.golang.org/grpc/reflection"
)
```

```
const (
  port     = ":50051"
  noOfSteps = 3
)

// server is used to create MoneyTransactionServer.
type server struct{}

// MakeTransaction implements MoneyTransactionServer.MakeTransaction
func (s *server) MakeTransaction(in *pb.TransactionRequest, stream
pb.MoneyTransaction_MakeTransactionServer) error {
  log.Printf("Got request for money transfer....")
  log.Printf("Amount: $%f, From A/c:%s, To A/c:%s", in.Amount, in.From,
in.To)
  // Send streams here
  for i := 0; i < noOfSteps; i++ {
    // Simulating I/O or Computation process using sleep........
    // Usually this will be saving money transfer details in DB or
    // talk to the third party API
    time.Sleep(time.Second * 2)
    // Once task is done, send the successful message back to the client
    if err := stream.Send(&pb.TransactionResponse{Status: "good",
      Step:        int32(i),
      Description: fmt.Sprintf("Description of step %d", int32(i))}); err
!= nil {
      log.Fatalf("%v.Send(%v) = %v", stream, "status", err)
    }
  }
  log.Printf("Successfully transfered amount $%v from %v to %v", in.Amount,
in.From, in.To)
  return nil
}

func main() {
  lis, err := net.Listen("tcp", port)
  if err != nil {
    log.Fatalf("Failed to listen: %v", err)
  }
  // Create a new GRPC Server
  s := grpc.NewServer()
  // Register it with Proto service
  pb.RegisterMoneyTransactionServer(s, &server{})
  // Register reflection service on gRPC server.
  reflection.Register(s)
  if err := s.Serve(lis); err != nil {
    log.Fatalf("Failed to serve: %v", err)
  }
}
```

`MakeTransaction` is the function that interests us. It takes a request and a stream as its arguments. In the function, we are looping through the number of steps (here, it is three), and performing the computation. The server is simulating the mock I/O or computation using the `time.Sleep` function:

```
stream.Send()
```

This function sends a stream response from the server to the client. Now, let us compose the client program. This is also a bit different to the basic GRPC client that we saw in the preceding code. Create a new directory for the client program:

```
mkdir $GOPATH/src/github.com/narenaryan/serverPush/grpcClient
vi $GOPATH/src/github.com/narenaryan/serverPush/grpcClient/cilent.go
```

Now, start writing the client logic in that file:

```go
package main

import (
  "io"
  "log"

  pb "github.com/narenaryan/serverPush/datafiles"
  "golang.org/x/net/context"
  "google.golang.org/grpc"
)

const (
  address = "localhost:50051"
)

// ReceiveStream listens to the stream contents and use them
func ReceiveStream(client pb.MoneyTransactionClient, request
*pb.TransactionRequest) {
  log.Println("Started listening to the server stream!")
  stream, err := client.MakeTransaction(context.Background(), request)
  if err != nil {
    log.Fatalf("%v.MakeTransaction(_) = _, %v", client, err)
  }
  // Listen to the stream of messages
  for {
    response, err := stream.Recv()
    if err == io.EOF {
      // If there are no more messages, get out of loop
      break
    }
    if err != nil {
```

```
      log.Fatalf("%v.MakeTransaction(_) = _, %v", client, err)
    }
    log.Printf("Status: %v, Operation: %v", response.Status,
response.Description)
  }
}

func main() {
  // Set up a connection to the server.
  conn, err := grpc.Dial(address, grpc.WithInsecure())
  if err != nil {
    log.Fatalf("Did not connect: %v", err)
  }
  defer conn.Close()
  client := pb.NewMoneyTransactionClient(conn)

  // Prepare data. Get this from clients like Front-end or Android App
  from := "1234"
  to := "5678"
  amount := float32(1250.75)

  // Contact the server and print out its response.
  ReceiveStream(client, &pb.TransactionRequest{From: from,
    To: to, Amount: amount})
}
```

Here, `ReceiveStream` is the custom function we wrote for the sake of sending a request and receiving a stream of messages. It takes two arguments: `MoneyTransactionClient` and `TransactionRequest`. It uses the first argument to create a stream and starts listening to it. Whenever the server exhausts all the messages, the client will stop listening and terminate. Then, an `io.EOF` error will be returned if the client tries to receive messages. We are logging the responses collected from the GRPC server. The second argument, `TransactionRequest`, is used to send the request to the server for the first time. Now, running it will make it more clear to us. On terminal one, run the GRPC server:

```
go run $GOPATH/src/github.com/narenaryan/serverPush/grpcServer/server.go
```

It will keep on listening for incoming requests. Now, run the client on the second terminal to see the action:

```
go run $GOPATH/src/github.com/narenaryan/serverPush/grpcClient/client.go
```

This outputs the following to the console:

```
2017/07/16 15:08:15 Started listening to the server stream!
2017/07/16 15:08:17 Status: good, Operation: Description of step 0
2017/07/16 15:08:19 Status: good, Operation: Description of step 1
2017/07/16 15:08:21 Status: good, Operation: Description of step 2
```

At the same time, the server also logs its own messages on terminal one:

```
2017/07/16 15:08:15 Got request for money Transfer....
2017/07/16 15:08:15 Amount: $1250.750000, From A/c:1234, To A/c:5678
2017/07/16 15:08:21 Successfully transfered amount $1250.75 from 1234 to
5678
```

This process happens in sync with the server. The client stays alive until all the streaming messages are sent back. The server can handle any number of clients at a given time. Every client request is considered as an individual entity. This is an example of the server sending a stream of responses. There are other cases that can also be implemented with protocol buffers and GRPC:

- The client sending streamed requests to get one final response from the server
- The client and server are both sending streamed requests and responses at the same time

The official GRPC team has provided a nice example of routing a taxi on GitHub. You can take a look at it to learn more about the functioning of bidirectional streams at
`https://github.com/grpc/grpc-go/tree/master/examples/route_guide.`

Summary

In this chapter, we started our journey by understanding the basics of protocol buffers. Then, we came across the protocol buffers language, which has many types such as scalar, enumeration, and repeated types. We saw a few analogies between JSON and protocol buffers. We learned why protocol buffers are more memory efficient than the plain JSON data format. We defined a sample protocol buffer by simulating a network interface. The `message` keyword is used to define messages in a protocol buffer.

Next, we installed the `protoc` compiler to compile our files written in the protocol buffer language. Then, we saw how to compile a `.proto` file to generate a `.go` file. This Go file has all the structs and interfaces for the main program to consume. Next, we wrote a protocol buffer for an address book and person. We saw how to use `grpc.Marshal` to serialize Go structs into binary, transmittable data. We also found out that the conversion from protocol buffer to JSON and vice versa is very easily achievable in Go.

We then moved to GRPC, an RPC technology from Google using protocol buffers. We saw the benefits of HTTP/2 and GRPC. We then defined a GRPC service and data in the form of protocol buffers. Next, we implemented a GRPC server and GRPC in respect to the file generated from `.proto`.

GRPC provides a bidirectional and multiplexed transport mechanism. This means that it can use a single TCP connection for all its message transmissions. We implemented one such scenario where the client sends a message to a server and the server replies back with a stream of messages.

7
Working with PostgreSQL, JSON, and Go

In this chapter, we are going to look at SQL in the big picture. In previous chapters, we discussed SQLite3, which is a small database for quick prototyping. But when it comes to a production grade application, people prefer MySQL or PostgreSQL. Both are well proven in the web application space. First, we will discuss the internals of PostgreSQL and then move on to writing database models in Go. We will then try to realize the URL shortening service with a solid example.

In this chapter, we will cover the following topics:

- Introduction to the PostgreSQL database
- Installing PostgreSQL and creating users and databases
- Learning about `pq`, a database driver in Go
- Implementing a URL shortening service with PostgreSQL and a Base62 algorithm
- Exploring the JSON store in PostgreSQL
- Introducing `gorm`, a powerful ORM for Go
- Implementation of an e-commerce REST API

Getting the code

You can get the code samples for this chapter at `https://github.com/narenaryan/gorestful/tree/master/chapter7`. In the previous chapter, we discussed protocol buffers and GRPC. But here, we come back to the REST API with JSON and see how PostgreSQL supplements JSON.

Installing the PostgreSQL database

PostgreSQL is an open-source database that can be installed on multiple platforms. On Ubuntu, it can be installed using the following commands:

To add the repo to the package list:

```
sudo sh -c 'echo "deb http://apt.postgresql.org/pub/repos/apt/ `lsb_release
-cs`-pgdg main" >> /etc/apt/sources.list.d/pgdg.list'

wget -q https://www.postgresql.org/media/keys/ACCC4CF8.asc -O - | sudo apt-
key add -
```

To update the package list:

```
sudo apt-get update
apt-get install postgresql postgresql-contrib
```

This installs the database on an Ubuntu machine and starts a server on port 5432. Now, in order to enter the database shell, use these commands. PostgreSQL creates a default user called postgres to log in. Take a look at the following command:

```
sudo su - postgres
```

Now the user has access to the database. Launch the PostgreSQL shell using the psql command:

```
psql
```

This shows that PostgreSQL follows a different approach for entering into the shell compared to other similar databases such as MySQL or SQLite3. On Windows, the installation is done by clicking the binary installer file. It is a GUI-based installation where the port and password for superuser should be supplied. Once the database is installed, we can check that using the **pgAdmin3** tool. The macOS X setup is similar to Ubuntu, except the installation is done through Homebrew. Take a look at the following command:

```
brew install postgresql
```

And then make the database server run even when the system is rebooted by using the following command:

```
pg_ctl -D /usr/local/var/postgres start && brew services start postgresql
```

Now, the PostgreSQL server starts running and is available to store and retrieve data on macOS X.

Adding users and databases in PostgreSQL

Now, we should know how to create a new user and database. For this, we are going to use Ubuntu/Mac as the general example. We do this in a shell called the `psql` shell. We can see all available commands in `psql` using the `\?` command. In order to enter into `psql`, first change to the `postgres` user. On Ubuntu, you can do that using the following command:

```
sudo su postgres
```

Now, it turns us into a user called `postgres`. Then, launch the `psql` shell using the `psql` command. If you type `\?` in there, you see the output of all available commands:

```
Informational
  (options: S = show system objects, + = additional detail)
  \d[S+]                  list tables, views, and sequences
  \d[S+]    NAME          describe table, view, sequence, or index
  \da[S]    [PATTERN]     list aggregates
  \dA[+]    [PATTERN]     list access methods
  \db[+]    [PATTERN]     list tablespaces
  \dc[S+]   [PATTERN]     list conversions
  \dC[+]    [PATTERN]     list casts
  \dd[S]    [PATTERN]     show object descriptions not displayed elsewhere
  \ddp      [PATTERN]     list default privileges
  \dD[S+]   [PATTERN]     list domains
  \det[+]   [PATTERN]     list foreign tables
  \des[+]   [PATTERN]     list foreign servers
  \deu[+]   [PATTERN]     list user mappings
```

To list all available users and their privileges, you will find a command in the `Informational` section of shell help, that is:

```
\du - List roles
```

A role is an access permission given to a user. The default role in that list is `postgres`:

```
postgres=# \du
                   List of roles
 Role name |                         Attributes                         | Member of
-----------+------------------------------------------------------------+--
-----------
 postgres  | Superuser, Create role, Create DB, Replication, Bypass RLS | {}
```

The preceding command lists roles (users) with their attributes (what a role is allowed to do) and other options. For adding a new user, we just type this `psql` command:

```
CREATE ROLE naren with LOGIN PASSWORD 'passme123';
```

This creates a new user with the name `naren` and the password `passme123`. Now, give the permission to the user to create databases and further roles, using the following command:

```
ALTER USER naren CREATEDB, CREATEROLE;
```

In order to delete a user, just use the `DROP` command in the same context:

```
DROP ROLE naren;
```

> Don't try to change the password for the default `postgres` user. It is intended to be a sudo account, and should not be kept as a normal user. Instead, create a role and give require permissions for it.

Now we know how to create a role. Let us see a few more CRUD commands, which are really SQL commands that we see in other relational databases too. Take a look at the following table:

Action	SQL command
Create database	`CREATE DATABASE mydb;`

Create table	`CREATE TABLE products (`
	`    product_no integer,`
	`    name text,`
	`    price numeric`
	`);`

Insert into table	`INSERT INTO products VALUES (1, 'Rice', 5.99);`
Update table	`UPDATE products SET price = 10 WHERE price = 5.99;`
Delete from table	`DELETE FROM products WHERE price = 5.99;`

Now, let us see from Go how we can talk to PostgreSQL and try to do the preceding operations using a simple example.

pq, a pure PostgreSQL database driver for Go

In the previous chapters when we dealt with SQLite3, we used an external library called `go-sqlite3`. In the same way, a database driver library is available to bridge both Go and PostgreSQL. That library is called `pq`. We can install that library using the command:

```
go get github.com/lib/pq
```

After getting this library, we need to use it in a similar way to SQLite3. The API will be in line to the `database/sql` package of Go. In order to create a new table, we should initialize the DB. To create a new database, just type this command from the `psql` shell, as shown in the following command; it is a one-time thing:

```
CREATE DATABASE mydb;
```

Now, we will write a small code illustration that explains the usage of the `pq` driver. Create a directory called `models` in your `$GOPATH`. Here, my `GOPATH` is `/home/naren/workspace/`. Similar to all the previous examples in the former chapters, we will create our packages and application sources in the `src/` directory:

```
mkdir github.com/narenaryan/src/models
```

Now, add a file called `web_urls.go`. This file is going to have the table creation logic:

```go
package models

import (
        "database/sql"
        "log"
        _ "github.com/lib/pq"
)


func InitDB() (*sql.DB, error) {
        var err error
        db, err := sql.Open("postgres",
"postgres://naren:passme123@localhost/mydb?sslmode=disable")
        if err != nil {
                return nil, err
        } else {
                // Create model for our URL service
                stmt, err := db.Prepare("CREATE TABLE WEB_URL(ID SERIAL
PRIMARY KEY, URL TEXT NOT NULL);")
```

```
if err != nil {
        log.Println(err)
        return nil, err
}
res, err := stmt.Exec()
log.Println(res)
if err != nil {
        log.Println(err)
        return nil, err
}
return db, nil
        }
}
```

We are importing the `pq` library here. We are using the `sql.Open` function to start a new database connection pool. If you observe the connection string, it consists of multiple parts. Take a look at the following diagram:

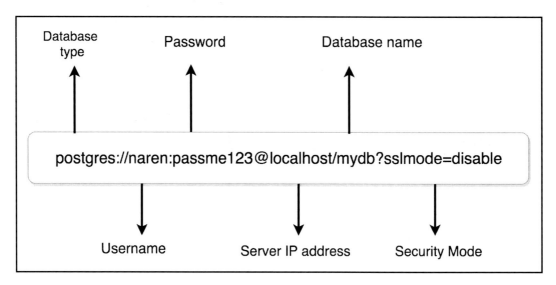

The connection string should consist of the database type, the `username:password` pair, the database server IP, and the sslmode settings. We are then creating a table called `web_url`. All the error handlers are there to specify if something goes wrong. The `InitDB` function returns the database connection object to whatever program imports the function. Let us write the main program to use this package:

```
package main

import (
```

```
        "log"
        "github.com/narenaryan/models"
)

func main() {
  db, err := models.InitDB()
  if err != nil {
    log.Println(db)
  }
}
```

This program imports the `models` package and uses the `InitDB` function from it. We are just printing that database connection, which will be an address. If you run the program, you will see the address of the object got printed:

go run main.go

This creates a `web_url` table in the `mydb` database. We can crosscheck that by entering into the `psql` shell and typing:

\c mydb \dt

It connects the user to `mydb` database and lists all available tables, as shown in the following code snippet:

```
You are now connected to database "mydb" as user "postgres".
 List of relations
 Schema | Name | Type | Owner
--------+---------+-------+-------
 public | web_url | table | naren
(1 row)
```

In PostgreSQL, the AUTO INCREMENT type needs to be replaced by SERIAL while providing a schema for a table creation.

Implementing a URL shortening service using Postgres and pq

Let us write the URL shortening service to explain all the concepts we discussed in the preceding section. Before that, let us design a package that implements the Base62 algorithm with encoding/decoding functions. The URL shortening technique needs the Base62 algorithm to convert a long URL to short, and vice versa. We then write a solid example to show how this encoding works. Create a directory called `base62` in the GOPATH:

```
mkdir $GOPATH/src/github.com/narenaryan/base62
```

Now, add a file called `encodeutils.go`, which houses our encode and decode functions.

Defining the Base62 algorithm

We saw how the Base62 algorithm works in the previous chapters. Here is the solid implementation of that algorithm. The logic is purely mathematical and can be found everywhere on the web. Take a look at the following code:

```
package base62

import (
    "math"
    "strings"
)

const base =
"0123456789abcdefghijklmnopqrstuvwxyzABCDEFGHIJKLMNOPQRSTUVWXYZ"
const b = 62

// Function encodes the given database ID to a base62 string
func ToBase62(num int) string{
    r := num % b
    res := string(base[r])
    div := num / b
    q := int(math.Floor(float64(div)))

    for q != 0 {
        r = q % b
        temp := q / b
        q = int(math.Floor(float64(temp)))
        res = string(base[int(r)]) + res
    }
```

```
        return string(res)
    }

    // Function decodes a given base62 string to datbase ID
    func ToBase10(str string) int{
        res := 0
        for _, r := range str {
            res = (b * res) + strings.Index(base, string(r))
        }
        return res
    }
```

In the preceding program, we defined two functions called `ToBase62` and `ToBase10`. The first one takes an integer and generates a `base62` string, and the latter one reverses the effect; that is, it takes a `base62` string and gives the original number. In order to illustrate this, let us create a simple program that uses both the functions to show encoding/decoding:

vi $GOPATH/src/github.com/narenaryan/usebase62.go

Add the following content to it:

```
package main

import (
        "log"
        base62 "github.com/narenaryan/base62"
)

func main() {
  x := 100
  base62String := base62.ToBase62(x)
  log.Println(base62String)
  normalNumber := base62.ToBase10(base62String)
  log.Println(normalNumber)
}
```

Here, we are using the functions from the `base62` package and trying to see the output. If we run this program (from `$GOPATH/src/github.com/narenaryan`) using the following command:

go run usebase62.go

It prints:

```
2017/08/07 23:00:05 1C
2017/08/07 23:00:05 100
```

`base62` encoding of `100` is `1C`. This is because the index 100 shrunk to `1C` in our `base62` logic:

```
const base =
"0123456789abcdefghijklmnopqrstuvwxyzABCDEFGHIJKLMNOPQRSTUVWXYZ"
```

The original number will be used to map the character in this base string. Then, the number is divided by 62 to find out the next characters. The beauty of this algorithm is creating a unique, shorter string for every given number. We use this technique to pass a database ID into the `ToBase62` algorithm and get a shorter string out. Whenever a URL shortening request comes to our server, it should perform the following steps:

1. Store the URL in the database and get the ID of that record inserted.
2. Pass this ID to the client as the API response.
3. Whenever a client loads the shortened URL, it hits our API server.
4. The API server then converts the short URL back to the database ID and fetches the record from the original URL.
5. Finally, the client can use this URL to redirect to the original site.

We are going to write a Go project here that implements the preceding steps. Let us compose the program. I am creating a directory structure for our project. We take files from the preceding illustrations for handling encoding/decoding `base62` and also for database logic. The directory structure looks like this:

```
urlshortener
├──── main.go
├──── models
│      └──── models.go
└──── utils
       └──── encodeutils.go

2 directories, 3 files
```

Copy this directory to `$GOPATH/src/github.com/narenaryan`. Once again, a small caution. Replace `narenaryan` with your username. Copy `encodeutils.go` and `models.go` from the preceding examples. Then, start writing the main program:

```go
package main

import (
    "database/sql"
    "encoding/json"
    "io/ioutil"
    "log"
    "net/http"
    "time"

    "github.com/gorilla/mux"
    _ "github.com/lib/pq"
    "github.com/narenaryan/urlshortener/models"
    base62 "github.com/narenaryan/urlshortener/utils"
)

// DB stores the database session imformation. Needs to be initialized once
type DBClient struct {
  db *sql.DB
}

// Model the record struct
type Record struct {
  ID  int    `json:"id"`
  URL string `json:"url"`
}

// GetOriginalURL fetches the original URL for the given encoded(short) string
func (driver *DBClient) GetOriginalURL(w http.ResponseWriter, r *http.Request) {
  var url string
  vars := mux.Vars(r)
  // Get ID from base62 string
  id := base62.ToBase10(vars["encoded_string"])
  err := driver.db.QueryRow("SELECT url FROM web_url WHERE id = $1", id).Scan(&url)
  // Handle response details
  if err != nil {
    w.Write([]byte(err.Error()))
  } else {
    w.WriteHeader(http.StatusOK)
    w.Header().Set("Content-Type", "application/json")
```

```go
    responseMap := map[string]interface{}{"url": url}
    response, _ := json.Marshal(responseMap)
    w.Write(response)
  }
}

// GenerateShortURL adds URL to DB and gives back shortened string
func (driver *DBClient) GenerateShortURL(w http.ResponseWriter, r
*http.Request) {
  var id int
  var record Record
  postBody, _ := ioutil.ReadAll(r.Body)
  json.Unmarshal(postBody, &record)
  err := driver.db.QueryRow("INSERT INTO web_url(url) VALUES($1) RETURNING
id", record.URL).Scan(&id)
  responseMap := map[string]interface{}{"encoded_string":
base62.ToBase62(id)}
  if err != nil {
    w.Write([]byte(err.Error()))
  } else {
    w.Header().Set("Content-Type", "application/json")
    response, _ := json.Marshal(responseMap)
    w.Write(response)
  }
}

func main() {
  db, err := models.InitDB()
  if err != nil {
    panic(err)
  }
  dbclient := &DBClient{db: db}
  if err != nil {
    panic(err)
  }
  defer db.Close()
  // Create a new router
  r := mux.NewRouter()
  // Attach an elegant path with handler
  r.HandleFunc("/v1/short/{encoded_string:[a-zA-Z0-9]*}",
dbclient.GetOriginalURL).Methods("GET")
  r.HandleFunc("/v1/short", dbclient.GenerateShortURL).Methods("POST")
  srv := &http.Server{
    Handler: r,
    Addr:    "127.0.0.1:8000",
    // Good practice: enforce timeouts for servers you create!
    WriteTimeout: 15 * time.Second,
    ReadTimeout:  15 * time.Second,
```

```
  }
  log.Fatal(srv.ListenAndServe())
}
```

First, we imported the `postgres` library and other necessary libraries. We imported our database session from the models. Next, we imported our encode/decode base62 algorithms to implement our logic:

```
// DB stores the database session imformation. Needs to be initialized once
type DBClient struct {
  db *sql.DB
}

// Model the record struct
type Record struct {
  ID  int    `json:"id"`
  URL string `json:"url"`
}
```

The `DBClient` is needed in order to pass the database driver between various functions. The record is the structure that resembles the record that gets inserted into the database. We defined two functions in our code called `GenerateShortURL` and `GetOriginalURL` for adding the URL to the database and then fetching it back from DB respectively. As we already explained the internal technique of URL shortening, the client that is using this service will get the necessary response back. Let us run the program and see the output before jumping into further details:

go run $GOPATH/src/github.com/narenaryan/urlshortener/main.go

If your `$GOPATH/bin` is already in the system `PATH` variable, we can first install the binary and run it like this:

go install github.com/narenaryan/urlshortener/main.go

And then just the program name:

urlshortener

It is a best practice to install the binary because it is available systemwide. But for smaller programs, we can run `main.go` by visiting the directory of the program.

Now it runs the HTTP server and starts collecting requests for the URL shortening service. Open the console and type these CURL commands:

```
curl -X POST \
  http://localhost:8000/v1/short \
  -H 'cache-control: no-cache' \
  -H 'content-type: application/json' \
  -d '{
  "url":
"https://www.forbes.com/forbes/welcome/?toURL=https://www.forbes.com/sites/
karstenstrauss/2017/04/20/the-highest-paying-jobs-in-tech-
in-2017/&refURL=https://www.google.co.in/&referrer=https://www.google.co.in
/"
}'
```

It returns the shortened string:

```
{
    "encoded_string": "1"
}
```

The encoded string is just `"1"`. Base62 algorithms start allocating shorter strings starting from one to a combination of alphanumeric letters. Now, if we need to retrieve the original URL we can perform a `GET` request:

```
curl -X GET \
  http://localhost:8000/v1/short/1 \
  -H 'cache-control: no-cache' \
```

It returns the following JSON:

```
{
"url":"https://www.forbes.com/forbes/welcome/?toURL=https://www.forbes.com/
sites/karstenstrauss/2017/04/20/the-highest-paying-jobs-in-tech-
in-2017/\u0026refURL=https://www.google.co.in/\u0026referrer=https://www.go
ogle.co.in/"}
```

So, the service can use this result to redirect the user to the original URL (site). Here, the generated string doesn't depend on the length of the URL because only the database ID is the criteria for encoding.

The RETURNING keyword needs to be added to the INSERT SQL command in PostgreSQL to fetch the last inserted database ID. This is not the case with MySQL or SQLite3 INSERT INTO web_url( ) VALUES($1) RETURNING id, record.URL. This DB query returns the last inserted record's ID. If we drop that RETURNING keyword, the query returns nothing.

Exploring the JSON store in PostgreSQL

PostgreSQL >9.2 has a prominent feature 9.2" dbid="254735" called the JSON store. PostgreSQL introduced a new data type for storing the JSON data. PostgreSQL allows users to insert a `jsonb` field type, which holds the JSON string. It is quite useful in modeling the real-world data that has to be more flexible with the structure. PostgreSQL draws the best of both worlds by allowing us to store JSON strings as well as relational types.

In this section, we will try to realize a few of the JSON models that we defined for e-commerce websites in the previous chapters. But here, we will use the JSON field to store and retrieve items in PostgreSQL. For accessing PostgreSQL's JSON store, the normal `pq` library is very tedious. So, in order to handle that better, we can use an **Object Relational Mapper (ORM)** called **GORM**.

GORM, a powerful ORM for Go

This ORM has the API for all operations that can be done in the `database/sql` package. We can install GORM using this command:

```
go get -u github.com/jinzhu/gorm
```

For full documentation about this ORM, visit, `http://jinzhu.me/gorm/`. Let us write a program that implements user and order type JSON models. A user can place an order. We will use the models that we defined in the previous chapter. We can create a new directory called `jsonstore` in `$GOPATH/src/github.com/narenaryan` and create a new directory for our model in it:

```
mkdir jsonstore
mkdir jsonstore/models
touch jsonstore/models/models.go
```

Now, edit the `models.go` file to this:

```go
package models

import (
  "github.com/jinzhu/gorm"
  _ "github.com/lib/pq"
)

type User struct {
  gorm.Model
  Orders []Order
  Data string `sql:"type:JSONB NOT NULL DEFAULT '{}'::JSONB" json:"-"`
}

type Order struct {
  gorm.Model
  User User
  Data string `sql:"type:JSONB NOT NULL DEFAULT '{}'::JSONB"`
}

// GORM creates tables with plural names. Use this to suppress it
func (User) TableName() string {
  return "user"
}

func (Order) TableName() string {
  return "order"
}


func InitDB() (*gorm.DB, error) {
  var err error
  db, err := gorm.Open("postgres",
"postgres://naren:passme123@localhost/mydb?sslmode=disable")
  if err != nil {
    return nil, err
  } else {
    /*
    // The below AutoMigrate is equivalent to this
    if !db.HasTable("user") {
      db.CreateTable(&User{})
    }

    if !db.HasTable("order") {
      db.CreateTable(&Order{})
    }
```

```
    */
    db.AutoMigrate(&User{}, &Order{})
    return db, nil
  }
}
```

This looks similar to the model we defined earlier in this chapter. Here, a lot of things are new for us. Every model (table) we create should be represented as a struct in GORM. That is the reason we created two structs, `User` and `Order`. The first line should be `gorm.Model`. The other fields are the fields of the table. By default, an incrementing ID will be created. In the previous model for the URL shortener, we manually checked the existence of table before operating on it. But here, there is a function:

```
    db.AutoMigrate(&User{}, &Order{})
```

This function creates the tables for structs passed as parameters. It makes sure that if tables exist already, it skips creation. If you observe carefully, we added a function for those structs, `TableName`. By default, all the table names that GORM creates are plural names (`users` is created for `User`). In order to force it to create the given names, we need to override that function. One more interesting thing is, in the structs, we used a field called `Data`. That is of type:

```
    `sql:"type:JSONB NOT NULL DEFAULT '{}'::JSONB" json:"-"`
```

Yes, it is a `jsonb` type string. We, for now, add its type as `string`. PostgreSQL and GORM takes care of handling it. We are then returning the database connection to whoever imports the `models` package.

Implementing the e-commerce REST API

Before jumping in, let us design the API specification table, which shows the REST API signatures for various URL endpoints. Refer to the following table:

Endpoint	Method	Description
`/v1/user/id`	GET	Get a user using ID
`/v1/user`	POST	Create a new user
`/v1/user?first_name=NAME`	GET	Get all users by the given first name
`/v1/order/id`	GET	Get an order with the given ID
`/v1/order`	POST	Create a new order

Now we come to the main program; let us add one more file to our `jsonstore` project. In this program, we will try to implement the first three endpoints. We suggest the implementation of the remaining two endpoints as an assignment for the reader. Take a look at the following command:

touch jsonstore/main.go

The program structure follows the same style as all the programs we have seen until now. We use Gorilla Mux as our HTTP router and import the database driver into our program:

```go
package main

import (
  "encoding/json"
  "io/ioutil"
  "log"
  "net/http"
  "time"

  "github.com/gorilla/mux"
  "github.com/jinzhu/gorm"
    _ "github.com/lib/pq"
  "github.com/narenaryan/jsonstore/models"
)

// DB stores the database session imformation. Needs to be initialized once
type DBClient struct {
  db *gorm.DB
}

// UserResponse is the response to be send back for User
type UserResponse struct {
  User models.User `json:"user"`
  Data interface{} `json:"data"`
}

// GetUsersByFirstName fetches the original URL for the given
encoded(short) string
func (driver *DBClient) GetUsersByFirstName(w http.ResponseWriter, r
*http.Request) {
  var users []models.User
  name := r.FormValue("first_name")
  // Handle response details
  var query = "select * from \"user\" where data->>'first_name'=?"
  driver.db.Raw(query, name).Scan(&users)
  w.WriteHeader(http.StatusOK)
  w.Header().Set("Content-Type", "application/json")
```

```go
    //responseMap := map[string]interface{}{"url": ""}
    respJSON, _ := json.Marshal(users)
    w.Write(respJSON)
}

// GetUser fetches the original URL for the given encoded(short) string
func (driver *DBClient) GetUser(w http.ResponseWriter, r *http.Request) {
    var user = models.User{}
    vars := mux.Vars(r)
    // Handle response details
    driver.db.First(&user, vars["id"])
    var userData interface{}
    // Unmarshal JSON string to interface
    json.Unmarshal([]byte(user.Data), &userData)
    var response = UserResponse{User: user, Data: userData}
    w.WriteHeader(http.StatusOK)
    w.Header().Set("Content-Type", "application/json")
    //responseMap := map[string]interface{}{"url": ""}
    respJSON, _ := json.Marshal(response)
    w.Write(respJSON)
}

// PostUser adds URL to DB and gives back shortened string
func (driver *DBClient) PostUser(w http.ResponseWriter, r *http.Request) {
    var user = models.User{}
    postBody, _ := ioutil.ReadAll(r.Body)
    user.Data = string(postBody)
    driver.db.Save(&user)
    responseMap := map[string]interface{}{"id": user.ID}
    var err string = ""
    if err != "" {
        w.Write([]byte("yes"))
    } else {
        w.Header().Set("Content-Type", "application/json")
        response, _ := json.Marshal(responseMap)
        w.Write(response)
    }
}

func main() {
    db, err := models.InitDB()
    if err != nil {
        panic(err)
    }
    dbclient := &DBClient{db: db}
    if err != nil {
        panic(err)
    }
```

```
      defer db.Close()
      // Create a new router
      r := mux.NewRouter()
      // Attach an elegant path with handler
      r.HandleFunc("/v1/user/{id:[a-zA-Z0-9]*}",
  dbclient.GetUser).Methods("GET")
      r.HandleFunc("/v1/user", dbclient.PostUser).Methods("POST")
      r.HandleFunc("/v1/user", dbclient.GetUsersByFirstName).Methods("GET")
      srv := &http.Server{
        Handler: r,
        Addr:    "127.0.0.1:8000",
        // Good practice: enforce timeouts for servers you create!
        WriteTimeout: 15 * time.Second,
        ReadTimeout:  15 * time.Second,
      }
      log.Fatal(srv.ListenAndServe())
  }
```

There are three important aspects here:

- We replaced the traditional driver with the GORM driver
- Used GORM functions for CRUD operations
- We inserted JSON into PostgreSQL and retrieved results in the JSON field

Let us explain all the elements in detail. First, we imported all the necessary packages. The interesting ones are:

```
"github.com/jinzhu/gorm"
 _ "github.com/lib/pq"
"github.com/narenaryan/jsonstore/models"
```

GORM internally uses the `database/sql` package to some extent. We imported models from the package we created in the preceding code. Next, we created three functions, implementing the first three API specifications. They are `GetUsersByFirstName`,60;`GetUser`, and `PostUser`. Each function is inheriting the database driver and passed as the handler functions for the URL endpoints in the `main` function:

```
      r.HandleFunc("/v1/user/{id:[a-zA-Z0-9]*}",
  dbclient.GetUser).Methods("GET")
      r.HandleFunc("/v1/user", dbclient.PostUser).Methods("POST")
      r.HandleFunc("/v1/user", dbclient.GetUsersByFirstName).Methods("GET")
```

Now, if we enter the first function, which is simple, these statements will grab our attention:

```
  driver.db.First(&user, vars["id"])
```

The preceding statement tells the DB to fetch the first record from the database with the given second parameter `ID`. It fills the data returned to the `user` struct. We are using `UserResponse` instead of the `User` struct in `GetUser` because `User` consists of the data field, which is a string. But, in order to return complete and proper JSON to the client, we need to convert the data into a proper struct and then marshal it:

```
// UserResponse is the response to be send back for User
type UserResponse struct {
  User models.User `json:"user"`
  Data interface{} `json:"data"`
}
```

Here, we are creating an empty interface that can hold any JSON data. When we call the first function using the driver, the user struct has a data field, which is a string. We need to convert that string to a struct and then send it along with other details in `UserResponse`. Now let us see this in action. Run the program using the following command:

```
go run jsonstore/main.go
```

And make a few CURL commands to see the API response:

Create user:

```
curl -X POST \
  http://localhost:8000/v1/user \
  -H 'cache-control: no-cache' \
  -H 'content-type: application/json' \
  -d '{
    "username": "naren",
    "email_address": "narenarya@live.com",
    "first_name": "Naren",
    "last_name": "Arya"
}'
```

It returns the inserted record in the DB:

```
{
  "id": 1
}
```

Now, if we `GET` the details of the inserted record:

```
curl -X GET http://localhost:8000/v1/user/1
```

It returns all the details about the user:

```
{"user":{"ID":1,"CreatedAt":"2017-08-27T11:55:02.974371+05:30","UpdatedAt":
"2017-08-27T11:55:02.974371+05:30","DeletedAt":null,"Orders":null},"data":{
"email_address":"narenarya@live.com","first_name":"Naren","last_name":"Arya
","username":"naren"}}
```

Insert one more record for checking the first name API:

```
curl -X POST \
  http://localhost:8000/v1/user \
  -H 'cache-control: no-cache' \
  -H 'content-type: application/json' \
  -d '{
    "username": "nareny",
    "email_address": "naren.yellavula@gmail.com",
    "first_name": "Naren",
    "last_name": "Yellavula"
}'
```

This inserts our second record. Let us test our third API, `GetUsersByFirstName`:

```
curl -X GET 'http://localhost:8000/v1/user?first_name=Naren'
```

This returns all the users with the given first name:

```
[{"ID":1,"CreatedAt":"2017-08-27T11:55:02.974371+05:30","UpdatedAt":"2017-0
8-27T11:55:02.974371+05:30","DeletedAt":null,"Orders":null},{"ID":2,"Create
dAt":"2017-08-27T11:59:41.84332+05:30","UpdatedAt":"2017-08-27T11:59:41.843
32+05:30","DeletedAt":null,"Orders":null}]
```

The core motto of this project is to show how JSON can be stored and retrieved out of PostgreSQL. The special thing here is that we queried on the JSON field instead of the normal fields in the `User` table.

Remember, PostgreSQL stores its users in a table called user. If you want to create a new user table, create it using `"user"` (double quotes). Even while retrieving use double quotes. Otherwise, the DB will fetch internal user details:

```
SELECT * FROM "user"; // Correct way
SELECT * FROM user; // Wrong way. It fetches database
users
```

This concludes our journey through PostgreSQL. There is a lot more to explore in Postgres. It brings the best of both worlds by allowing us to store relational as well as JSON data in the same table.

Summary

In this chapter, we started our journey by installing PostgreSQL. We introduced PostgreSQL formally and tried to see all possible SQL queries for CRUD operations. We then saw how to add users and databases in PostgreSQL. We then installed and explained `pq`, a Postgres driver for the Go language. We explained how the driver API performs raw SQL queries.

Then came the implementation part of the URL shortening service; that REST service takes the original URL and returns a shortened string. It also takes the shortened URL and returns the original URL. We wrote a sample program to illustrate the Base62 algorithm that powers our service. We leveraged this algorithm in our service next and created a REST API.

GORM is a well-known object-relational mapper for Go. Using an ORM, one can easily manage the database operations. GORM provides a few useful functions, such as `AutoMigrate` (create a table if one doesn't exist), for writing intuitive Go code over the traditional `database/sql` driver.

PostgreSQL also allows JSON storage (called the JSON store) past version 9.2. It allows developers to get the benefits of relational databases with the JSON format. We can create indexes on JSON fields, query on JSON fields, and so on. We implemented a REST API for the e-commerce model we defined in the previous chapters using GORM. PostgreSQL is a well established, open-source relational database that can suffice our enterprise needs. The driver support for Go is exceptional with `pq` and `gorm`.

8
Building a REST API Client in Go and Unit Testing

In this chapter, we are going to discuss how Go client applications work in depth. We will explore `grequests`, a Python request-style library that allows us to make API calls from the Go code. Then, we will write a client software that uses the GitHub API. In the course of this, we will try to learn about two wonderful libraries called `cli` and `cobra`. After these fundamentals, we will try to use the knowledge to write an API testing tool on the command line. Then we will see about Redis, an in-memory database which we can use to cache the API responses to backup the data.

In this chapter, we will cover the following topics:

- What is a client software?</li>
- Basics for writing a command-line tool in Go
- Introducing `grequests`, a Python request-like library in Go
- Inspecting GitHub REST API from a Go client
- Creating an API client in Go
- Caching an API for later use
- Creating a unit testing tool for the API

Getting the code

You can get the code samples for this chapter at the GitHub repository link `https://github.com/narenaryan/gorestful/tree/master/chapter8`. This chapter has examples that are a combination of single programs, as well as projects. So, copy the respective directory to your `GOPATH` to run the code samples properly. For the last example of unit testing the URL shortening service, the tests are available at `https://github.com/narenaryan/gorestful/tree/master/chapter7`.

Plan for building a REST API client

Till now, we mainly focused on writing server-side REST APIs. Basically, they are server programs. In a few cases, such as GRPC, we also needed the client. But a true client program takes input from the user and executes some logic. For working with a Go client, we should know the `flag` library in Go. Before that, we should know how to make requests for an API from a Go program. In previous chapters, we assumed the clients could be CURL, Browser, Postman, and so on. But how do we consume an API from Go?

Command-line tools are equally important as web user interfaces to perform system tasks. In **business-to-business** (**B2B**) companies, the software is packaged as a single binary instead of having multiple different pieces. As a Go developer, you should know how to achieve the goal of writing apps for the command line. Then, that knowledge can be leveraged to create REST API-related web clients very easily and elegantly.

Basics for writing a command-line tool in Go

Go provides a basic library called `flag`. It refers to the command-line flags. Since it is already packed with the Go distribution, there is no need to install anything externally. We can see the absolute basics of writing the command-line tool. The `flag` package has multiple functions, such as `Int` and `String`, to handle the input given as command-line flags. Suppose we need to take a name from the user and print it back to the console. We use the `flag.String` method, as shown in the following code snippet:

```
import "flag"
var name = flag.String("name", "No Namer", "your wonderful name")
```

Let us write a short program for clear details. Create a file called `flagExample.go` in your `$GOPATH/src/github.com/narenaryan` and add the following content:

```
package main

import (
  "flag"
  "log"
  )

var name = flag.String("name", "stranger", "your wonderful name")

func main(){
  flag.Parse()
  log.Printf("Hello %s, Welcome to the command line world", *name)
}
```

In this program, we are creating a flag called `name`. It is a string pointer. `flag.String` takes three arguments. The first one is the name of the argument. The second and third are the default values of that flag and the help text, respectively. We then ask the program to parse all flag pointers. When we run the program, it actually fills the values from the command line to the respective variables. To access the value of a pointer, we use `*`. First build and then run the program using the following commands:

go build flagExample.go

This creates a binary in the same directory. We can run it like a normal executable:

`./flagExample`

It gives the following output:

Hello stranger, Welcome to the command line world

Here, we didn't give any argument called `name`. But we have assigned the default value to that argument. Go's flag takes the default value and proceeds further. Now, in order to see what options are available and to know about them, ask for help:

./flagExample -h

```
Output
========
Usage of ./flagExample:
  -name string
        your wonderful name (default "stranger")
```

This is the reason we passed help text as the third argument for the flag command.

 In Windows, `flagExample.exe` will be generated when we build a `.go` file. After that, from the command line, we can run the program by calling the program name.

Now try to add the argument, and it prints the given name:

```
./flagExample -name Albert
(or)
./flagExample -name=Albert
```

Both work fine as arguments which give the output:

```
Hello Albert, Welcome to the command line world
```

If we need multiple parameters to collect, we need to modify the preceding program to this:

```go
package main

import (
  "flag"
  "log"
  )

var name = flag.String("name", "stranger", "your wonderful name")
var age = flag.Int("age", 0, "your graceful age")

func main(){
  flag.Parse()
  log.Printf("Hello %s (%d years), Welcome to the command line world",
*name, *age)
}
```

This takes two parameters, just one more addition of a different type. If we run this, we see the output:

```
./flagExampleMultiParam -name Albert -age 24

Hello Albert (24 years), Welcome to the command line world
```

This is exactly what we expected. Instead of using the pointers, we can bind a variable to the parsed output. This binding is done through the `init()` function, which will run in a Go program irrespective of whether main exists or not:

```
var name String
func init() {
    flag.IntVar(&name, "name", "stranger", "your wonderful name")
}
```

In this way, the value will directly come and sit in the variable. The complete rewrite of the preceding program using the `init()` function is shown in the following code snippet:

```
initFlag.go:
package main

import (
  "flag"
  "log"
  )

var name string
var age int

func init() {
    flag.StringVar(&name, "name", "stranger", "your wonderful name")
    flag.IntVar(&age, "age", 0, "your graceful age")
}

func main(){
    flag.Parse()
    log.Printf("Hello %s (%d years), Welcome to the command line world",
name, age)
}
```

The output is exactly the same as the preceding program. Here, instead of using pointers, we are able to load data directly into our variables.

In Go, execution starts from the main program. But a Go program can have any number of `init` functions. If a package has an `init` function in it, that will be executed.

This `flag` library is very basic to work. But in order to write advanced client applications, we need to take the help of the library. In the next section, we look at such a library.

CLI – a library for building beautiful clients

This is the next step for a Go developer after playing with the `flag` package. It provides an intuitive API for creating command-line applications with ease. It allows us to collect arguments and flags. It could be quite handy for designing complex applications. To install the package, use the following command:

```
go get github.com/urfave/cli
```

After that, let us write a program that does exactly the same job as the preceding programs:

`cli/cliBasic.go`:

```go
package main

import (
  "log"
  "os"

  "github.com/urfave/cli"
)

func main() {
  // Create new app
  app := cli.NewApp()

  // add flags with three arguments
  app.Flags = []cli.Flag {
    cli.StringFlag{
      Name: "name",
      Value: "stranger",
      Usage: "your wonderful name",
    },
    cli.IntFlag{
      Name: "age",
      Value: 0,
      Usage: "your graceful age",
```

```
        },
    }
    // This function parses and brings data in cli.Context struct
    app.Action = func(c *cli.Context) error {
        // c.String, c.Int looks for value of given flag
        log.Printf("Hello %s (%d years), Welcome to the command line world",
c.String("name"), c.Int("age"))
        return nil
    }
    // Pass os.Args to cli app to parse content
    app.Run(os.Args)
}
```

This is lengthier than the one before, but it is more expressive. We created a new app using the `cli.NewApp` function. It creates a new struct. We need to attach a few parameters to this struct. They are the `Flags` struct and the `Action` function. The `Flags` struct is a list that defines all possible flags for this application. The structure of `Flag` from **GoDoc** (`https://godoc.org/github.com/urfave/cli#Flag`) is:

```
type Flag interface {
    fmt.Stringer
    // Apply Flag settings to the given flag set
    Apply(*flag.FlagSet)
    GetName() string
}
```

The inbuilt structs, such as `StringFlag` and `IntFlag`, implement this `Flag` interface. `Name`, `Value`, and `Usage` are straightforward. They are similar to the ones used in the `flag` package. The `Action` function takes the argument `cli.Context`. That context object holds all of the information about flags and command-line arguments. We can use them and apply logic to them. The `c.String`, `c.Int`, and other functions are used to look up the flag variables. For example, in the preceding program, `c.String("name")` fetches a flag variable whose name is `name`. This program runs the same as the previous programs:

```
go build cli/cliBasic.go
```

Collecting command-line arguments in CLI

There is a difference between command-line arguments and flags. The following diagram clearly specifies the distinction between them:

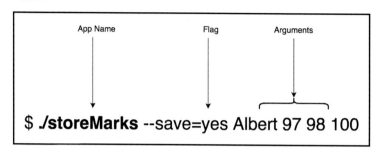

Suppose that we have a command-line app called storeMarks for saving the marks of a student. It has a flag (called `save`) to specify whether details should be pushed to DB or not. The arguments that are given are the name and actual marks of the student. We already saw how to collect the flag values in the program. In this section, we will see how to collect program arguments in an expressive way.

For collecting arguments, we use the `c.Args` function, where `c` is the `cli` context of the `Action` function. Create a directory called `cli` and add a new program, `cli/storeMarks.go`:

```go
package main

import (
    "github.com/urfave/cli"
    "log"
    "os"
)

func main() {
    app := cli.NewApp()
    // define flags
    app.Flags = []cli.Flag{
        cli.StringFlag{
            Name:  "save",
            Value: "no",
            Usage: "Should save to database (yes/no)",
        },
    }

    app.Version = "1.0"
```

```
// define action
app.Action = func(c *cli.Context) error {
  var args []string
  if c.NArg() > 0 {
    // Fetch arguments in a array
    args = c.Args()
    personName := args[0]
    marks := args[1:len(args)]
    log.Println("Person: ", personName)
    log.Println("marks", marks)
  }
  // check the flag value
  if c.String("save") == "no" {
    log.Println("Skipping saving to the database")
  } else {
    // Add database logic here
    log.Println("Saving to the database", args)
  }
  return nil
}

app.Run(os.Args)
}
```

`c.Args` keeps all of the arguments we entered. Since we know the order of the arguments, we deduced that the first argument is the name and the remaining values are the marks. We are checking a flag called `save` to save those details in a database or not (we don't have database logic here, for simplicity). `app.Version` sets the version of the tool. All other things remain the same as the last program.

Let us run this program and see the output:

```
go build cli/storeMarks.go
```

Run the program:

```
./storeMarks --save=yes Albert 89 85 97

2017/09/02 21:02:02 Person: Albert
2017/09/02 21:02:02 marks [89 85 97]
2017/09/02 21:02:02 Saving to the database [Albert 89 85 97]
```

If we don't give any flag, the default is `save=no`:

```
./storeMarks Albert 89 85 97

2017/09/02 21:02:59 Person: Albert
2017/09/02 21:02:59 marks [89 85 97]
2017/09/02 21:02:59 Skipping saving to the database
```

Everything looks good till now. But how can the tool display help when a user needs it? The `cli` library already creates a nice help section for the given app. Type any of these commands and help text will be autogenerated:

- `./storeMarks -h` (or)
- `./storeMarks -help` (or)
- `./storeMarks --help`
- `./storeMarks help`

A nice help section appears, like this one showing version details and available flags (global options), commands, and arguments:

```
NAME:
    storeMarks - A new cli application

USAGE:
    storeMarks [global options] command [command options] [arguments...]

VERSION:
    1.0

COMMANDS:
      help, h Shows a list of commands or help for one command

GLOBAL OPTIONS:
    --save value Should save to database (yes/no) (default: "no")
    --help, -h show help
    --version, -v print the version
```

This actually makes building client applications easier. It is way faster and more intuitive than the internal `flag` package.

> Command-line tools are binaries that are generated after building the program. They need to be run with the options. It is like any system program and not related to Go compiler anymore

grequests – a REST API package for Go

The developers who worked on Python know about the `Requests` library. It is a clean, short library that is not included in the standard library of Python. The Go package `grequests` is inspired by that library. It provides a simple set of functions, using which we can make API requests such as `GET`, `POST`, `PUT`, and `DELETE` from our Go code. Using `grequests` allows us to encapsulate the inbuilt HTTP request and response. To install the `grequests` package for your Go, run the following command:

```
go get -u github.com/levigross/grequests
```

Now, see this basic program illustrating the use of the `grequests` library to make a `GET` request to a REST API. Create a directory called `grequests` in your Go source directory and add a file called `basicRequest.go`, as shown in the following code snippet:

```go
package main

import (
    "github.com/levigross/grequests"
    "log"
)

func main() {
    resp, err := grequests.Get("http://httpbin.org/get", nil)
    // You can modify the request by passing an optional RequestOptions
struct
    if err != nil {
        log.Fatalln("Unable to make request: ", err)
    }
    log.Println(resp.String())
}
```

The `grequests` package has methods for performing all REST actions. The preceding program uses the `Get` function from the package. It takes two function arguments. The first one is the URL of the API, and the second one is the request parameters object. Since we are not passing any request parameters, the second argument is `nil` here. `resp` is returned from the request, and it has a function called `String()` that returns the response body:

```
go run grequests/basicRequest.go
```

The output is the JSON response returned by the `httpbin`:

```
{
    "args": {},
    "headers": {
```

```
        "Accept-Encoding": "gzip",
        "Connection": "close",
        "Host": "httpbin.org",
        "User-Agent": "GRequests/0.10"
    },
    "origin": "116.75.82.9",
    "url": "http://httpbin.org/get"
}
```

API overview of grequests

The most important thing to explore in `grequests` is not the HTTP functions, but the `RequestOptions` struct. It is a very big struct that holds various kinds of information on the type of API method. If the REST method is `GET`, the `RequestOptions` holds the `Params` property. If the method is a `POST`, the struct will have a `Data` property. Whenever we make a request, we get a response back. Let us see the structure of the response. From the official documentation, the response looks like this:

```
type Response struct {
    Ok bool
    Error error
    RawResponse *http.Response
    StatusCode int
    Header http.Header
}
```

The `Ok` property of response holds the information about whether a request is successful or not. If something went wrong, an error will be filled into the `Error` property. `RawResponse` is the Go HTTP response that will be used by other functions of the `grequests` response. `StatusCode` and `Header` store the status codes of the response and header details, respectively. There are a few functions in `Response` that are useful:

- JSON
- XML
- String
- Bytes

These can be called on the obtained response by passing an empty interface to the functions—`grequests/jsonRequest.go`:

```go
package main

import (
  "github.com/levigross/grequests"
  "log"
)

func main() {
  resp, err := grequests.Get("http://httpbin.org/get", nil)
  // You can modify the request by passing an optional RequestOptions
struct
  if err != nil {
    log.Fatalln("Unable to make request: ", err)
  }
  var returnData map[string]interface{}
  resp.JSON(&returnData)
  log.Println(returnData)

}
```

We declared an interface to hold the JSON values. We then populated the `returnData` (empty interface) using the `resp.JSON` function. This program prints the map instead of plain JSON.

Getting comfortable with the GitHub REST API

GitHub provides a well-written REST API to consume from the users. It opens up the data about users, repositories, repository statistics, and so on, to the clients through the API. The current stable version is v3. The API documentation can be found at `https://developer.github.com/v3/`. The root endpoint of the API is:

```
curl https://api.github.com
```

The other API will be added to this base API. Now let us see how to make a few queries and get data related to various elements. For the unauthenticated user, the rate limit is 60/hour, whereas for clients who are passing `client_id` (which one can get from the GitHub account), it is 5,000/hour.

If you have a GitHub account (if not, it is recommended you create one), you can find access tokens in the **Your Profile | Personal Access Tokens** area or by visiting `https://github.com/settings/tokens`. Create a new access token using the **Generate new token** button. It asks for various permissions for types for the resource. Tick all of them. A new string will be generated. Save it to some private place. The token we have generated can be used to access the GitHub API (for longer rate limits).

The next step is to save that access token to an environment variable, `GITHUB_TOKEN`. To do that, open your `~/.profile` or `~/.bashrc` file and add this as the last line:

```
export GITHUB_TOKEN=YOUR_GITHUB_ACCESS_TOKEN
```

`YOUR_GITHUB_ACCESS_TOKEN` is what was generated and saved previously from the GitHub account. Let us create a program for fetching all the repos of the given user. Create a new directory called `githubAPI` and create a program file called `getRepos.go`:

```go
package main

import (
  "github.com/levigross/grequests"
  "log"
  "os"
)

var GITHUB_TOKEN = os.Getenv("GITHUB_TOKEN")
var requestOptions = &grequests.RequestOptions{Auth: []string{GITHUB_TOKEN,
"x-oauth-basic"}}

type Repo struct {
  ID int `json:"id"`
  Name string `json:"name"`
  FullName string  `json:"full_name"`
  Forks int `json:"forks"`
  Private bool `json:"private"`
}

func getStats(url string) *grequests.Response{
  resp, err := grequests.Get(url, requestOptions)
  // You can modify the request by passing an optional RequestOptions
struct
  if err != nil {
    log.Fatalln("Unable to make request: ", err)
  }
  return resp
}
```

```
func main() {
  var repos []Repo
  var repoUrl = "https://api.github.com/users/torvalds/repos"
  resp := getStats(repoUrl)
  resp.JSON(&repos)
  log.Println(repos)
}
```

Run the program, and you will see the following output:

```
2017/09/03 17:59:41 [{79171906 libdc-for-dirk torvalds/libdc-for-dirk 10
false} {2325298 linux torvalds/linux 18274 false} {78665021 subsurface-for-
dirk torvalds/subsurface-for-dirk 16 false} {86106493 test-tlb
torvalds/test-tlb 25 false}]
```

The printed output is not JSON but a list of the Go Repo `struct`. The preceding program illustrates how we can query the GitHub API and load that data into our custom struct:

```
type Repo struct {
  ID int `json:"id"`
  Name string `json:"name"`
  FullName string  `json:"full_name"`
  Forks int `json:"forks"`
  Private bool `json:"private"`
}
```

This is the struct we used for saving the details of our repository. The JSON returned has many fields, but for simplicity's sake, we are just plucking a few important fields out of them:

```
var GITHUB_TOKEN = os.Getenv("GITHUB_TOKEN")
var requestOptions = &grequests.RequestOptions{Auth: []string{GITHUB_TOKEN,
"x-oauth-basic"}}
```

In the first line, we are fetching the environment variable called `GITHUB_TOKEN`. The `os.Getenv` function returns the value of an environment variable by the given name. For GitHub to assume the origin of the `GET` request, we should set the authentication. For that, pass an argument to the `RequestOptions` struct. That argument should be a list of the username and password.

Creating a CLI tool as an API client for the GitHub REST API

After looking at this example, we are able to easily access the GitHub API from our Go client. We can combine both of the techniques we learned in this chapter so far to come up with a command-line tool that consumes the GitHub API. Let us create a new command-line application which:

- Provides options to get repo details by username
- Uploads any file to GitHub gists (text snippets) with a given description
- Authenticates using a personal access token

 Gists are snippets provided by GitHub to store text content. For more details, visit `https://gist.github.com`.

Create a program called `gitTool.go` in the `githubAPI` directory. This will be the logic for the preceding program specification:

```go
package main

import (
  "encoding/json"
  "fmt"
  "github.com/levigross/grequests"
  "github.com/urfave/cli"
  "io/ioutil"
  "log"
  "os"
)

var GITHUB_TOKEN = os.Getenv("GITHUB_TOKEN")
var requestOptions = &grequests.RequestOptions{Auth: []string{GITHUB_TOKEN,
"x-oauth-basic"}}

// Struct for holding response of repositories fetch API
type Repo struct {
  ID       int    `json:"id"`
  Name     string `json:"name"`
  FullName string `json:"full_name"`
  Forks    int    `json:"forks"`
  Private  bool   `json:"private"`
}
```

```go
// Structs for modelling JSON body in create Gist
type File struct {
  Content string `json:"content"`
}

type Gist struct {
  Description string           `json:"description"`
  Public      bool             `json:"public"`
  Files       map[string]File  `json:"files"`
}

// Fetches the repos for the given Github users
func getStats(url string) *grequests.Response {
  resp, err := grequests.Get(url, requestOptions)
  // you can modify the request by passing an optional RequestOptions
struct
  if err != nil {
    log.Fatalln("Unable to make request: ", err)
  }
  return resp
}

// Reads the files provided and creates Gist on github
func createGist(url string, args []string) *grequests.Response {
  // get first teo arguments
  description := args[0]
  // remaining arguments are file names with path
  var fileContents = make(map[string]File)
  for i := 1; i < len(args); i++ {
    dat, err := ioutil.ReadFile(args[i])
    if err != nil {
      log.Println("Please check the filenames. Absolute path (or) same
directory are allowed")
      return nil
    }
    var file File
    file.Content = string(dat)
    fileContents[args[i]] = file
  }
  var gist = Gist{Description: description, Public: true, Files:
fileContents}
  var postBody, _ = json.Marshal(gist)
  var requestOptions_copy = requestOptions
  // Add data to JSON field
  requestOptions_copy.JSON = string(postBody)
  // make a Post request to Github
  resp, err := grequests.Post(url, requestOptions_copy)
  if err != nil {
```

```
      log.Println("Create request failed for Github API")
   }
   return resp
}

func main() {
   app := cli.NewApp()
   // define command for our client
   app.Commands = []cli.Command{
      {
        Name:     "fetch",
        Aliases: []string{"f"},
        Usage:    "Fetch the repo details with user. [Usage]: goTool fetch
user",
        Action: func(c *cli.Context) error {
           if c.NArg() > 0 {
              // Github API Logic
              var repos []Repo
              user := c.Args()[0]
              var repoUrl =
fmt.Sprintf("https://api.github.com/users/%s/repos", user)
              resp := getStats(repoUrl)
              resp.JSON(&repos)
              log.Println(repos)
           } else {
              log.Println("Please give a username. See -h to see help")
           }
           return nil
        },
      },
      {
        Name:     "create",
        Aliases: []string{"c"},
        Usage:    "Creates a gist from the given text. [Usage]: goTool name
'description' sample.txt",
        Action: func(c *cli.Context) error {
           if c.NArg() > 1 {
              // Github API Logic
              args := c.Args()
              var postUrl = "https://api.github.com/gists"
              resp := createGist(postUrl, args)
              log.Println(resp.String())
           } else {
              log.Println("Please give sufficient arguments. See -h to see
help")
           }
           return nil
        },
```

```
      },
   }

   app.Version = "1.0"
   app.Run(os.Args)
}
```

Let us run the program before jumping into the details of explanation. It makes clear how we implemented the program:

```
go build githubAPI/gitTool.go
```

It creates a binary in the same directory. If you type ./gitTool -h, it shows:

```
NAME:
   gitTool - A new cli application

USAGE:
   gitTool [global options] command [command options] [arguments...]

VERSION:
   1.0

COMMANDS:
      fetch, f Fetch the repo details with user. [Usage]: goTool fetch user
      create, c Creates a gist from the given text. [Usage]: goTool name
'description' sample.txt
      help, h Shows a list of commands or help for one command

GLOBAL OPTIONS:
   --help, -h show help
   --version, -v print the version
```

If you see the help commands, there are two commands, fetch and create. fetch fetches the repositories of a given user and create creates a gist with the supplied files. Let us create two sample files in the same directory of the program to test the create command:

```
echo 'I am sample1 file text' > githubAPI/sample1.txt
echo 'I am sample2 file text' > githubAPI/sample2.txt
```

Run the tool with the first command:

```
./gitTool f torvalds
```

It returns all repositories belonging to the great Linus Torvalds. The log message prints the struct that filled:

```
[{79171906 libdc-for-dirk torvalds/libdc-for-dirk 10 false} {2325298 linux
torvalds/linux 18310 false} {78665021 subsurface-for-dirk
torvalds/subsurface-for-dirk 16 false} {86106493 test-tlb torvalds/test-tlb
25 false}]
```

Now, let us check the second command. It creates the `gist` with the given description and a set of files as arguments:

```
./gitTool c "I am doing well" sample1.txt sample2.txt
```

It returns the JSON details about the created `gist`. It is a very lengthy JSON, so the output is skipped here. Then, open your `gist.github.com` account, and you will see the created `gist`:

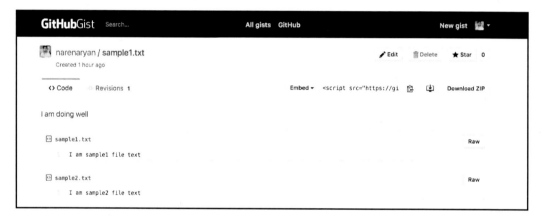

Now, coming to the explanation, we first imported `grequests` for making API calls and `cli` for building the command-line tool. Other imports are necessary to read files, log to the console, and encode JSON. We then defined three structs: `Repo`, `File`, and `Gist`. The GitHub `gists` API expects a JSON data to create:

```json
{
  "description": "the description for this gist",
  "public": true,
  "files": {
    "file1.txt": {
      "content": "String file contents"
    }
  }
}
```

The `grequests POST` request takes `requestOptions` that have `Data` as the field. But the signature of it is `Map[string]string`, which is not enough to create the preceding structure. `grequests` allows us to pass a JSON string with any structure to the API. We created structs so that data can be filled and marshalled into proper JSON to `POST` request get succeeded.

Then, we created two functions: `getStats` (that returns all repo details of a given user) and `createGist` (that creates new `gist` files with the given description and filenames). The second function is more interesting. We are passing a URL for the `POST` request, description, and `file_names` in the form of an `args` array. Then, we are iterating on each and every file and getting the content. We are adjusting our structs so that the final JSON body for the `POST` request will be in the same structure. Finally, we are making a `POST` request with the `requestOptions` that have our JSON.

In this way, we combined both of the libraries to build an API client which can do any task. The beauty of Go is that we can ship the final binary in which both the logic for the command-line tool and the REST API calling the logic were buried.

> For any Go program to read and understand soon, follow the `main` function and then step into the other functions. In that way, we can come across imported packages and their APIs.

Using Redis for caching the API data

Redis is an in-memory database that can store key/value pairs. It best suits the caching use cases where we need to store information temporarily but for huge traffic. For example, sites such as BBC and The Guardian show the latest articles on the dashboard. Their traffic is so high, if documents (articles) are fetched from the database, they need to maintain a huge cluster of databases all the time. Since the given set of articles does not change (at least for hours), the BBC can maintain a cache which saves the articles. When the first customer visits the page, a copy is pulled from the DB, sent to the browser, and placed in the Redis cache. The next time a customer appears, the BBC application server reads content from Redis instead of going to the DB. Since Redis runs in primary memory, latency is reduced. The customer sees his page loaded in a flash. The benchmarks on the web can tell more about how efficiently a site can optimize its contents.

What if data is no longer relevant in Redis? (For example, the BBC updated its top stories.) Redis provides a way to expire the `keys:values` stored in it. We can run a scheduler that updates the Redis whenever the expiration time has passed.

Similarly, we can cache the third-party API responses for the given request (`GET`). We need to do it, because third-party systems like GitHub are giving us a rate limit (telling us to be conservative). For a given `GET URL`, we can store the `URL` as key and the `Response` as value. Whenever the same request is given within the next time (before key expiration), just pull the response out of Redis instead of hitting the GitHub servers. This method is applicable to our REST API, too. The most frequent and unchanged REST API can be cached in order to reduce the load on the primary database.

There is a wonderful library available for Go to talk to Redis. It is `https://github.com/go-redis/redis`. It is a well-known library which many developers suggest you use. The following diagram illustrates the concept very well:

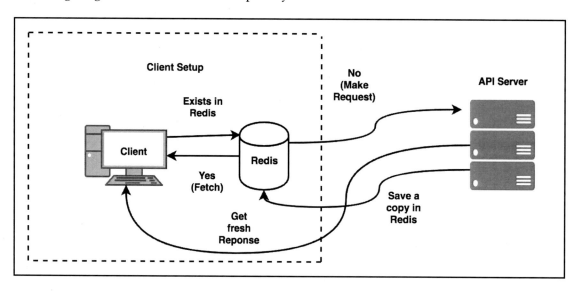

One caveat to note here is the expiration of the API. A real-time API should not be cached because of its dynamic nature. Caching brings performance optimization to our plate, as well as a few headaches. Be careful while caching. There are many better practices available globally. Please go through them to get an understanding of various architectures.

Creating a unit testing tool for our URL shortening service

In the previous chapter, we created a URL shortening service. The structure of the URL shortener project we worked on previously looks like this:

```
├──── main.go
├──── models
│     └──── models.go
└──── utils
      └──── encodeutils.go

2 directories, 3 files
```

In the `main.go` file, we created two API handlers: one for `GET` and one for `POST`. We are going to write the unit tests for both of those handlers. Add a file called `main_test.go` in the root directory of the project:

touch main_test.go

In order to test our API, we need to test our API handlers:

```go
package main_test

import (
  "testing"
  "net/http"
)

func TestGetOriginalURL(t *testing.T) {
  // make a dummy reques
  response, err := http.Get("http://localhost:8000/v1/short/1")

    if http.StatusOK != response.StatusCode {
      t.Errorf("Expected response code %d. Got %d\n", http.StatusOK,
response.StatusCode)
    }

    if err != nil {
      t.Errorf("Encountered an error:", err)
    }
}
```

There is a testing package in Go named `testing`. It allows us to create a few assertions and lets us make a pass or fail test. We are testing the API `TestGetOriginalURL` by making a simple HTTP request. Make sure you have at least one record inserted in the database. The advanced testing topics of database connections are out of the scope of this book. We can test this using Go test command inside the project directory.

Summary

We started our chapter with understanding client software: how a software client works and how we can create a few. We saw the basics of writing a command-line application. CLI is a third-party package that enables us to create beautiful command-line applications. After installing it, we saw how to collect command-line arguments through the tool. We also explored commands and flags in our CLI application. Next, we looked into `grequests`, a package similar to Python requests to make API requests from Go code. We saw how to make `GET`, `POST`, and so on, requests from the client programs.

We next explored the GitHub API on how to fetch details like repositories. With the knowledge of both concepts, we developed a client that lists the repositories for a given user and also creates a `gist` (a text file on GitHub). We introduced Redis architecture on how caching could help handle rate-limited API. Finally, we wrote a unit test for the URL shortening service we created in the previous chapter.

9
Scaling Our REST API Using Microservices

Building a REST API is easy in terms of concepts. But scaling them to accept huge traffic is a challenge. Till now, we looked into the details of creating REST API structures and sample REST APIs. In this chapter, we are going to explore the Go Kit, a wonderful, idiomatic Go package for building microservices. This is the microservices age, where startups are turning into enterprises in no time. The microservice architecture allows companies to quickly iterate in parallel. We will start by defining microservices and then move on to Go Kit by creating REST-style microservices.

In this chapter, we will cover the following topics:

- The difference between monolith and microservices
- The need for microservices
- Introducing Go Kit, a microservice toolkit in Go
- Creating a REST API with Go Kit
- Adding logging to the API
- Adding instrumentation to the API

Getting the code

You can get the code samples for this chapter at the GitHub repository link `https://github.com/narenaryan/gorestful/tree/master/chapter9`. In the previous chapter, we discussed Go API clients. Here, we come back to the REST API with microservice architecture.

What are microservices?

What are microservices? This is the question the enterprise world is asking the computing world. Because of the bigger teams, the companies are ready to embrace microservices for breaking down tasks. Microservice architecture replaces the traditional monolith with granular services that talk to each other with some kind of agreement.

Microservices bring the following benefits to the plate:

- If the team is big, people can work on chunks of applications
- Adaptability is easy for the new developers
- Adopting best practices, such as **Continuous Integration (CI)** and **Continuous Delivery (CD)**
- Easily replaceable software with loosely coupled architecture

In a monolith application (traditional application), a single huge server serves the incoming requests by multiplexing the computing power. It is good because we have everything, such as an application server, database, and other things, in a single place. It also has disadvantages. When a piece of software breaks, everything breaks. Also, developers need to set up an entire application to develop a small piece.

The disadvantage list of a monolithic application could be:

- Tightly coupled architecture
- Single point of failure
- Velocity of adding new features and components
- Fragmentation of work is limited to teams
- Continuous deployment is very tough because an entire application needs to be pushed

Looking at the monolith application, the entire stack is treated as a single entity. If the database fails, the app fails. If a bug in the code crashes the software application, the entire connectivity with clients goes down. This actually led to the emergence of microservices.

Let us take a scenario. A company run by Bob uses the traditional **Service Oriented Architecture** (**SOA**), where developers work around the clock to add new features. If there is a release, people need to test the code overall for every small component. The project moves from development to testing when all changes are done. Another company on the next street, run by Alice, uses the microservices architecture. All software developers in Alice's company work on individual services, that get tested by a continuous build pipeline that notifies things pretty quickly. The developers talk with each other's REST/RPC APIs to add new features. They can easily shift their stack from one technology to another, as compared to Bob's developers. This example shows that Alice's company's flexibility and velocity is greater than Bob's.

Microservices also create a platform that allows us to use containers (docker, and so on). In microservices, orchestration and service discovery are very important to track the loosely coupled elements. A tool such as Kubernetes is used to manage the docker containers. Generally, it is a good practice to have a docker container for a microservice. Service discovery is the automatic detection of an IP address and other details on the fly. This removes the potential threat of hardcoding the stuff that is needed for microservices to consult each other.

Monolith versus microservices

Industry experts suggest starting a software application as a monolith and then breaking it down into microservices in the long run. This actually helps us focus on the application delivery, instead of studying the microservices patterns. Once the product is stabilized, then developers should find a way to loosely couple functionalities. Take a look at the following diagram:

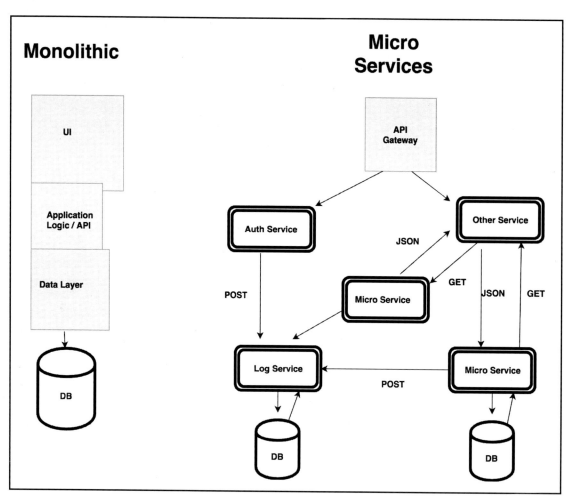

This diagram depicts the structure of monolith and microservice architectures. A monolith has everything wrapped in the form of an onion. It is called a tightly coupled system. In contrast, microservices are individual, easy to replace and modify. Each microservice can talk to each other through various transport mechanisms, such as HTTP and RPC. The format could be either JSON or Protocol Buffers.

Go Kit, a package for building microservices

In the enterprise world, people know about Netflix's Eureka and Spring Boot from the Java community. In Go, a package that tries to reach that level of implementation is obviously **Go kit**. It is a toolkit for building microservices.

It has a Go style of adding services, which makes us feel good. It comes with a procedure for adding the microservices. In the upcoming sections, we will see how to create a microservice with the steps defined by Go Kit. It mainly consists of many layers. There are three layers where request and response flow in Go Kit:

- **Transport layer**: This takes care of transferring data from one service to another
- **Endpoint layer**: This takes care of building endpoints for the given services
- **Service layer**: This is the actual business logic for the API handlers

Install Go Kit using this command:

```
go get github.com/go-kit/kit
```

Let us lay down the plan for our first microservice. We all know the encryption of messages. A message string can be encrypted using a key that outputs a gibberish message that can be passed over the wire. The recipient decrypts the message and gets back the original string. This process is called encryption in cryptography. We will try to implement this as part of our microservice illustration:

- First, develop logic for encryption
- Then, integrate it with Go Kit

Go comes with packages for encrypting messages. We need to import encrypting algorithms from those packages and use them. As part of the first step, we will write a project that uses an **Advanced Encryption Standard (AES)**.

Create a directory called `encryptString` in your `GOPATH/src/user` directory:

```
mkdir $GOPATH/src/github.com/narenaryan/encryptString
cd $GOPATH/src/github.com/narenaryan/encryptString
```

Now let us add one more in the new directory, called utils. Add two files, `main.go` in the project directory and `utils.go` in the new directory called `utils`. The directory structure looks like this:

```
└── encryptString
    ├── main.go
    └── utils
        └── utils.go
```

Now let us add the logic of encryption in our `utils.go` file. We create two functions, one for encrypting and another for decrypting the messages, as shown in the following code:

```go
package utils
import (
    "crypto/aes"
    "crypto/cipher"
    "encoding/base64"
)
```

The AES algorithm takes the initialization vector. Let us define that first:

```go
// Implements AES encryption algorithm(Rijndael Algorithm)
/* Initialization vector for the AES algorithm
More details visit this link
https://en.wikipedia.org/wiki/Advanced_Encryption_Standard */
var initVector = []byte{35, 46, 57, 24, 85, 35, 24, 74, 87, 35, 88, 98, 66,
32, 14, 05}
```

Now, let us implement the logic for encryption and decryption:

```go
// EncryptString encrypts the string with given key
func EncryptString(key, text string) string {
    block, err := aes.NewCipher([]byte(key))
    if err != nil {
        panic(err)
    }
    plaintext := []byte(text)
    cfb := cipher.NewCFBEncrypter(block, initVector)
    ciphertext := make([]byte, len(plaintext))
    cfb.XORKeyStream(ciphertext, plaintext)
    return base64.StdEncoding.EncodeToString(ciphertext)
}
```

In the `EncryptString` function, we are creating a new cipher block using a key. Then we are passing that block to a cipher block encryptor function. That encryptor takes the block and initialization vector. Then we generate ciphertext (an encrypted message) by doing a `XORKeyStream` on the cipher block. It fills the ciphertext. Then we need to do a Base64 encoding to generate the protected string:

```go
// DecryptString decrypts the encrypted string to original
func DecryptString(key, text string) string {
    block, err := aes.NewCipher([]byte(key))
    if err != nil {
        panic(err)
    }
    ciphertext, _ := base64.StdEncoding.DecodeString(text)
    cfb := cipher.NewCFBEncrypter(block, initVector)
    plaintext := make([]byte, len(ciphertext))
    cfb.XORKeyStream(plaintext, ciphertext)
    return string(plaintext)
}
```

In the `DecryptString` function, decode Base64 encoding and create a cipher block with the key. Pass this cipher block with the initialization vector to `NewCFBEncrypter`. Next, use `XORKeyStream` to load content from cipher text to plain text. Basically, it is a process of swapping the encrypted and decrypted messages in `XORKeyStream`. This finishes the `utils.go` file.

Now let us edit the `main.go` file to leverage the preceding `utils` package:

```go
package main
import (
    "log"
    "github.com/narenaryan/encryptString/utils"
)
// AES keys should be of length 16, 24, 32
func main() {
    key := "111023043350789514532147"
    message := "I am A Message"
    log.Println("Original message: ", message)
    encryptedString := utils.EncryptString(key, message)
    log.Println("Encrypted message: ", encryptedString)
    decryptedString := utils.DecryptString(key, encryptedString)
    log.Println("Decrypted message: ", decryptedString)
}
```

Here, we are importing the encrypting/decrypting functions from the `utils` package and using them to show an example.

If we run this program, we see the following output:

```
go run main.go

Original message: I am A Message
Encrypted message: 8/+JCfTb+ibIjzQtmCo=
Decrypted message: I am A Message
```

It shows how we can use the AES algorithm to encrypt a message and get it back using the same secret key. This algorithm is also called the **Rijndael** (pronounced rain-dahl) algorithm.

Building a REST microservice with Go Kit

With this knowledge, we are ready to build our first microservice that provides the API for encryption/decryption. We use Go Kit and our encryption `utils` to write that microservice. As we discussed in the previous section, a Go-Kit microservice should be built in a step-wise manner. To create a service, we need to design a few things upfront. They are:

- Service implementation
- Endpoints
- Request/response models
- Transport

Sit tight. This terminology seems alien for now. We will be quite comfortable with it soon. Let us create a directory with the following directory structure. Every Go Kit project can be in this project structure. Let us call our project `encryptService`. Create these files in the same tree structure in the `encryptService` directory:

```
├─── helpers
│    ├─── endpoints.go
│    ├─── implementations.go
│    ├─── jsonutils.go
│    └─── models.go
└─── main.go
```

We will go through each and every file and see how things should be built. First, in Go Kit, create the interface that tells all functions our microservice performs. In this case, those functions are `Encrypt` and `Decrypt`. `Encrypt` takes the key and converts the text to a cipher message. `Decrypt` converts the cipher message back to the text using the key. Take a look at the following code:

```
import (
  "context"
)
// EncryptService is a blueprint for our service

type EncryptService interface {
  Encrypt(context.Context, string, string) (string, error)
  Decrypt(context.Context, string, string) (string, error)
}
```

The service needs to implement these functions to satisfy the interface. Next, create models for your services. Models specify what data a service can receive and produce back. Create a `models.go` file in the `helpers` directory of the project:

encryptService/helpers/models.go

```
package helpers

// EncryptRequest strctures request coming from client
type EncryptRequest struct {
  Text string `json:"text"`
  Key  string `json:"key"`
}

// EncryptResponse strctures response going to the client
type EncryptResponse struct {
  Message string `json:"message"`
  Err     string `json:"error"`
}

// DecryptRequest strctures request coming from client
type DecryptRequest struct {
  Message string `json:"message"`
  Key     string `json:"key"`
}

// DecryptResponse strctures response going to the client
type DecryptResponse struct {
  Text string `json:"text"`
  Err  string `json:"error"`
}
```

Since we have two service functions, there are four functions mapped to the request and response. The next step is to create a struct that implements the preceding defined interface, `EncryptService`. So, create that logic in an implementations file in the following path:

```
encryptService/helpers/implementations.go
```

First, let us import all necessary packages. Also, give the package name:

```go
package helpers
import (
    "context"
    "crypto/aes"
    "crypto/cipher"
    "encoding/base64"
    "errors"
)
// EncryptServiceInstance is the implementation of interface for micro
service
type EncryptServiceInstance struct{}
// Implements AES encryption algorithm(Rijndael Algorithm)
/* Initialization vector for the AES algorithm
More details visit this link
https://en.wikipedia.org/wiki/Advanced_Encryption_Standard */
var initVector = []byte{35, 46, 57, 24, 85, 35, 24, 74, 87, 35, 88, 98, 66,
32, 14, 05}
// Encrypt encrypts the string with given key
func (EncryptServiceInstance) Encrypt(_ context.Context, key string, text
string) (string, error) {
    block, err := aes.NewCipher([]byte(key))
    if err != nil {
        panic(err)
    }
    plaintext := []byte(text)
    cfb := cipher.NewCFBEncrypter(block, initVector)
    ciphertext := make([]byte, len(plaintext))
    cfb.XORKeyStream(ciphertext, plaintext)
    return base64.StdEncoding.EncodeToString(ciphertext), nil
}
// Decrypt decrypts the encrypted string to original
func (EncryptServiceInstance) Decrypt(_ context.Context, key string, text
string) (string, error) {
    if key == "" || text == "" {
        return "", errEmpty
    }
    block, err := aes.NewCipher([]byte(key))
    if err != nil {
```

```
            panic(err)
    }
    ciphertext, _ := base64.StdEncoding.DecodeString(text)
    cfb := cipher.NewCFBEncrypter(block, initVector)
    plaintext := make([]byte, len(ciphertext))
    cfb.XORKeyStream(plaintext, ciphertext)
    return string(plaintext), nil
}
var errEmpty = errors.New("Secret Key or Text should not be empty")
```

This is leveraging the same AES encryption we saw in the previous example. In this file, we are creating a struct called `EncyptionServiceInstance` that has two methods, `Encrypt` and `Decrypt`. So it satisfies the preceding interface. Now, how can we link these actual service implementations with service requests and responses? We need to define endpoints for that. So, add the following endpoints to link service requests with service business logic.

 We are using the `Capitalized` function and variable names because in Go, any function or variable that is Capital is exported from that package name. In `main.go`, to use all these functions, we need to export them first. Giving capital names makes them visible to the main program.

Create `endpoints.go` in the `helpers` directory:

```
package helpers
import (
    "context"
    "github.com/go-kit/kit/endpoint"
)
// EncryptService is a blueprint for our service
type EncryptService interface {
    Encrypt(context.Context, string, string) (string, error)
    Decrypt(context.Context, string, string) (string, error)
}
// MakeEncryptEndpoint forms endpoint for request/response of encrypt
function
func MakeEncryptEndpoint(svc EncryptService) endpoint.Endpoint {
    return func(ctx context.Context, request interface{}) (interface{},
error) {
        req := request.(EncryptRequest)
        message, err := svc.Encrypt(ctx, req.Key, req.Text)
        if err != nil {
            return EncryptResponse{message, err.Error()}, nil
        }
        return EncryptResponse{message, ""}, nil
    }
}
```

```
// MakeDecryptEndpoint forms endpoint for request/response of decrypt
function
func MakeDecryptEndpoint(svc EncryptService) endpoint.Endpoint {
    return func(ctx context.Context, request interface{}) (interface{},
error) {
        req := request.(DecryptRequest)
        text, err := svc.Decrypt(ctx, req.Key, req.Message)
        if err != nil {
            return DecryptResponse{text, err.Error()}, nil
        }
        return DecryptResponse{text, ""}, nil
    }
}
```

Here, we are clubbing the previous interface definition code with the endpoints definition code. Endpoints take a service as the argument and return a function. This function, in turn, takes a request and returns a response. These things are the same as what we defined in our models.go file. We check the errors, then return back the struct for a response.

Now, things fit nicely. In the previous REST API examples we worked on, we always tried to unmarshal the JSON string into the Go structs. For a response, we converted the struct back into the JSON string by marshaling. Here, we unmarshal and marshal request and response, respectively. For that, we write one more file for encoding/decoding logic. Let us call that file jsonutils.go and add it in the helpers directory:

```
package helpers
import (
    "context"
    "encoding/json"
    "net/http"
)
// DecodeEncryptRequest fills struct from JSON details of request
func DecodeEncryptRequest(_ context.Context, r *http.Request) (interface{},
error) {
    var request EncryptRequest
    if err := json.NewDecoder(r.Body).Decode(&request); err != nil {
        return nil, err
    }
    return request, nil
}
// DecodeDecryptRequest fills struct from JSON details of request
func DecodeDecryptRequest(_ context.Context, r *http.Request) (interface{},
error) {
    var request DecryptRequest
    if err := json.NewDecoder(r.Body).Decode(&request); err != nil {
        return nil, err
```

```
    }
    return request, nil
}
// EncodeResponse is common for both the reponses from encrypt and decrypt
services
func EncodeResponse(_ context.Context, w http.ResponseWriter, response
interface{}) error {
    return json.NewEncoder(w).Encode(response)
}
```

EncodeResponse is common for marshaling the response of EncyptService and
DecryptService, but while decoding JSON into structs we need two different methods.
We defined them as DecodeEncryptRequest and DecodeDecryptRequest. These
functions use Go's internal JSON package to marshal and unmarshal data.

Now we have all helper files that have the constructs needed to create a microservice. Let us
design the main function that import the existing things and wire microservice to a server:

```
package main
import (
    "log"
    "net/http"
    httptransport "github.com/go-kit/kit/transport/http"
    "github.com/narenaryan/encryptService/helpers"
)
func main() {
    svc := helpers.EncryptServiceInstance{}
    encryptHandler :=
httptransport.NewServer(helpers.MakeEncryptEndpoint(svc),
        helpers.DecodeEncryptRequest,\
        helpers.EncodeResponse)
    decryptHandler :=
httptransport.NewServer(helpers.MakeDecryptEndpoint(svc),
        helpers.DecodeDecryptRequest,
        helpers.EncodeResponse)
    http.Handle("/encrypt", encryptHandler)
    http.Handle("/decrypt", decryptHandler)
    log.Fatal(http.ListenAndServe(":8080", nil))
}
```

We are importing Go Kit's transport/http as `httptransport` to create handlers. A handler attaches the endpoints, JSON decoder, and JSON encoder. Then, using Go's net/http, we are handling the HTTP requests for the given URL endpoint. `httptransport.NewServer` takes a few arguments: an endpoint, the JSON decoder, and the JSON encoder. Where is the logic for the service execution? It lies in the endpoint. An endpoint takes the request model and spits out the response model. Now, let us run this project within the `encryptService` directory:

```
go run main.go
```

We can make curl POST requests to check the output:

```
curl -XPOST -d'{"key":"111023043350789514532147", "text": "I am A
Message"}' localhost:8080/encrypt

{"message":"8/+JCfTb+ibIjzQtmCo=","error":""}
```

We provided the key and message to the microservice. It returned the cipher message back. It means the service encrypted the text. Make one more request to decrypt the message by passing the same key along with the cipher message:

```
curl -XPOST -d'{"key":"111023043350789514532147", "message":
"8/+JCfTb+ibIjzQtmCo="}' localhost:8080/decrypt

{"text":"I am A Message","error":""}
```

It returns us the exact message we passed initially. Hurray! We wrote our first microservice for encrypting/decrypting messages. Apart from handling normal HTTP requests, Go Kit provides many other useful constructs, such as middleware for:

- Transport logging
- Application logging
- Application instrumentation
- Service discovery

In the upcoming sections, we discuss a few important constructs from the preceding list.

Adding logging to your microservice

In this section, let us learn how to add transport-level logging and application-level logging to our Go Kit microservices. We use the above example but modify it a little bit. Let us call our new project `encryptServiceWithLogging`. In the GitHub project of this book, you will find this directory. We visited the concepts of middleware many times in this book. For revision, a middleware is a function that tampers the request/response before/after it reaches the respective request handlers. Go Kit allows us to create logging middleware, which we attach to our service. That middleware will have the logging logic. In this example, we try to log to the Stderr (console). Add one new file called `middleware.go` to the `helpers` directory, as shown in the following code:

```go
package helpers
import (
    "context"
    "time"
    log "github.com/go-kit/kit/log"
)
// LoggingMiddleware wraps the logs for incoming requests
type LoggingMiddleware struct {
    Logger log.Logger
    Next EncryptService
}
// Encrypt logs the encyption requests
func (mw LoggingMiddleware) Encrypt(ctx context.Context, key string, text string) (output string, err error) {
    defer func(begin time.Time) {
        _ = mw.Logger.Log(
            "method", "encrypt",
            "key", key,
            "text", text,
            "output", output,
            "err", err,
            "took", time.Since(begin),
        )
    }(time.Now())
    output, err = mw.Next.Encrypt(ctx, key, text)
    return
}
// Decrypt logs the encyption requests
func (mw LoggingMiddleware) Decrypt(ctx context.Context, key string, text string) (output string, err error) {
    defer func(begin time.Time) {
        _ = mw.Logger.Log(
            "method", "decrypt",
            "key", key,
```

```
                "message", text,
                "output", output,
                "err", err,
                "took", time.Since(begin),
        )
    }(time.Now())
    output, err = mw.Next.Decrypt(ctx, key, text)
    return
}
```

We need to create a struct that has a logger and our service instance. Then, define a few methods on that whose names are similar to the service methods (in this case, they are `encrypt` and `decrypt`). The **Logger** is the Go Kit's logger that has a `Log` function. This `Log` function takes a few arguments. It takes a pair of arguments. The first and second are one set. The third and fourth are another set. Refer to the following code snippet:

```
mw.Logger.Log(
        "method", "decrypt",
        "key", key,
        "message", text,
        "output", output,
        "err", err,
        "took", time.Since(begin),
    )
```

We need to maintain the order in which the log should print. After logging our request details, we make sure to allow the request to go to the next middleware/handler using this function. `Next` is of the type `EncryptService`, which is our actual implementation:

```
mw.Next.(Encrypt/Decrypt)
```

For the encryption function, middleware logs a request for encryption and passes it to the implementation of the service. In order to hook this created middleware into our service, modify `main.go` to this:

```
package main
import (
    "log"
    "net/http"
    "os"
    kitlog "github.com/go-kit/kit/log"
    httptransport "github.com/go-kit/kit/transport/http"
    "github.com/narenaryan/encryptService/helpers"
)
func main() {
    logger := kitlog.NewLogfmtLogger(os.Stderr)
```

```
        var svc helpers.EncryptService
        svc = helpers.EncryptServiceInstance{}
        svc = helpers.LoggingMiddleware{Logger: logger, Next: svc}
        encryptHandler :=
httptransport.NewServer(helpers.MakeEncryptEndpoint(svc),
            helpers.DecodeEncryptRequest,
            helpers.EncodeResponse)
        decryptHandler :=
httptransport.NewServer(helpers.MakeDecryptEndpoint(svc),
            helpers.DecodeDecryptRequest,
            helpers.EncodeResponse)
        http.Handle("/encrypt", encryptHandler)
        http.Handle("/decrypt", decryptHandler)
        log.Fatal(http.ListenAndServe(":8080", nil))
}
```

We imported the log from Go Kit as `kitlog`. We created a new logger
using `NewLogfmtLogger(os.Stderr)`. This attaches the logging to the console. Now, pass
this logger and service to the `LoggingMiddleware`. It returns the service that can be passed
to the HTTP server. Now, let us run the program from `encryptServiceWithLogging` and
see what output logs on the console:

```
go run main.go
```

It starts our microservice. Now, fire client requests from the CURL command:

```
curl -XPOST -d'{"key":"111023043350789514532147", "text": "I am A
Message"}' localhost:8080/encrypt

curl -XPOST -d'{"key":"111023043350789514532147", "message":
"8/+JCfTb+ibIjzQtmCo="}' localhost:8080/decrypt
{"text":"I am A Message","error":""}
```

That logs the following messages on the server console:

```
method=encrypt key=111023043350789514532147 text="I am A Message"
output="8/+JCfTb+ibIjzQtmCo=" err=null took=11.32μs

method=decrypt key=111023043350789514532147 message="8/+JCfTb+ibIjzQtmCo="
output="I am A Message" err=null took=6.773μs
```

This is to log the messages per application/service. System-level logging is also available
and can be approached from the Go Kit's documentation.

Adding instrumentation to your microservice

For any microservice, along with logging, instrumentation is vital. The `metrics` package of Go Kit records statistics about your service's runtime behavior: counting the number of jobs processed, recording the duration of requests after they have finished, and so on. This is also a middleware that tampers the HTTP requests and collects metrics. To define a middleware, simply add one more struct, similar to the logging middleware. Metrics are useless unless we monitor. **Prometheus** is a metrics monitoring tool that can collect latency, number of requests for a given service, and so on. Prometheus scrapes the data from the metrics that Go Kit generates.

You can download the latest stable version of Prometheus from this site. Before using Prometheus, make sure you install these packages, that are needed by the Go Kit:

```
go get github.com/prometheus/client_golang/prometheus
go get github.com/prometheus/client_golang/prometheus/promhttp
```

Once these are installed, try to copy the last discussed logging service project into a directory called `encryptServiceWithInstrumentation`. The directory is exactly the same, except we add one more file called `instrumentation.go` to the `helpers` directory and modify our `main.go` to import the instrumentation middleware. The project structure looks like this:

```
├── helpers
│   ├── endpoints.go
│   ├── implementations.go
│   ├── instrumentation.go
│   ├── jsonutils.go
│   ├── middleware.go
│   └── models.go
└── main.go
```

Instrumentation can measure the number of requests per service and the latency in terms of parameters such as `Counter` and `Histogram`, respectively. We try to create a middleware that has these two measurements (requests count, latency) and implements the functions for the given services. In those middleware functions, we try to call the Prometheus client API to increment the number of requests, log the latency, and so on. The core Prometheus client library tries to increment a request count in this way:

```
// Prometheus
c := prometheus.NewCounter(stdprometheus.CounterOpts{
    Name: "request_duration",
    ...
}, []string{"method", "status_code"})
c.With("method", "MyMethod", "status_code", strconv.Itoa(code)).Add(1)
```

NewCounter creates a new counter struct that expects counter options. These options are the name of the operation and other details. Then, we need to call the With function on the struct with the method, method name, and error code. This particular signature is demanded by Prometheus to generate the counter metric. Finally, we are incrementing the counter with the Add(1) function call.

The newly added file instrumentation.go implementation looks like this:

```go
package helpers
import (
    "context"
    "fmt"
    "time"
    "github.com/go-kit/kit/metrics"
)
// InstrumentingMiddleware is a struct representing middleware
type InstrumentingMiddleware struct {
    RequestCount metrics.Counter
    RequestLatency metrics.Histogram
    Next EncryptService
}
func (mw InstrumentingMiddleware) Encrypt(ctx context.Context, key string,
text string) (output string, err error) {
    defer func(begin time.Time) {
        lvs := []string{"method", "encrypt", "error", fmt.Sprint(err !=
nil)}
        mw.RequestCount.With(lvs...).Add(1)
        mw.RequestLatency.With(lvs...).Observe(time.Since(begin).Seconds())
    }(time.Now())
    output, err = mw.Next.Encrypt(ctx, key, text)
    return
}
func (mw InstrumentingMiddleware) Decrypt(ctx context.Context, key string,
text string) (output string, err error) {
    defer func(begin time.Time) {
        lvs := []string{"method", "decrypt", "error", "false"}
        mw.RequestCount.With(lvs...).Add(1)
        mw.RequestLatency.With(lvs...).Observe(time.Since(begin).Seconds())
    }(time.Now())
    output, err = mw.Next.Decrypt(ctx, key, text)
    return
}
```

This is exactly the same as the logging middleware code. We created a struct with a few fields. We attached the functions for both the encrypt and decrypt services. Inside the middleware function, we are looking for two metrics; one is count and the second one is latency. When a request is passed through this middleware:

```
mw.RequestCount.With(lvs...).Add(1)
```

This line increments the counter. Now see the other line:

```
mw.RequestLatency.With(lvs...).Observe(time.Since(begin).Seconds())
```

This line observes the latency by calculating the difference between the request arrival time and final time (since the defer keyword is used, this will be executed after the request and response cycle is completed). In simple words, the preceding middleware logs the request count and latency to the metrics provided by the Prometheus client. Now let us modify our `main.go` file to look like this:

```go
package main
import (
    "log"
    "net/http"
    "os"
    stdprometheus "github.com/prometheus/client_golang/prometheus"
    "github.com/prometheus/client_golang/prometheus/promhttp"
    kitlog "github.com/go-kit/kit/log"
    httptransport "github.com/go-kit/kit/transport/http"
    "github.com/narenaryan/encryptService/helpers"
    kitprometheus "github.com/go-kit/kit/metrics/prometheus"
)
func main() {
    logger := kitlog.NewLogfmtLogger(os.Stderr)
    fieldKeys := []string{"method", "error"}
    requestCount := kitprometheus.NewCounterFrom(stdprometheus.CounterOpts{
        Namespace: "encryption",
        Subsystem: "my_service",
        Name: "request_count",
        Help: "Number of requests received.",
    }, fieldKeys)
    requestLatency :=
kitprometheus.NewSummaryFrom(stdprometheus.SummaryOpts{
        Namespace: "encryption",
        Subsystem: "my_service",
        Name: "request_latency_microseconds",
        Help: "Total duration of requests in microseconds.",
    }, fieldKeys)
    var svc helpers.EncryptService
    svc = helpers.EncryptServiceInstance{}
```

```
    svc = helpers.LoggingMiddleware{Logger: logger, Next: svc}
    svc = helpers.InstrumentingMiddleware{RequestCount: requestCount,
RequestLatency: requestLatency, Next: svc}
    encryptHandler :=
httptransport.NewServer(helpers.MakeEncryptEndpoint(svc),
        helpers.DecodeEncryptRequest,
        helpers.EncodeResponse)
    decryptHandler :=
httptransport.NewServer(helpers.MakeDecryptEndpoint(svc),
        helpers.DecodeDecryptRequest,
        helpers.EncodeResponse)
    http.Handle("/encrypt", encryptHandler)
    http.Handle("/decrypt", decryptHandler)
    http.Handle("/metrics", promhttp.Handler())
    log.Fatal(http.ListenAndServe(":8080", nil))
}
```

We are importing the kit Prometheus package for initializing the metrics template, and the client Prometheus package for providing the option structs. We are creating `requestCount` and `requestLatency` metrics-type structs and passing them to our `InstrumentingMiddleware`, which is imported from `helpers`. If you see this line:

```
    requestCount := kitprometheus.NewCounterFrom(stdprometheus.CounterOpts{
        Namespace: "encryption",
        Subsystem: "my_service",
        Name:      "request_count",
        Help:      "Number of requests received.",
    }, fieldKeys)
```

It is how we create a template that matches with the `RequestCount` in the `InstrumentingMiddleware` struct in `helpers.go`. The options that we pass will be appended to a single string while generating the metrics:

```
encryption_my_service_request_count
```

This is a uniquely identifiable service instrumentation that tells us, *This is a request count operation for my microservice called Encryption*. There is one more interesting line we added to the server part of the code in `main.go`:

```
"github.com/prometheus/client_golang/prometheus/promhttp"
...
http.Handle("/metrics", promhttp.Handler())
```

This actually creates an endpoint that can generate a page with collected metrics. This page can be scraped (parsed) by Prometheus to store, plot, and display metrics. If we run the program and make 5 HTTP requests to the encrypt service and 10 HTTP requests to the decrypt service, the metrics page logs the count of requests and their latencies:

```
go run main.go # This starts the server
```

Make 5 CURL requests to the encrypt service in a loop from another bash shell (in Linux):

```
for i in 1 2 3 4 5; do curl -XPOST -d'{"key":"11102304335078951453214 7",
"text": "I am A Message"}' localhost:8080/encrypt; done

{"message":"8/+JCfTb+ibIjzQtmCo=","error":""}
{"message":"8/+JCfTb+ibIjzQtmCo=","error":""}
{"message":"8/+JCfTb+ibIjzQtmCo=","error":""}
{"message":"8/+JCfTb+ibIjzQtmCo=","error":""}
{"message":"8/+JCfTb+ibIjzQtmCo=","error":""}
```

Make 10 CURL requests in a loop for the decrypt service (the output is hidden for brevity):

```
for i in 1 2 3 4 5 6 7 8 9 10; do curl -XPOST -
d'{"key":"11102304335078951453214 7", "message": "8/+JCfTb+ibIjzQtmCo="}'
localhost:8080/decrypt; done
```

Now, visit the URL http://localhost:8080/metrics and you will see a page that the Prometheus Go client is generating for us. The content of the page will have this information:

```
# HELP encryption_my_service_request_count Number of requests received.
# TYPE encryption_my_service_request_count counter
encryption_my_service_request_count{error="false",method="decrypt"} 10
encryption_my_service_request_count{error="false",method="encrypt"} 5
# HELP encryption_my_service_request_latency_microseconds Total duration of
requests in microseconds.
# TYPE encryption_my_service_request_latency_microseconds summary
encryption_my_service_request_latency_microseconds{error="false",method="de
crypt",quantile="0.5"} 5.4538e-05
encryption_my_service_request_latency_microseconds{error="false",method="de
crypt",quantile="0.9"} 7.6279e-05
encryption_my_service_request_latency_microseconds{error="false",method="de
crypt",quantile="0.99"} 8.097e-05
encryption_my_service_request_latency_microseconds_sum{error="false",method
="decrypt"} 0.000603101
encryption_my_service_request_latency_microseconds_count{error="false",meth
od="decrypt"} 10
encryption_my_service_request_latency_microseconds{error="false",method="en
crypt",quantile="0.5"} 5.02e-05
```

```
encryption_my_service_request_latency_microseconds{error="false",method="en
crypt",quantile="0.9"} 8.8164e-05
encryption_my_service_request_latency_microseconds{error="false",method="en
crypt",quantile="0.99"} 8.8164e-05
encryption_my_service_request_latency_microseconds_sum{error="false",method
="encrypt"} 0.000284823
encryption_my_service_request_latency_microseconds_count{error="false",meth
od="encrypt"} 5
```

As you can see, there are two types of metrics:

- `encryption_myservice_request_count`
- `encryption_myservice_request_latency_microseconds`

If you see the number of requests to the `encrypt` method and `decrypt` method, they match with the CURL requests we made.

 The `encryption_myservice` metrics type has count and latency metrics for both the encrypt and decrypt microservices. The method parameter tells from which microservice the metrics are drawn.

These kinds of metrics give us key insights, such as which microservice is being used heavily and how the latency trends are over time, and so on. But in order to see the data in action, you need to install the Prometheus server and write a configuration file for Prometheus to scrape metrics from your Go Kit service. For more information about creating targets (hosts generating metrics pages) in Prometheus, visit `https://prometheus.io/docs/operating/configuration/`.

We can also pass data from Prometheus to Grafana, a graphing and monitoring tool for nice real-time charts of metrics. Go Kit provides many other features, such as service discovery. Scaling microservices is only possible if the system is loosely coupled, monitored, and optimized.

Summary

In this chapter, we started with the definition of microservices. The main difference between a monolith application and a microservice is the way tightly coupled architecture is broken into loosely coupled architecture. Microservices talk to each other using either REST-based JSON or RPC-based protocol buffers. Using microservices, we can break business logic into multiple chunks. Each service does one job pretty well. This approach comes with a disadvantage. Monitoring and managing microservices is painful. Go provides a wonderful toolkit called Go Kit. It is a microservices framework using which we can generate boilerplate code for microservices.

We need to define a few things in Go Kit. We need to create implementations, endpoints, and models for a Go-Kit service. Endpoints take requests and return responses. Implementations have the actual business logic of services. Models are a nice way to decode and encode request and response objects. Go Kit provides various middleware for performing vital tasks such as logging, instrumentation (metrics), and service discovery.

The small organizations can start with a monolith, but in bigger organizations with huge teams, microservices suit better. In the next chapter, we can see how to deploy our Go services using Nginx. A service needs to be deployed for it to be exposed to the outside world.

10
Deploying Our REST services

In this chapter, we are going to see how to deploy our Go applications using a few tools such as Nohup and Nginx. To make a website visible to the internet, we need to have a **Virtual Private Server** (**VPS**) and deployment tools. We will first see how to run a Go executable and make it a background process using Nohup. Next, we will install Nginx and configure it to proxy the Go server.

In this chapter, we will cover the following topics:

- What is an Nginx proxy server?
- Learning Nginx server blocks
- Load balancing strategies in Nginx
- Deploying our Go service using Nginx
- Rate limiting and securing our Nginx proxy server
- Monitoring our Go service using a tool called Supervisord

Getting the code

The code for this chapter is available at `https://github.com/narenaryan/gorestful/tree/master/chapter10`. Copy it to `GOPATH` and run according to the instructions given in the chapter.

Installing and configuring Nginx

Nginx is a high performant web server and load balancer, and is well suited to deploying high traffic websites. Even though this decision is opinionated, Python and Node developers usually use this.

Nginx can also act as an upstream proxy server that allows us to redirect the HTTP requests to multiple application servers running on the same server. The main contender of Nginx is Apache's httpd. Nginx is an excellent static file server that can be used by the web clients. Since we are dealing with APIs, we will look into aspects of dealing with HTTP requests.

On Ubuntu 16.04, use these commands to install Nginx:

```
sudo apt-get update
sudo apt-get install nginx
```

On macOS X, you can install it with `brew`:

```
brew install nginx
```

`https://brew.sh/` is a very useful software packaging system for macOS X users. My recommendation is to use it for installing software. Once it is successfully installed, you can check it by opening the machine IP in the browser. Open `http://localhost/` on your web browser. You will see this:

> # Welcome to nginx!
>
> If you see this page, the nginx web server is successfully installed and working. Further configuration is required.
>
> For online documentation and support please refer to nginx.org. Commercial support is available at nginx.com.
>
> *Thank you for using nginx.*

This means that Nginx is installed successfully. It is serving on port 80 and serving the default page. On macOS, the default Nginx listening port will be 8000:

```
sudo vi /usr/local/etc/nginx/nginx.conf
```

On Ubuntu (Linux), the file will be on this path:

```
sudo vi /etc/nginx/nginx.conf
```

Open the file, and search for a server and modify port 80 to 8000:

```
server {
        listen 8080; # Change this to 80
        server_name localhost;
        #charset koi8-r;
        #access_log logs/host.access.log main;
        location / {
            root html;
            index index.html index.htm;
        }
        ...
}
```

Now everything is ready. The server runs on the 80 HTTP port, which means a client can access it using a URL (http://localhost/) and no port (http://localhost:3000). This basic server serves static files from a directory called html. The root parameter can be modified to any directory where we place our web assets. You can check the status of Nginx with the following command:

```
service nginx status
```

Nginx for the Windows operating system is quite basic and not really intended for production-grade deployments. Open-source developers usually prefer Debian or Ubuntu servers for deploying the API servers with Nginx.

What is a proxy server?

A proxy server is a server that holds the information of original servers in it. It acts as the front block for the client request. Whenever a client makes an HTTP request, it can directly go the application server. But, if the application server is written in a programming language, you need a translator that can turn the application response into a client-understandable response. **Common Gateway Interface (CGI)** does the same thing. For Go, we can run a simple HTTP server and it can work as a normal server (no translation required). So, why are we using another server called Nginx? We are using Nginx because it brings a lot of things into the picture.

The benefits of having a proxy server (Nginx):

- It can act as a load balancer
- It can sit in front of cluster of applications and redirect HTTP requests
- It can serve a filesystem with a good performance
- It streams media very well

If the same machine is running multiple applications, then we can bring all those under one umbrella. Nginx can also act as the API gateway that can be the starting point for multiple API endpoints. We will see about a specially dedicated API gateway in the next chapter, but Nginx can also work as one. Refer to the following diagram:

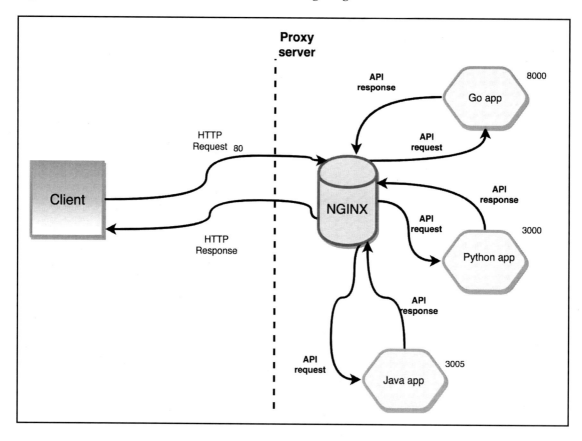

If you see, the illustration client is talking directly to Nginx instead of the ports where other applications are running. In the diagram, Go is running on port `8000` and other applications are running on different ports. It means the different servers are providing different API endpoints. If the client wishes to call those APIs, it needs to access three ports. Instead, if we have Nginx, it can act as a proxy server for all three and simplifies the client request-response cycle.

Nginx is also called an upstream server because it serves the requests from the other server. From the illustration, a Python app can request an API endpoint from a Go app smoothly.

Important Nginx paths

There are a few important Nginx paths we need to know about to work with the proxy server. In Nginx, we can host multiple sites (`www.example1.com`, `www.exampl2.com`, and so on) at the same time. Take a look at the following table:

Type	Path	Description
Configuration	`/etc/nginx/nginx.con`	This is the base Nginx configuration file. It can be used as the default file.
Configuration	`/etc/nginx/sites-available/`	If we have multiple sites running within Nginx, we can have multiple configuration files.
Configuration	`/etc/nginx/sites-enabled/`	These are the sites activated currently on Nginx.
Log	`/var/log/nginx/access.log`	This log file records the server activity, such as timestamp and API endpoints.
Log	`/var/log/nginx/error.log`	This log file logs all proxy server-related errors, such as disk space, file system permissions, and so on.

These paths are in the Linux operating system. For macOS X, use `/usr/local/nginx` as the base path.

Using server blocks

Server blocks are the actual configuration pieces that tell the server what to serve and on which port to listen. We can define multiple server blocks in the `sites-available` folder. On Ubuntu, the location will be:

> `/etc/nginx/sites-available`

On macOS X, the location will be:

> `/usr/local/etc/nginx/sites-avaiable`

Until we copy the `sites-available` to the `sites-enabled` directory, the configuration has no effect. So, always create a soft link for `sites-available` to `sites-enabled` for every new configuration you create.

Creating a sample Go application and proxying it

Now, let us create a bare application server in Go with logging:

```
mkdir -p $GOPATH/src/github.com/narenaryan/basicServer
vi $GOPATH/src/github.com/narenaryan/basicServer/main.go
```

This file is a basic Go server to illustrate the proxy server's functioning. Then, we add a configuration to Nginx to proxy port 8000 (Go running port) to HTTP port (80). Now, let us write the code:

```
package main
import (
    "encoding/json"
    "fmt"
    "log"
    "net/http"
    "os"
    "time"
)
// Book holds data of a book
type Book struct {
    ID int
    ISBN string
    Author string
    PublishedYear string
}
func main() {
    // File open for reading, writing and appending
```

```
    f, err := os.OpenFile("app.log", os.O_RDWR|os.O_CREATE|os.O_APPEND,
0666)
    if err != nil {
        fmt.Printf("error opening file: %v", err)
    }
    defer f.Close()
    // This attache sprogram logs to file
    log.SetOutput(f)
    // Function handler for handling requests
    http.HandleFunc("/", func(w http.ResponseWriter, r *http.Request) {
        log.Printf("%q", r.UserAgent())
        // Fill the book details
        book := Book{
            ID: 123,
            ISBN: "0-201-03801-3",
            Author: "Donald Knuth",
            PublishedYear: "1968",
        }
        // Convert struct to JSON using Marshal
        jsonData, _ := json.Marshal(book)
        w.Header().Set("Content-Type", "application/json")
        w.Write(jsonData)
    })
    s := &http.Server{
        Addr: ":8000",
        ReadTimeout: 10 * time.Second,
        WriteTimeout: 10 * time.Second,
        MaxHeaderBytes: 1 << 20,
    }
    log.Fatal(s.ListenAndServe())
}
```

This is a simple server that returns book details as an API (dummy data here). Run the program and it runs on port 8000. Now, open a shell and make a CURL command:

```
CURL -X GET "http://localhost:8000"
```

It returns the data:

```
{
  "ID":123,
  "ISBN":"0-201-03801-3",
  "Author":"Donald Knuth",
  "PublishedYear":"1968"
}
```

But the client needs to request to `8000` port here. How can we proxy this server using Nginx? As we previously discussed, we need to edit the default sites-available server block, called `default`:

`vi /etc/nginx/sites-available/default`

Edit this file, find the server block, and add one line to it:

```
server {
        listen 80 default_server;
        listen [::]:80 default_server ipv6only=on;

        root /usr/share/nginx/html;
        index index.html index.htm;

        # Make site accessible from http://localhost/
        server_name localhost;

        location / {
                # First attempt to serve request as file, then
                # as directory, then fall back to displaying a 404.
                try_files $uri $uri/ =404;
                # Uncomment to enable naxsi on this location
                # include /etc/nginx/naxsi.rules
                proxy_pass http://127.0.0.1:8000;
        }
}
```

This section of the `config` file is called the server block. This controls the setting up of the proxy server where `listen` says where `nginx` should listen. `root` and `index` point to the static files if we need to serve any. `server_name` is the domain name of yours. Since we don't have a domain ready, it is just localhost. The `location` is the key section here. In `location`, we can define our `proxy_pass`, which can proxy a given URL:PORT. Since our Go application is running on `8000` port, we mentioned it there. If we are running it on a different machine, such as:

```
http://example.com:8000
```

We can give the same thing as a parameter to `proxy_pass`. In order to take this configuration into effect, we need to restart the Nginx server. Do that using:

`service nginx restart`

Now, make CURL request to `http://localhost` and you will see the Go application's output:

```
CURL -X GET "http://localhost"
{
  "ID":123,
  "ISBN":"0-201-03801-3",
  "Author":"Donald Knuth",
  "PublishedYear":"1968"
}
```

`location` is a directive that defines a **Unified Resource Identifier (URI)** that can proxy a given `server:port` combination. It means that by defining various URIs, we can proxy multiple applications running on the same server. It looks like:

```
server {
    listen ...;
    ...
    location / {
        proxy_pass http://127.0.0.1:8000;
    }
    location /api {
        proxy_pass http://127.0.0.1:8001;
    }
    location /mail {
        proxy_pass http://127.0.0.1:8002;
    }
    ...
}
```

Here, three applications are running on different ports. These, after being added to our configuration file, can be accessed by the client as:

```
http://localhost/
http://localhost/api/
http://localhost/mail/
```

Load balancing with Nginx

In practical cases, we use multiple servers instead of one for handling huge sets of incoming requests for APIs. But who needs to forward an incoming client request to a server instance? Load balancing is a process where the central server distributes the load to various servers based on certain criteria. Refer to the following diagram:

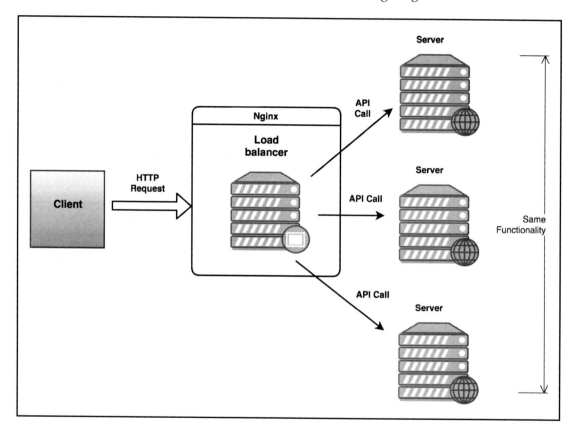

Those requesting criteria are called load balancing methods. Let us see what each does in a simple table:

Load balancing method	Description
Round Robin	Requests are distributed evenly across servers and server weights are taken into consideration.
Least Connection	Requests are sent to the server that is currently serving the least number of clients.
IP Hash	This is used to send the requests from a given client's IP to the given server. Only when that server is not available is it given to another server.
Least Time	A request from the client is sent to the machine with the lowest average latency (time to serve client) and least number of active connections.

We now see how load balancing is practically achieved in Nginx for our Go API servers. The first step in this process is to create an `upstream` in the `http` section of the Nginx configuration file:

```
http {
    upstream cluster {
        server site1.mysite.com weight=5;
        server site2.mysite.com weight=2;
        server backup.mysite.com backup;
    }
}
```

Here, servers are the IP addresses or domain names of the servers running the same code. We are defining an `upstream` called `backend` here. It is a server group that we can refer to in our location directive. Weights should be given in proportion to the resources available. In the preceding code, `site1` is given a higher weight because it may be a bigger instance (memory and disk). Now, in the location directive, we can specify the server group with the `proxy_pass` command:

```
server {
    location / {
        proxy_pass http://cluster;
    }
}
```

Now, the proxy server that is running will pass requests to the machines in the cluster for all API endpoints hitting /. The default request routing algorithm will be Round Robin, which means all the servers' turns will be repeated one after the other. If we need to change it, we mention that in the upstream definition. Take a look at the following code snippet:

```
http {
    upstream cluster {
        least_conn;
        server site1.mysite.com weight=5;
        server site2.mysite.com;
        server backup.mysite.com backup;
    }
}

server {
    location / {
        proxy_pass http://cluster;
    }
}
```

The preceding configuration says to *create a cluster of three machines, and add load balancing method as least connections.* least_conn is the string we used to mention the load balancing method. The other values could be ip_hash or least_time. You can try this by having a set of machines in the **Local Area Network (LAN)**. Or else, we can have Docker installed with multiple virtual containers as different machines to test out load balancing.

 We need to add that http block in the /etc/nginx/nginx.conf file, whereas the server block is in /etc/nginx/sites-enabled/default. It is better to separate these two settings.

Rate limiting our REST API

We can also limit the rate of access to our Nginx proxy server by rate limiting. It provides a directive called limit_conn_zone (http://nginx.org/en/docs/http/ngx_http_limit_conn_module.html#limit_conn_zone). The format of it is this:

```
limit_conn_zone client_type zone=zone_type:size;
```

client_type can be of two types:

- IP address (limit requests from a given IP address)
- Server name (limit requests from a server)

`zone_type` also changes in correspondence to the `client_type`. It takes values as per the following table:

Client type	Zone type
`$binary_remote_address`	`addr`
`$server_name`	`servers`

Nginx needs to save a few things to memory to remember the IP addresses and servers for rate limiting. `size` is the storage that we allocate for Nginx to perform its memorizing. It takes values such as 8m (8MB) or 16m (16MB). Now, let us see where to add these settings. The preceding one should be added as a global setting to the `http` directive in the `nginx.conf` file:

```
http {
    limit_conn_zone $server_name zone=servers:10m;
}
```

This allocates the shared memory for Nginx to use. Now, in the server directive of sites-available/default, add the following:

```
server {
    limit_conn servers 1000;
}
```

The total number of connections for the given server will not exceed 1K in the preceding configuration using `limit_conn`. If we try to put the rate limit from a given IP address to the client, then use this:

```
server {
  location /api {
      limit_conn addr 1;
  }
}
```

This setting stops a client (IP address) from opening more than one connection to the server (for example, railway booking online). If we have a file that the client downloads and need to set a bandwidth constraint, use `limit_rate`:

```
server {
  location /download {
      limit_conn addr 10;
      limit_rate 50k;
  }
}
```

In this way, we can control the client's interaction with our services that are proxied under Nginx. If we use Go binary directly to run the service, we lose all these features.

Securing our Nginx proxy server

This is the most important piece in the Nginx set up. In this section, we will see how to restrict access to our server using basic authentication. This will be very important for our REST API servers because, let us suppose we have servers X, Y, and Z that talk to each other. X can serve clients directly, but X talks to Y and Z for some information by calling an internal API. Since we know that clients should not access Y or Z, we can make it so that only X is allowed to access the resources. We can allow or deny the IP addresses using the nginx access module. It looks like this:

```
location /api {
    ...
    deny 192.168.1.2;
    allow 192.168.1.1/24;
    allow 127.0.0.1;
    deny all;
}
```

This configuration tells Nginx to allow requests from clients ranging 192.168.1.1/24, excluding 192.168.1.2. The next line says to allow requests from the same host and block all other requests from any other client. The complete server block looks like this:

```
server {
    listen 80 default_server;
    root /usr/share/nginx/html;

    location /api {

        deny 192.168.1.2;
        allow 192.168.1.1/24;
        allow 127.0.0.1;
        deny all;
    }
}
```

For more information regarding this, see the documentation at `nginx_http_access_module`. We can also add password-secured access to our Nginx served static files. It is mostly not applicable to the API because there, the application takes care of authenticating the user.

Monitoring our Go API server with Supervisord

It is fine that Nginx is sitting in front of our Go API server, it just proxies a port. However, sometimes that web application may stop due to the operating system restarting or crashing. Whenever your web server gets killed, it is someone's job to automatically bring it back to life. Supervisord is such a task runner. To make our API server run all the time, we need to monitor it. Supervisord is a tool that can monitor running processes (system) and can restart them when they were terminated.

Installing Supervisord

We can easily install Supervisord using Python's `pip` command. On Ubuntu 16.04, just use the `apt-get` command:

```
sudo apt-get install -y supervisor
```

This installs two tools, `supervisor` and `supervisorctl`. Supervisorctl is intended to control the supervisor and add tasks, restart tasks, and so on. Let us use the sample `basicServre.go` program we created for illustrating Nginx for this too. Install the binary to the `$GOPATH/bin` directory. Here, suppose my `GOPATH` is `/root/workspace`:

```
go install github.com/narenaryan/basicServer
```

 Always add the `bin` folder of your current `GOPATH` to the system path. Whenever you install the project binary, it is available as a normal executable from the overall system environment. You can do it adding this line to the `~/.profile` file: `export  PATH=$PATH:/usr/local/go/bin`.

Now, create a configuration file at:

```
/etc/supervisor/conf.d/goproject.conf
```

You can add any number of configuration files and supervisord treats them as separate processes to run. Add the following content to the preceding file:

```
[supervisord]
logfile = /tmp/supervisord.log
[program:myserver]
command=/root/workspace/bin/basicServer
autostart=true
autorestart=true
redirect_stderr=true
```

By default, we have a file called supervisord.conf at /etc/supervisor/. Look at it for further reference:

- The [supervisord] section gives the location of the log file for supervisord.
- [program:myserver] is the task block that traverses to a given directory and executes the command given.

Now, we can ask our supervisorctl to re-read the configuration and restart the task (process). For that, just say:

```
supervisorctl reread
supervisorctl update
```

Then, launch our supervisorctl with:

```
supervisorctl
```

You will see something like this:

```
root@ubuntu:~# supervisorctl
myserver                         RUNNING    pid 6886, uptime 0:00:47
supervisor> help

default commands (type help <topic>):
=====================================
add     clear  fg        open  quit    remove  restart   start   stop  update
avail   exit   maintail  pid   reload  reread  shutdown  status  tail  version

supervisor> 
```

So, our book service is getting monitored by `Supervisor`. Let us try to kill the process and see what `Supervisor` does:

```
kill 6886
```

Now, as soon as possible, `Supervisor` starts a new process (different `pid`) by running the binary:

```
root@ubuntu:~# kill 6886
root@ubuntu:~# supervisorctl
myserver                         RUNNING     pid 6903, uptime 0:00:10
supervisor> help

default commands (type help <topic>):
```

This is very useful in production scenarios where a service needs to be up in case of any crash or OS restart. One question here, how do we start/stop an application service? Use the `start` and `stop` commands from `supervisorctl` for smooth operations:

```
supervisorctl> stop myserver
supervisorctl> start myserver
```

For more details about the Supervisor, visit `http://supervisord.org/`.

Summary

This chapter is dedicated to showing how we can deploy our API services into production. One way is to run the Go binary and access it through the `IP: Port` combination directly from the client. That IP will be the **Virtual Private Server** (**VPS**) IP address. Instead, we can have a domain name registered and pointed to the VPS. The second and better way is to hide it behind a proxy server. Nginx is such a proxy server, using which we can have multiple application servers under one umbrella.

We saw how to install Nginx and start configuring it. Nginx provides features such as load balancing and rate limiting, which could be crucial while giving APIs to clients. Load balancing is the process of distributing loads among similar servers. We saw what types of loading mechanisms are available. Some of them are Round Robin, IP Hash, Least Connection, and so on. Then, we added authentication to our servers by allowing and denying a few sets of IP addresses.

Finally, we need a process monitor that can bring our crashed application back to life. Supervisord is a very good tool for the job. We saw how to install Supervisord and also launch supervisorctl, a command-line application to control running servers.

In the next chapter, we are going to see how to make our API production-grade using an API gateway. We will discuss deeply how we can put our API behind an entity that takes care of authentication and rate limiting.

11
Using an API Gateway to Monitor and Metricize REST API

Once we have developed our API, we need to expose it to the outside world. In that journey, we deploy them. But is that sufficient? Don't we need to track our API? Which clients are connecting? What is the latency of requests, and so on and so forth? There are many other post-API development steps that one should follow to make their API production grade. They are authentication, logging, rate limiting, and so on. The best way to add those features is to use an API gateway. In this chapter, we will explore an open-source API gateway called **Kong**. Open-source software is preferable to cloud providers because of the reduced risk of vendor lock. All the API gateways differ in the implementation but perform the same task.

In this chapter, we will cover the following topics:

- Why is an API gateway needed?
- Introducing Kong, an open-source API gateway
- Example illustration in Docker
- Adding developed API to Kong
- Logging in Kong
- Authentication and rate limiting in Kong
- Important commands from Kong CLI

Getting the code

You can get the code samples for this chapter at `https://github.com/narenaryan/` `gorestful/tree/master/chapter11`. The usage of the files in the chapter is explained in the respective sections. You can also import the Postman client collection (JSON file) from the repository to test the API, which we will walk through in this chapter.

Why is an API gateway required?

Suppose a company named XYZ developed the API for its internal purpose. There are two ways in which it exposes that API for external use:

- Exposes it using authentication from known clients
- Exposes it as an API as a service

In the first case, this API is consumed by the other services inside the company. Since they are internal, we don't restrict the access. But in the second case, since API details are given to the outside world, we need a broker in between to check and validate the requests. This broker is the API gateway. An API gateway is a broker that sits in between the client and the server and forwards the request to the server on passing specific conditions.

Now, XYZ has an API written in Go and also in Java. There are a few common things that apply to any API:

- Authentication
- Logging of requests and responses

Without an API gateway, we need to write another server that tracks things such as requests and authentication of the API. It is hectic to implement and maintain when new APIs keep being added to the organization. To take care of these basic things, an API gateway is a fine piece of middleware.

Basically, an API getaway does these things:

- Logging
- Security
- Traffic control
- Transformations

Logging is the way to track the requests and responses. If we need an organization-level logging in contrast to application level-logging in Go kit, we should enable logging in an API gateway. Security is how authentication works. It can be basic auth, token-based authentication, OAuth2.0, and so on. It is essential to restrict access to the API for the valid customers/clients.

Traffic control comes into play when an API is a paid service. When an organization sells the data as an API, It needs to limit the operations per client. For example, a client can make 10,000 API requests per month. The rate can be set according to the plan the client has opted for. This is a very important feature. Transformations are like modifying the request before it hits the application server or modifying the response before it is sent back to the client. Take a look at the following diagram:

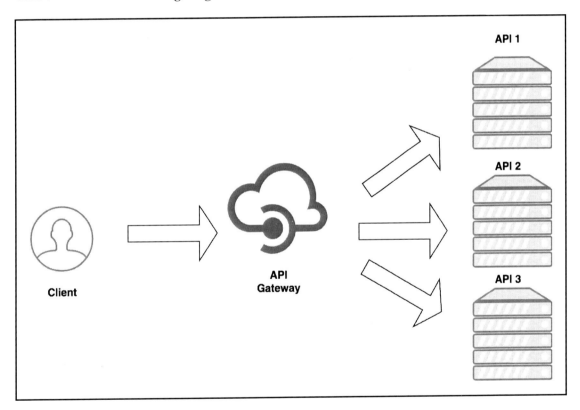

We can see how we are able to add the preceding features to our web services. From the diagram, the API gateway can redirect requests to any given internal servers. The client sees all the APIs are under a single entity of the organization.

Kong, an open-source API gateway

Kong is an open-source API gateway and a microservices management layer, delivering high performance and reliability. It is a combination of two libraries worth mentioning. One is **OpenResty** and another one is **Nginx**. Kong is a wrapper around these two main components. OpenResty is a fully-fledged web platform that integrates Nginx and Lua. Lua is another programming language similar to Go. Kong is written in Lua. We use Kong as a tool for deploying our Go REST services. The main topics we cover are:

- Installation of Kong and the Kong database
- Adding our API to Kong
- Using the plugins
- Logging in Kong
- Rate limiting in Kong

Kong needs a database to run. It could be either Cassandra or PostgreSQL. Since we are already familiar with PostgreSQL, we chose it. Where to install them? For illustration, we can install them on our local machine, but there is a drawback; it can screw up our machine. In order to test the setup, we are going to use Docker. Docker can create containerized applications and run them in a predictable, isolated environment.

Using Kong, we can hide our API under a gateway. We can create consumers (clients) for our API. Kong does everything through a REST API. Kong has two kinds of API:

- Application API (runs on port `8000`)
- Admin API (runs on port `8001`)

Using an application API, we can access our web services. An admin API allows us to add/remove APIs under the gateway. We will see these things in more detail in upcoming sections. For more details about Kong, visit `https://getkong.org/`.

Introducing Docker

Docker is a virtualization tool that can create operating systems in the form of tiny containers. It is like multiple OS on a single host. Developers usually complain saying *working in my box* while facing deployment problems. Docker removes those situations by defining an OS environment in the form of images. A Docker image has all the information about a given OS at a given time. It allows us to replicate that environment any number of times.

It was available for Linux initially but is now available for macOS X and Windows. For downloading and installing Docker, visit `https://docs.docker.com/engine/installation/`. For Windows and Mac, the binaries are available on the Docker website and can be easily installed. After installing, verify the Docker installation with the following command:

```
docker -v
Docker version 17.09.0-ce, build afdb6d4
```

It will give the version number; always choose the latest Docker. Now that Docker is ready, let us run a few commands to install Kong. The upcoming section requires some knowledge of Docker. Please go through the wonderful articles on the web explaining the fundamentals of Docker if not confident enough.

Our final goal is to create three containers:

- Kong database
- Go container
- Kong application

When these three containers run, it sets the stage for setting up a web service behind an API gateway.

Installing a Kong database and Kong

First, install the PostgreSQL DB. One condition is that we need to expose the 5432 port. The user and database name should be kong, and that should be passed as environment variables to the container:

```
docker run -d --name kong-database \
          -p 5432:5432 \
          -e "POSTGRES_USER=kong" \
          -e "POSTGRES_DB=kong" \
          postgres:9.4
```

This command works in this way:

1. Get me an image from the Docker repository called postgres:9.4.
2. Give a name to the image called kong-database.
3. Set environment variables in the container called POSTGRES_USER and POSTGRES_DB.

This creates a Docker container by pulling a PostgreSQL image, which is hosted on the **DockerHub** (https://hub.docker.com/) repository. Now, apply the migrations required by Kong by running one more Docker command:

```
docker run --rm \
    --link kong-database:kong-database \
    -e "KONG_DATABASE=postgres" \
    -e "KONG_PG_HOST=kong-database" \
    kong:latest kong migrations up
```

It applies the migrations on the previously created PostgreSQL DB container. The command has an option called --rm, which says, *remove this container once migrations are done*. Before installing the Kong container, let us prepare our Go service. It will be a simple project with a health check GET API.

Now, go to any directory on the host machine and create a project called kongExample:

```
mkdir kongExample
```

Create a program called main.go inside that directory, which fetches the health check (date and time) for a GET request:

```
package main
import (
    "fmt"
    "github.com/gorilla/mux"
```

```
    "log"
    "net/http"
    "time"
)
func HealthcheckHandler(w http.ResponseWriter, r *http.Request) {
    w.WriteHeader(http.StatusOK)
    fmt.Fprintf(w, time.Now().String())
}
func main() {
    // Create a new router
    r := mux.NewRouter()
    // Attach an elegant path with handler
    r.HandleFunc("/healthcheck", HealthcheckHandler)
    srv := &http.Server{
        Handler: r,
        Addr: "0.0.0.0:3000",
        // Good practice: enforce timeouts for servers you create!
        WriteTimeout: 15 * time.Second,
        ReadTimeout: 15 * time.Second,
    }
    log.Fatal(srv.ListenAndServe())
}
```

This program returns the date and time when requested. Now, we need to Dockerize this application. Dockerizing means creating a running container. Add a Dockerfile to the current directory (in the same level `kongExample`):

```
FROM golang
ADD kongExample /go/src/github.com/narenaryan/kongExample
RUN go get github.com/gorilla/mux
RUN go install github.com/narenaryan/kongExample
ENTRYPOINT /go/bin/kongExample
```

We build a container with the help of this Dockerfile. It says to pull the `golang` container from DockerHub (installing the Go compiler and setting the `GOPATH` is automatically taken care of) and copy this `kongExample` project to the container. Install necessary packages for the project (in this case it is Gorilla Mux), then compile the binary and start the server. Run this command to create the container:

```
docker build . -t gobuild
```

Notice the `.` after the `docker build` command. The `-t` option is to tag the image with the name. It tells Docker to look at the Dockerfile in the current directory and create a Docker image with the given instructions. We need to actually run this image to create a container:

```
docker run  -p 3000:3000 --name go-server -dit gobuild
```

It creates a container called `go-server` and starts the Go web server on port `3000`. Now install Kong container, like this:

```
docker run -d --name kong \
    --link kong-database:kong-database \
    --link go-server:go-server \
    -e "KONG_DATABASE=postgres" \
    -e "KONG_PG_HOST=kong-database" \
    -e "KONG_PROXY_ACCESS_LOG=/dev/stdout" \
    -e "KONG_ADMIN_ACCESS_LOG=/dev/stdout" \
    -e "KONG_PROXY_ERROR_LOG=/dev/stderr" \
    -e "KONG_ADMIN_ERROR_LOG=/dev/stderr" \
    -p 8000:8000 \
    -p 8443:8443 \
    -p 8001:8001 \
    -p 8444:8444 \
    kong:latest
```

This command is similar to the first one except we are exposing many other ports for Kong to function. We are also pulling the `kong:latest` image from DockerHub. Others are environment variables that are required by Kong. We are linking `kong-database` to a hostname called `kong-database` and `go-server` to `go-server`. A hostname is a helpful entity in a Docker environment to identify and reach to one container from another. Docker maintains an internal **Domain Name Space** (**DNS**) that keeps track of IP addresses of Docker containers to the linked names. This starts the Kong container and starts the Kong service with a default file called `kong.conf.default`.

Now, if we look at the running containers, it lists three container IDs:

```
docker ps -q
b6cd3ad39f75
53d800fe3b15
bbc9d2ba5679
```

Docker containers are nothing but isolated environments for running applications. It is a best practice to run microservices in different containers as they are loosely coupled and one environment won't interfere with the other.

It means we successfully set up the infrastructure for the Kong API gateway. Let's see how to add the API from `go-server` in Kong. In order to check the status of Kong, just make a `GET` request to this URL:

```
curl -X GET http://localhost:8001/status
```

It returns the status of the database and also the stats for Kong:

```
{
    "database": {
        "reachable": true
    },
    "server": {
        "connections_writing": 1,
        "total_requests": 13,
        "connections_handled": 14,
        "connections_accepted": 14,
        "connections_reading": 0,
        "connections_active": 2,
        "connections_waiting": 1
    }
}
```

Adding API to Kong

Kong provides an intuitive REST API to add a custom API to the gateway. In order to add the aforementioned healthcheck API, we need to make a `POST` request to the Kong admin API, which runs on port `8001`. From now on we use the Postman REST client to show all API requests. These API requests are also available as a JSON file collection in the chapter's repository for readers to download and import in their Postman clients respectively. For more information on exporting and importing Postman collections, visit `https://www.getpostman.com/docs/postman/collections/data_formats`.

Make a `POST` request from Postman to the Kong admin URL `http://localhost:8001/apis` with these fields in the JSON body:

```
{
    "name": "myapi",
    "hosts": "server1",
    "upstream_url": "http://go-server:3000",
    "uris":["/api/v1"],
    "strip_uri": true,
    "preserve_host": false
}
```

It adds our health check API to Kong. The Postman screen looks like the following screenshot with all the changes. Postman is a wonderful tool that allows Windows, macOS X, and Linux users to make/test HTTP API requests. You can download it here `https://www.getpostman.com/`.

Once we make this, we get the response JSON with details of the API. This new `myapi` will be given an ID:

```
{
  "created_at": 1509195475000,
  "strip_uri": true,
  "id": "795409ae-89ae-4810-8520-15418b96161f",
  "hosts": [
    "server1"
  ],
  "name": "myapi",
  "http_if_terminated": false,
  "preserve_host": false,
  "upstream_url": "http://go-server:3000",
  "uris": [
    "/api/v1"
  ],
  "upstream_connect_timeout": 60000,
  "upstream_send_timeout": 60000,
  "upstream_read_timeout": 60000,
  "retries": 5,
  "https_only": false
}
```

A `GET` request to this URL, `http://localhost:8001/apis/myapi` returns the metadata of newly added `myapi`.

Coming to the fields that we posted to the `POST` API, the `name` is the unique name of the API. We need to use this to identify an API on the gateway. `hosts` is the list of hosts from which the gateway can accept and forward requests. Upstream URL is the actual address to which Kong forward requests. Since we linked the `go-server` container, in the beginning, we can directly refer `http://go-server:3000` from the Kong. The `uris` field is intended to specify the path relative to the upstream proxy (Go server) to fetch resources.

For example, if the URI is `/api/v1` and the Go server's API is `/healthcheck`, the resulting gateway API will be:

```
http://localhost:8000/api/v1/healthcheck
```

`preserve_host` is the property that says whether Kong should change the request's host field to the hostname of the upstream server. For more information, see `https://getkong.org/docs/0.10.x/proxy/#the-preserve_host-property`. Other settings such as `upstream_connect_timeout` are straightforward.

We added our API to Kong. Let us verify if it is forwarding our health check request to the Go server or not. Don't forget to add a header called `Host` with the value `server1` for all the API requests. This is very important. The API call looks like the following screenshot:

We received the response successfully. This is the response returned by our `HealthcheckHandler` in our `main.go` program.

If you receive a 404 error, please try the procedure from the beginning. The problem could be the containers not running or the upstream URL not being accessible from the Kong container. Another critical error may arise from not adding host in the request headers. This is the host given while adding the API.

This health check API is actually running as a Go service. We made a request for the API gateway and it is forwarding that to the Go. It proves that we successfully linked our API with an API gateway.

This is the addition of the API, the tip of the iceberg. What about other things? We will be going through each and every feature of the API gateway and try to implement them for our API.

In Kong, apart from this basic routing, additional things such as logging and rate limiting are available. We need to enable them to our API using plugins. A Kong plugin is an inbuilt component that allows us to plug any functionality easily. There are many types of plugins available. Out of them, we will discuss a few interesting ones in the next section. Let us start with the logging plugin.

API logging in Kong

Many plugins are available in Kong to log requests to multiple targets. A target is a system that collects the log and persists it somewhere. These are the important plugins available for logging:

- File log
- Syslog
- HTTP log

The first one is file logging. If we need the Kong server to store the request and response logs in the form of JSON to a file, use this plugin. We should call on Kong's admin REST API (`http://localhost:8001/apis/myapi/plugins`) to do that:

Hit the **Send** button and the gateway returns the response, like this:

```
{
  "created_at": 1509202704000,
  "config": {
    "path": "/tmp/file.log",
    "reopen": false
  },
  "id": "57954bdd-ee11-4f00-a7aa-1a48f672d36d",
  "name": "file-log",
  "api_id": "795409ae-89ae-4810-8520-15418b96161f",
  "enabled": true
}
```

It basically tells Kong that, for the given API called `myapi`, log every request to a file called /tmp/file.log. Now, make one more request for the health check (`http://localhost:8000/api/v1/healthcheck`) to the API gateway. The log for this request will be saved in the given file path.

How do we watch these logs? Those logs will be saved in the /tmp folder of the container. Open a new tab of a terminal and enter the Kong container using this command:

```
docker exec -i -t kong /bin/bash
```

This takes you into the container's bash shell. Now, inspect the log file:

```
cat /tmp/file.log
```

And you will see a lengthy JSON written to the file:

```
{"api":{"created_at":1509195475000,"strip_uri":true,"id":"795409ae-89ae-481
0-8520-15418b96161f","hosts":["server1"],"name":"myapi","headers":{"host":[
"server1"]},"http_if_terminated":false,"https_only":false,"retries":5,"uris
":["\/api\/v1"],"preserve_host":false,"upstream_connect_timeout":60000,"ups
tream_read_timeout":60000,"upstream_send_timeout":60000,"upstream_url":"htt
p:\/\/go-
server:3000"},"request":{"querystring":{},"size":"423","uri":"\/api\/v1\/he
althcheck","request_uri":"http:\/\/server1:8000\/api\/v1\/healthcheck","met
hod":"GET","headers":{"cache-control":"no-
cache","cookie":"session.id=MTUwODY2NTE3MnxOd3dBBTkZaUVNqVTBURmRTU1lRSVRsUlp
RMHhGU2xkQlZVNDFVMFFVMFJNVmxmjMlRFNDJUVXhhDTWpaWE1rOUNORXBFVkRJMlExSX1SMEU9fNFxTx
KgoEsN2IWvrF-sJgH4tSLxTw8o52lfgj2DwnHI","postman-token":"b70b1881-
d7bd-4d8e-b893-494952e44033","user-agent":"PostmanRuntime\/3.0.11-
hotfix.2","accept":"*\/*","connection":"keep-alive","accept-
encoding":"gzip,
deflate","host":"server1"}},"client_ip":"172.17.0.1","latencies":{"request"
:33,"kong":33,"proxy":0},"response":{"headers":{"content-
```

```
type":"text\/plain; charset=utf-8","date":"Sat, 28 Oct 2017 15:02:05
GMT","via":"kong\/0.11.0","connection":"close","x-kong-proxy-
latency":"33","x-kong-upstream-latency":"0","content-
length":"58"},"status":200,"size":"271"},"tries":[{"balancer_latency":0,"po
rt":3000,"ip":"172.17.0.3"}],"started_at":1509202924971}
```

IP addresses logged here are the internal IP assigned by the Docker to the containers. This
log also has a breakdown of latency information about the Kong proxy, Go server, and so
on. You can learn more about the format of logged fields at `https://getkong.org/plugins/`
`file-log/`. Kong admin API for enabling the other logging types is similar to the `file-`
`log`.

 The POST requests we are making from Postman to the admin API has the
header of `Content-Type: "application/json"`.

API authentication in Kong

As we mentioned, an API gateway should take care of authentication for the multiple APIs
running behind the gateway. Many plugins are available to provide authentication on the
fly in Kong. In the next chapter, we will see the authentication concept in detail. For now,
using these plugins, we can add authentication for a given API by calling the Kong admin
API.

An API key-based authentication is becoming famous these days. Kong provides the
following authentication patterns:

- API key-based authentication
- OAuth2 authentication
- JWT authentication

For the sake of simplicity, let us implement API key-based authentication. In simple words,
key-based authentication allows an external client to consume the REST API with a unique
token. For that in Kong, enable the key authentication plugin first. To enable the plugin,
make a POST request to the `http://localhost:8001/apis/myapi/plugins` URL with
two things in the JSON body:

1. The `name` is `key-auth`.
2. `config.hide_credentials` is `true`.

The second option is to strip/hide the credential to get passed to the Go API server. Take a look at the following screenshot:

It returns the JSON response with the created `api_id`:

```
{
    "created_at": 1509212748000,
    "config": {
        "key_in_body": false,
        "anonymous": "",
        "key_names": [
            "apikey"
        ],
        "hide_credentials": true
    },
    "id": "5c7d23dd-6dda-4802-ba9c-7aed712c2101",
    "enabled": true,
    "api_id": "795409ae-89ae-4810-8520-15418b96161f",
    "name": "key-auth"
}
```

Now, if we try to make a health check API request, we receive a 401 Unauthorized error:

```
{
    "message": "No API key found in request"
}
```

Then how can we consume an API? We need to create a consumer and give permissions for him to access the API. That permission is an API key. Let us see how to do that.

For creating a consumer, we need to create a consumer that represents a user consuming the API. Make an API call to the Kong admin API for consumers. The URL endpoint will be `http://localhost:8001/consumers`. Refer to the following screenshot:

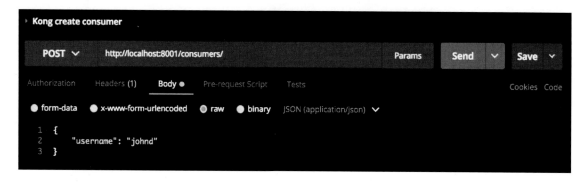

The `POST` body should have the `username` field. The response will be JSON with the created consumer:

```
{
    "created_at": 1509213840000,
    "username": "johnd",
    "id": "df024acb-5cbd-4e4d-b3ed-751287eafd36"
}
```

Now, if we need to grant the API permission to `johnd`, make a `POST` request to the `http://localhost:8001/consumers/johnd/key-auth` admin URL:

This returns the API key:

```
{
    "id": "664435b8-0f16-40c7-bc7f-32c69eb6c39c",
    "created_at": 1509214422000,
    "key": "89MH58EXzc4xHBO8WZB9axZ4uhZ1vW9d",
    "consumer_id": "df024acb-5cbd-4e4d-b3ed-751287eafd36"
}
```

We can use this API key generated in the subsequent API calls. Now, remake the health check with `apikey` in header whose value is the key from the preceding response, and it successfully returns the date and time with a `200 OK`. Refer to the following screenshot:

API rate limiting in Kong

We can limit the rate of an API for a given consumer. For example, GitHub limits clients to make 5000 requests per hour. After that, it throws an API rate limit exceeded error. We can add similar rate limiting constraints for our API using Kong's `rate-limiting` plugin.

We can enable it using this API: `http://localhost:8001/apis/myapi/plugins`, with `POST name`, `config.hour`, and `consumer_id` as body parameters:

This API call is creating a rate limiting rule. The `consumer_id` is the id of the username `johnd`. This JSON response has an `ID`

```
{
   "created_at": 1509216578000,
   "config": {
      "hour": 5000,
      "redis_database": 0,
      "policy": "cluster",
      "hide_client_headers": false,
      "redis_timeout": 2000,
      "redis_port": 6379,
      "limit_by": "consumer",
      "fault_tolerant": true
   },
   "id": "b087a740-62a2-467a-96b5-9cee1871a368",
   "enabled": true,
   "name": "rate-limiting",
   "api_id": "795409ae-89ae-4810-8520-15418b96161f",
   "consumer_id": "df024acb-5cbd-4e4d-b3ed-751287eafd36"
}
```

Now, the consumer (`johnd`) has the rate limit on the API. He will only be allowed to make 5000 requests per hour to our health check API. If he exceeds it, he receives the following error:

```
{"message":"API rate limit exceeded"}
```

How should a client know how many requests are remaining as part of rate control? Kong sets a few headers on the response when a client makes a request to the API. Try to make 10 health check requests and check the response headers; you will find the following in the response headers, which proves that rate limiting is working:

```
X-RateLimit-Limit-hour →5000
X-RateLimit-Remaining-hour →4990
```

In this way, Kong provides many good features to take our API to the next level. It doesn't mean that an API gateway is absolutely necessary, but it can give you the pleasure of having many cool features without writing a single line of code. It is an open-source software developed to avoid rewriting the universally defined API gateway functionality within the web service business logic. For more features such as load balancing and request transformations, go through the documentation of Kong at `https://konghq.com/plugins/`.

Kong CLI

Kong comes with a command-line tool for changing the behavior of Kong. It has a set of commands to start, stop, and modify Kong. Kong by default uses a configuration file. If we need to modify it, we need to restart Kong for those changes to be applied. So, all these housekeeping jobs are already wired into the Kong CLI tool. The basic functions are:

- `kong start`: For starting the Kong server
- `kong reload`: For reloading the Kong server
- `kong stop`: For stopping the Kong server
- `kong check`: For validating the given Kong configuration file
- `kong health`: For checking necessary services, such as the database, are running

Please go through the documentation of Kong CLI for more commands at `https://getkong.org/docs/0.9.x/cli/`.

Other API gateways

There are many other API gateway providers available in the market. As we mentioned earlier, all gateways perform the same kinds of functions. Enterprise gateway service providers such as Amazon API Gateway plays nice with EC2 and Lambdas. Apigee is another well-known API gateway technology that is a part of Google Cloud. The problem with cloud providers is that they can cause vendor lock (cannot easily migrate to another platform). Because of that reason, open-source alternatives are always good for startup companies.

Summary

In this chapter, we started with the basics of an API gateway. An API gateway tries to do a few things; it acts as a proxy for our API. By being a proxy, it forwards requests to the multiple APIs from different domains. In that process of forwarding, a gateway can block requests, rate limit them, and also transform requests/responses.

Kong is a good open-source API gateway available for the Linux platform. It has many features such as authentication, logging, and rate limiting. We saw how to install Kong, a Kong database, and our REST service inside the Docker containers. We used Docker instead of host machine because containers can be destroyed and created at will. It gives less chance for screwing up our host system. After learning about the installation, we learned that Kong has two types of REST API. One is the admin API, and the other is the app API. The admin API is the one we use to add our API to the gateway. The app API is our application's API. We saw how to add an API to Kong. Then, we came to know about Kong plugins. Kong plugins are the functional pieces that can plug into a Kong. Logging plugins are available. Authentication plugins and rate limiting plugins are also available in Kong.

We made requests with the Postman client and saw the sample JSON returned. For authentication, we used the `apikey` based consumer. We then simulated GitHub's 5000 requests per hour with a `key-auth` plugin of Kong.

Finally, we introduced the Kong CLI and also inspected other enterprise API gateways such as Apigee and Amazon API Gateway. In the next chapter, we will see in more detail how authentication works and try to secure our API when there is no API gateway present.

12
Handling Authentication for Our REST Services

In this chapter, we are going to explore authentication patterns in Go. Those patterns are `session-based authentication,` `JSON Web Tokens (JWT),` and `Open Authentication 2 (OAuth2).` We will try to leverage the Gorilla package's sessions library to create basic sessions. Then, we will try to move onto advanced REST API authentication strategies such as using stateless JWT. Finally, we will see how to implement our own OAuth2 and also learn what packages are available to provide us out-of-box OAuth2 implementations. In the previous chapter, the API gateway implemented authentication (using plugins) for us. If the API gateway is not present in our architecture, how do we secure our API? You will find the answer in this chapter.

In this chapter, we will cover the following topics:

- How authentication works
- Introducing Postman, a visual client for testing APIs
- Session-based authentication in Go
- Introducing Redis to store user sessions
- Introduction to JSON Web Tokens (JWT)
- OAuth2 architecture and basics

Getting the code

You can get the code samples for this chapter at `https://github.com/narenaryan/gorestful/tree/master/chapter12`. Since the example programs are not packages, the reader needs to create the project files by following the GOPATH way of writing projects.

How authentication works

Traditionally, authentication or simple authentication works in a session-centric way. A client that is requesting resources from the server tries to prove that it is the right consumer for any given resource. The flow starts like this. A client sends an authentication request to the server using user credentials. The server takes those credentials and matches them with the credentials stored on the server. If a match is successful, it writes something called a cookie in the response. This cookie is a small piece of information that is transferred to and from subsequent requests. The modern **user interfaces (UI)** of websites are **single-page applications (SPAs)**. There, the static web assets like HTML, JS are served from a CDN to render the web page initially. From next time, the communication between the web page and application server happens only through REST API/Web services.

A session is a nice way to record the user communication in a given period of time. The session is a concept that is usually stored in a cookie. The following diagram can sum up the entire process of authentication (simply auth):

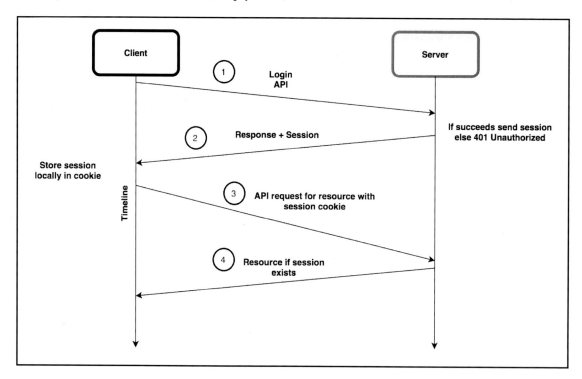

Now see the practical approach. A client (for example, a browser) sends a request to the **Login API** of the server. The server tries to check those credentials with the database and if credentials exist, writes a cookie back onto the response saying this user is authenticated. A cookie is a message to be consumed by the server at the later point of time. When the client receives the response, it stores that cookie locally. If the web browser is the client, it stores it in the cookie storage. From next time, the client can freely ask for resources from the server by showing the cookie as the key for passage. When a client decides to terminate the session, it calls the Logout API on the server. The server destroys the session in the response. This process continues. The server can also keep an expiration on cookies so that the authentication window is valid for a certain time if there is no activity. This is how all websites work.

Now, we will try to implement one such system using the Gorilla kit's `sessions` package. We already saw how the Gorilla kit provides an HTTP router in the initial chapters. This sessions package is one of them. We need to install the package first by using the following command:

```
go get github.com/gorilla/sessions
```

Now, we can create a new session using this statement:

```
var store = sessions.NewCookieStore([]byte("secret_key"))
```

That `secret_key` should be the key that Gorilla sessions use to encrypt the session cookies. If we add a session as a normal text, anyone can read it. So, the server needs to encrypt a message to a random string. For that, it asks to provide a secret key. This secret key can be any randomly generated string. Keeping secret keys in code is not a good idea, so we try to store it as an environment variable and read it in code on the fly. We will see how we can implement one such system.

Session-based authentication

Create a project called `simpleAuth` in GOPATH and add a `main.go` file, which holds the logic for our program:

```
mkdir simpleAuth
touch main.py
```

In this program, we are going to see how we can create a session-based authentication using the Gorilla sessions package. Refer to the following code snippet:

```
package main
import (
```

```go
        "log"
        "net/http"
        "os"
        "time"
        "github.com/gorilla/mux"
        "github.com/gorilla/sessions"
)
var store =
sessions.NewCookieStore([]byte(os.Getenv("SESSION_SECRET")))
var users = map[string]string{"naren": "passme", "admin": "password"}
// HealthcheckHandler returns the date and time
func HealthcheckHandler(w http.ResponseWriter, r *http.Request) {
        session, _ := store.Get(r, "session.id")
        if (session.Values["authenticated"] != nil) &&
session.Values["authenticated"] != false {
                w.Write([]byte(time.Now().String()))
        } else {
                http.Error(w, "Forbidden", http.StatusForbidden)
        }
}
// LoginHandler validates the user credentials
func LoginHandler(w http.ResponseWriter, r *http.Request) {
        session, _ := store.Get(r, "session.id")
        err := r.ParseForm()
        if err != nil {
                http.Error(w, "Please pass the data as URL form encoded",
http.StatusBadRequest)
                return
        }
        username := r.PostForm.Get("username")
        password := r.PostForm.Get("password")
        if originalPassword, ok := users[username]; ok {
                if password == originalPassword {
                        session.Values["authenticated"] = true
                        session.Save(r, w)
                } else {
                        http.Error(w, "Invalid Credentials", http.StatusUnauthorized)
                        return
                }
        } else {
                http.Error(w, "User is not found", http.StatusNotFound)
                return
        }
        w.Write([]byte("Logged In successfully"))
}
// LogoutHandler removes the session
func LogoutHandler(w http.ResponseWriter, r *http.Request) {
        session, _ := store.Get(r, "session.id")
```

```
        session.Values["authenticated"] = false
        session.Save(r, w)
        w.Write([]byte(""))
    }
    func main() {
        r := mux.NewRouter()
        r.HandleFunc("/login", LoginHandler)
        r.HandleFunc("/healthcheck", HealthcheckHandler)
        r.HandleFunc("/logout", LogoutHandler)
        http.Handle("/", r)
        srv := &http.Server{
            Handler: r,
            Addr: "127.0.0.1:8000",
            // Good practice: enforce timeouts for servers you create!
            WriteTimeout: 15 * time.Second,
            ReadTimeout: 15 * time.Second,
        }
        log.Fatal(srv.ListenAndServe())
    }
```

It is a REST API that allows one to access the health condition (up or not) of the system. In order to authenticate, one needs to call the login endpoint first. The program imported two main packages called mux and sessions from the Gorilla kit. Mux is used to link the URL endpoints of HTTP requests to a function handler, and sessions is used to create new sessions and validate existing ones on the fly.

In Go, we need to store sessions in the program memory. We can do that by creating CookieStore. This line explicitly tells the program to create one by picking the secret key from the environment variable called SESSION_SECRET:

```
    var store = sessions.NewCookieStore([]byte(os.Getenv("SESSION_SECRET")))
```

sessions has a new function called NewCookieStore that returns a store. We need to use this store to manage cookies. We can get a cookie session with this statement. If the session doesn't exist, it returns an empty one:

```
    session, _ := store.Get(r, "session.id")
```

session.id is a custom name that we gave to the session. With this name, a cookie will be sent back in the client response. LoginHandler tries to parse the form that was supplied by the client as multipart form data. This step is essential in the program:

```
    err := r.ParseForm()
```

This fills the `r.PostForm` map with the parsed key-value pairs. That API requires both username and password for its authentication. So, we are interested in scraping `username` and `password`. Once `LoginHandler` receives the data, it tries to check it with the details in a map called **users**. In a practical scenario, we use the database to validate those details. For simplicity's sake, we hardcoded values and tried to authenticate from it. If the username doesn't exist, return an error saying resource not found. If the username exists and the password is incorrect, return an `UnAuthorized` error message. If everything goes well, return a 200 response by setting the cookie value, like this:

```
session.Values["authenticated"] = true
session.Save(r, w)
```

The first statement sets the cookie key called `"authenticated"` to `true`. The second statement actually saves the session on the response. It takes request and response writers as the arguments. If we remove this statement, the cookie will not have any effect. Now, coming to the `HealthCheckHandler`, it does the same thing as `LoginHandler` initially, like this:

```
session, _ := store.Get(r, "session.id")
```

Then, it checks whether a given request has a cookie that has the key called `"authenticated"`. If that key exists and is true, it means it is the user that the server authenticated previously. But, if that key does not exist or the `"authenticated"` value is `false`, then the session is not valid, hence it returns a `StatusForbidden` error.

There should be a way for the client to invalidate a login session. It can do that by calling the logout API of the server. The API just sets the `"authenticated"` value to `false`. This tells the server that the client is not authenticated:

```
session, _ := store.Get(r, "session.id")
session.Values["authenticated"] = false
session.Save(r, w)
```

In this way, a simple authentication can be implemented using the sessions in any programming language, including Go.

Don't forget to add this statement, as it is the actual one that modifies and saves the cookie: `session.Save(r, w)`.

Now, let us see the execution of this program. Instead of CURL, we can use a wonderful tool called Postman. The main benefit is that it runs on all platforms including Microsoft Window; no need for CURL anymore.

The error codes can mean different things. For example, Forbidden (403) is issued when the user tries to access a resource without authentication, whereas Resource Not Found (404) is issued when the given resource does not exist on the server.

Introducing Postman, a tool for testing REST API

Postman is a wonderful tool that allows Windows, macOS X, and Linux users to make HTTP API requests. You can download it at `https://www.getpostman.com/`.

After installing Postman, enter a URL in the **Enter request URL** input text. Select the type of request (`GET`, `POST`, and so on). For each request, we can have many settings such as headers, `POST` body, and other details. Please go through the Postman documentation for more details. The basic usage of Postman is straightforward. Take a look at the following screenshot:

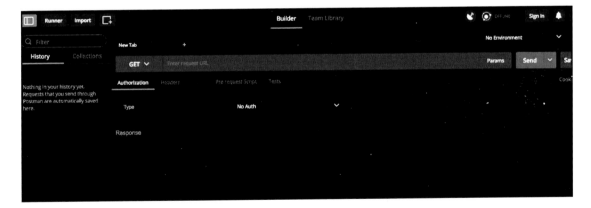

The builder is the window where we can add/edit requests. The preceding screenshot shows the empty builder where we try to make requests. Run the `main.go` in the preceding `simpleAuth` project and try to call the health check API, like this. Click on the **Send** button and you will see the response is forbidden:

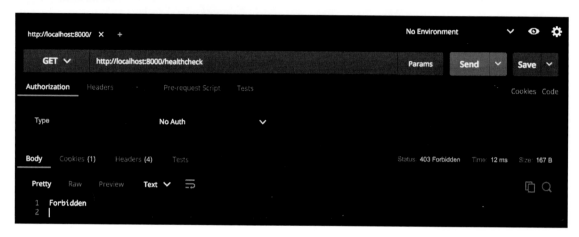

This is because we didn't log in yet. Postman automatically saves the cookie once authentication is successful. Now, call the login API by changing the method type from GET to POST and URL to `http://localhost:8000/login`. We should also pass the auth details as multipart form data. It looks like the following screenshot:

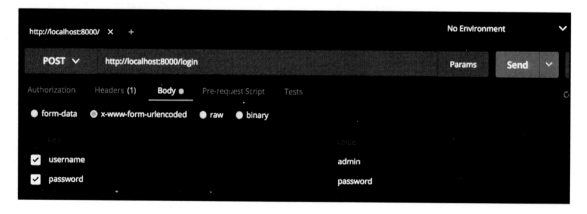

Now, if we hit send, it authenticates and receives the cookie. It returns a message saying **Logged In successfully**. We can also inspect the cookies by clicking on the **Cookies** link just below the **Send** and **Save** buttons on right-hand side. It shows the list of cookies saved and you will find a cookie called `session.id` there for localhost. The content will look like this:

```
session.id=MTUwODYzNDcwN3xEdi1CQkFFQ180SUFBUkFCRUFBQUpmLUNBUVVHYzNSeWFXNW5E
QThBRFdGMWRHaGxibJwWTJGMFpXUUVZbT12YkFJQ0FFBRT189iF-ruBQmyTdtAOaMR-
Rr9lNtsf1OJgirBDkcBpdEa0=; path=/; domain=localhost; Expires=Tue Nov 21
2017 01:11:47 GMT+0530 (IST);
```

Try to call the health check API again, and it returns us the system date and time:

```
2017-10-22 06:54:36.464214959 +0530 IST
```

If a client makes a GET request to the logout API:

```
http://localhost:8000/logout
```

The session will be invalidated and access to the resource will be forbidden until another login request is done.

Persisting client sessions with Redis

The sessions we created until now are stored in the program memory. It means if the program crashes or restarts, all the logged sessions will be lost. It needs the client to re-authenticate once again to get a new session cookie. It can be an annoying thing sometimes. In order to save sessions in some place, we chose **Redis**. Redis is a key-value storage that is very fast because it lives in primary memory.

The Redis server stores any key-value pairs we supply. It provides basic data types such as strings, lists, hashes, sets, and so on. For more details, visit `https://redis.io/topics/data-types`. We can install Redis with the following command on Ubuntu 16.04:

```
sudo apt-get install redis-server
```

On macOS X, we can just say:

```
brew install redis
```

For Windows too, binaries are available on the Redis website. Once Redis is installed, we can start the Redis server with this command:

```
redis-server
```

It starts the server on default port 6379. Now, we can store anything in that using Redis CLI (command-line tool). Open a new terminal and type `redis-cli`. Once the shell is launched, we can perform Redis commands to store and retrieve data into the user-defined type variables:

```
[7:30:30] naren:~ $ redis-cli
127.0.0.1:6379> SET Foo  1
OK
127.0.0.1:6379> GET Foo
"1"
```

We can store a key value using the `SET` Redis command. It stores the value as a string. If we try to perform `GET`, it returns us the string. It is our responsibility to convert them to numbers. Redis provides us handy functions to operate on those keys. For example, we can increment a key like this:

```
127.0.0.1:6379> INCR Foo
(integer) 2
```

Redis treats integers as integers internally. If you try to increment a non-number string, Redis throws an error:

```
127.0.0.1:6379> SET name "redis"
OK
127.0.0.1:6379> INCR name
(error) ERR value is not an integer or out of range
```

Why are we discussing Redis here? Because we are showing how Redis works and introducing a few basic commands on the Redis server. We are going to modify our project from `simpleAuth` to `simpleAuthWithRedis`.

In that project, instead of storing sessions in program memory, we use Redis. Even though the program crashes, sessions are not lost since they are saved in the external server. Who writes the bridging logic for that? We should. Luckily, we have a package that takes care of that coordination between Redis and the Go sessions package.

Install that package with the following command:

```
go get gopkg.in/boj/redistore.v1
```

And create a new program with a few modifications. Here, instead of using the sessions library, we use the `redistore` package. `redistore` has a function called `NewRediStore` that takes Redis configuration as the arguments along with the secret key. All other functions remain same. Now, add a `main.go` file in the `simpleAuthWithRedis` directory:

```go
package main
import (
    "log"
    "net/http"
    "os"
    "time"
    "github.com/gorilla/mux"
    redistore "gopkg.in/boj/redistore.v1"
)
var store, err = redistore.NewRediStore(10, "tcp", ":6379", "",
[]byte(os.Getenv("SESSION_SECRET")))
var users = map[string]string{"naren": "passme", "admin": "password"}
// HealthcheckHandler returns the date and time
func HealthcheckHandler(w http.ResponseWriter, r *http.Request) {
    session, _ := store.Get(r, "session.id")
    if (session.Values["authenticated"] != nil) &&
session.Values["authenticated"] != false {
        w.Write([]byte(time.Now().String()))
    } else {
        http.Error(w, "Forbidden", http.StatusForbidden)
    }
}
// LoginHandler validates the user credentials
func LoginHandler(w http.ResponseWriter, r *http.Request) {
    session, _ := store.Get(r, "session.id")
    err := r.ParseForm()
    if err != nil {
        http.Error(w, "Please pass the data as URL form encoded",
http.StatusBadRequest)
        return
    }
    username := r.PostForm.Get("username")
    password := r.PostForm.Get("password")
    if originalPassword, ok := users[username]; ok {
        if password == originalPassword {
            session.Values["authenticated"] = true
            session.Save(r, w)
        } else {
```

```
                http.Error(w, "Invalid Credentials", http.StatusUnauthorized)
                return
            }
        } else {
            http.Error(w, "User is not found", http.StatusNotFound)
            return
        }
        w.Write([]byte("Logged In successfully"))
    }
    // LogoutHandler removes the session
    func LogoutHandler(w http.ResponseWriter, r *http.Request) {
        session, _ := store.Get(r, "session.id")
        session.Options.MaxAge = -1
        session.Save(r, w)
        w.Write([]byte(""))
    }
    func main() {
        defer store.Close()
        r := mux.NewRouter()
        r.HandleFunc("/login", LoginHandler)
        r.HandleFunc("/healthcheck", HealthcheckHandler)
        r.HandleFunc("/logout", LogoutHandler)
        http.Handle("/", r)
        srv := &http.Server{
            Handler: r,
            Addr: "127.0.0.1:8000",
            // Good practice: enforce timeouts for servers you create!
            WriteTimeout: 15 * time.Second,
            ReadTimeout: 15 * time.Second,
        }
        log.Fatal(srv.ListenAndServe())
    }
```

One interesting change is that we removed the session instead of setting its value to `false`:

```
    session.Options.MaxAge = -1
```

This improved program works exactly the same as the previous one, except the session is saved in Redis. Open the Redis CLI and type this command to get all available keys:

```
[15:09:48] naren:~ $ redis-cli
127.0.0.1:6379> KEYS *
1) "session_VPJ54LWRE4DNTYCLEJWAUN5SDLVW6LN6MLB26W2OB4JDT26CR2GA"
127.0.0.1:6379>
```

That lengthy `"session_VPJ54LWRE4DNTYCLEJWAUN5SDLVW6LN6MLB26W2OB4JDT26CR2GA"` is the key stored by the `redistore`. If we delete that key, the client will automatically be forbidden from accessing resources. Now, stop the running program and restart it. You will see the session is not lost. In this way, we can save the client session. We can also persist sessions on the SQLite database. Many third-party packages are written to make that much easier.

Redis can serve the purpose of caching for your web applications. It can store temporary data such as sessions, frequently requested user content, and so on. It is usually compared to **memcached**.

Introduction to JSON Web Tokens (JWT) and OAuth2

The previous style of authentication is a plain username/password and session-based. It has a limitation of managing sessions by saving them in the program memory or Redis/SQLite3. The modern REST API implements token-based authentication. Here, tokens can be any strings generated by the server, which allows the client to access resources by showing the token. Here, the token is computed in such a way that the client and the server only know how to encode/decode the token. **JWT** tries to solve this problem by enabling us to create tokens that we can pass around.

Whenever a client passes the authentication details to the server, the server generates a token and passes it back to the client. The client saves that in some kind of storage, such as a database or local storage (in case of browser). The client uses that token to ask for resources from any API defined by the server:

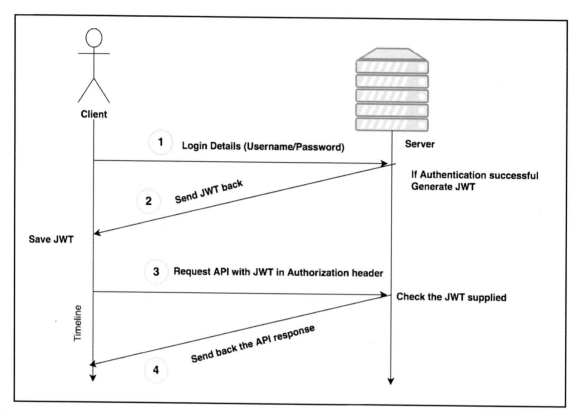

The steps can be summarized more briefly as follows:

1. The client passes the username/password in a POST request to the login API.
2. The server authenticates the details and if successful, it generates a JWT and returns it back instead of creating a cookie. It is the client's responsibility to store this token.
3. Now, the client has the JWT. It needs to add this in subsequent REST API calls such as GET, POST, PUT, and DELETE in the request headers.
4. Once again, the server checks the JWT and if it is successfully decoded, the server sends the data back by looking at the username supplied as part of the token.

JWT ensures that the data is sent from the correct client. The technique for creating a token takes cares of that logic. JWT leverages the secret key-based encryption.

JSON web token format

All we discussed in the preceding section was circling around a JWT token. We are going to see here what it really looks like and how it is produced. JWT is a string that is generated after performing few a steps. They are as follows:

1. Create a JWT header by doing **Base64Url** encoding on the header JSON.
2. Create a JWT payload by doing **Base64Url** encoding on the payload JSON.
3. Create a signature by encrypting the appended header and payload using a secret key.
4. JWT string can be obtained by appending the header, payload, and signature.

A header is a simple JSON object. It looks like the following code snippet in Go:

```
`{
  "alg": "HS256",
  "typ": "JWT"
}`
```

`"alg"` is a short form for the algorithm (HMAC with SHA-256) used for creating a signature. The message type is `"JWT"`. This will be common for all the headers. The algorithm may change depending on the system.

A payload looks like this:

```
`{
  "sub": "1234567890",
  "username": "Indiana Jones",
  "admin": true
}`
```

Keys in payload object are called claims. A claim is a key that specifies some special meaning to the server. There are three types of claims:

- Public claims
- Private claims (more important)
- Reserved claims

Reserved claims

Reserved claims are the ones defined by the JWT standard. They are:

- iat: issued at the time
- iss: issuer name
- sub: subject text
- aud: audience name
- exp: expiration time

For example, the server, while generating a token, can set an `exp` claim in the payload. The client then uses that token to access API resources. The server validates the token each time. When the expiration time is passed, the server will no longer validate the token. The client needs to generate a new token by logging in again.

Private claims

Private claims are the names used to identify one token from another. It can be used for authorization. Authorization is a process of identifying which client made the request. Multi-tenancy is having multiple clients in a system. The server can set a private claim called `username` on the payload of the token. Next time, the server can read this payload back and get the username, and then use that username to authorize and customize the API response.

`"username": "Indiana Jones"` is the private claim on the preceding sample payload. **Public claims** are the ones similar to private claims, but they should be registered with the IANA JSON Web Token Registry to make it as a standard. We limit the use of these.

A signature can be created by performing this (this is not code, just an illustration):

```
signature = HMACSHA256(
  base64UrlEncode(header) + "." +
  base64UrlEncode(payload),
  secret)
```

It is simply performing an encryption algorithm on the Base64URL encoded header and payload with a secret. This secret can be any string. It is exactly similar to the secret we used in the previous cookie session. This secret is usually saved in the environment variable and loaded into the program.

Now we append the encoded header, encoded payload, and signature to get our token string:

```
tokenString = base64UrlEncode(header) + "." + base64UrlEncode(payload) +
"." + signature
```

This is how a JWT token is generated. Are we going to do all this stuff manually in Go? No. In Go, or any other programming language, a few packages are available to wrap this manual creation of a token and verification. Go has a wonderful, popular package called `jwt-go`. We are going to create a project in the next section that uses `jwt-go` to sign a JWT and also validate them. One can install the package using the following command:

go get github.com/dgrijalva/jwt-go

This is the official GitHub page for the project: `https://github.com/dgrijalva/jwt-go`. The package provides a few functions that allow us to create tokens. There are many other packages with different additional features. You can see all available packages and features supported at `https://jwt.io/#libraries-io`.

Creating a JWT in Go

The `jwt-go` package has a function called `NewWithClaims` that takes two arguments:

1. Signing method such as HMAC256, RSA, and so on
2. Claims map

For example, it looks like the following code snippet:

```
token := jwt.NewWithClaims(jwt.SigningMethodHS256, jwt.MapClaims{
    "username": "admin",
    "iat":time.Now().Unix(),
})
```

`jwt.SigningMethodHS256` is an encryption algorithm that is available within the package. The second argument is a map with claims such as private (here username) and reserved (issued at). Now we can generate a `tokenString` using the `SignedString` function on a token:

```
tokenString, err := token.SignedString("my_secret_key")
```

This `tokenString` then should be passed back to the client.

Reading a JWT in Go

`jwt-go` also gives us the API to parse a given JWT string. The `Parse` function takes a string and key function as arguments. The `key` function is a custom function that validates whether the algorithm is proper or not. Let us say this is a sample token string generated by the preceding encoding:

```
tokenString =
"eyJhbGciOiJIUzI1NiIsInR5cCI6IkpXVCJ9.eyJ1c2VybmFtZSI6ImFkbWluIiwiaWF0IjoiM
TUwODc0MTU5MTQ2NiJ9.5m6KkuQFCgyaGS_xcVy4xWakwDgtAG3ILGGTBgYVBmE"
```

We can parse and get back the original JSON using:

```go
token, err := jwt.Parse(tokenString, func(token *jwt.Token) (interface{},
error) {
    // key function
    if _, ok := token.Method.(*jwt.SigningMethodHMAC); !ok {
        return nil, fmt.Errorf("Unexpected signing method: %v",
token.Header["alg"])
    }
    return "my_secret_key", nil
})

if claims, ok := token.Claims.(jwt.MapClaims); ok && token.Valid {
    // Use claims for authorization if token is valid
    fmt.Println(claims["username"], claims["iat"])
} else {
    fmt.Println(err)
}
```

`token.Claims` is implemented by a map called `MapClaims`. We can get the original JSON key-value pairs from that map.

OAuth 2 architecture and basics

OAuth 2 is an authentication framework that is used to create authentication pattern between different systems. In this, the client, instead of making a request to the resource server, makes an initial request for some entity called resource owner. This resource owner gives back the authentication grant for the client (if credentials are successful). The client now sends this authentication grant to another entity called an authentication server. This authentication server takes the grant and returns an access token. This token is the key thing for a client to access API resources. It needs to make an API request to the resource server with this access token and the response is served. In this entire flow, the second part can be done using JWT. Before that, let us learn the difference between authentication and authorization.

Authentication versus authorization

Authentication is the process of identifying whether a client is genuine or not. When a server authenticates a client, it checks the username/password pair and creates session cookie/JWT.

Authorization is the process of differentiating one client from another after a successful authentication. In cloud services, the resources requested by a client need to be served by checking that the resources belong to that client but not the other client. The permissions and access to resources vary for different clients. For example, the admin has the highest privileges of resources. A normal user's access is limited.

OAuth2 is a protocol for authenticating multiple clients to a service, whereas the JWT is a token format. We need to encode/decode JWT tokens to implement the second stage (dashed lines in the following screenshot) of OAuth 2.

Take a look at the following diagram:

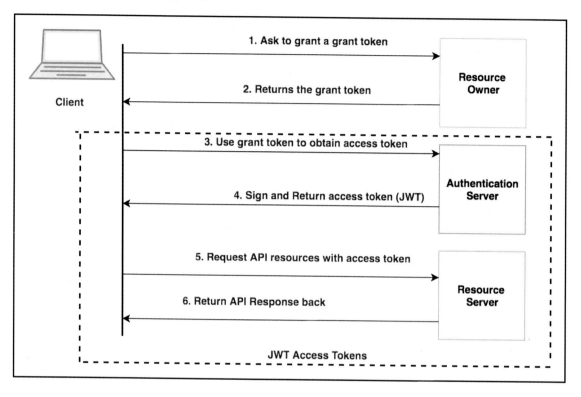

In this diagram, we can implement the dashed section using JWT. Authentication is happening at the authentication server level and authorization happens at the resource server level.

In the next section, let us write a program that does two things:

1. Authenticates the client and returns a JWT string.
2. Authorizes client API requests by validating JWT.

Create a directory called `jwtauth` and add `main.go`:

```go
package main
import (
    "encoding/json"
    "fmt"
    "log"
    "net/http"
    "os"
    "time"
    jwt "github.com/dgrijalva/jwt-go"
    "github.com/dgrijalva/jwt-go/request"
    "github.com/gorilla/mux"
)
var secretKey = []byte(os.Getenv("SESSION_SECRET"))
var users = map[string]string{"naren": "passme", "admin": "password"}
// Response is a representation of JSON response for JWT
type Response struct {
    Token string `json:"token"`
    Status string `json:"status"`
}
// HealthcheckHandler returns the date and time
func HealthcheckHandler(w http.ResponseWriter, r *http.Request) {
    tokenString, err :=
request.HeaderExtractor{"access_token"}.ExtractToken(r)
    token, err := jwt.Parse(tokenString, func(token *jwt.Token)
(interface{}, error) {
        // Don't forget to validate the alg is what you expect:
        if _, ok := token.Method.(*jwt.SigningMethodHMAC); !ok {
            return nil, fmt.Errorf("Unexpected signing method: %v",
token.Header["alg"])
        }
        // hmacSampleSecret is a []byte containing your secret, e.g.
[]byte("my_secret_key")
        return secretKey, nil
    })
    if err != nil {
        w.WriteHeader(http.StatusForbidden)
        w.Write([]byte("Access Denied; Please check the access token"))
        return
    }
    if claims, ok := token.Claims.(jwt.MapClaims); ok && token.Valid {
        // If token is valid
        response := make(map[string]string)
        // response["user"] = claims["username"]
        response["time"] = time.Now().String()
        response["user"] = claims["username"].(string)
```

```go
        responseJSON, _ := json.Marshal(response)
        w.Write(responseJSON)
    } else {
        w.WriteHeader(http.StatusForbidden)
        w.Write([]byte(err.Error()))
    }
}
// LoginHandler validates the user credentials
func getTokenHandler(w http.ResponseWriter, r *http.Request) {
    err := r.ParseForm()
    if err != nil {
        http.Error(w, "Please pass the data as URL form encoded",
http.StatusBadRequest)
        return
    }
    username := r.PostForm.Get("username")
    password := r.PostForm.Get("password")
    if originalPassword, ok := users[username]; ok {
        if password == originalPassword {
            // Create a claims map
            claims := jwt.MapClaims{
                "username": username,
                "ExpiresAt": 15000,
                "IssuedAt": time.Now().Unix(),
            }
            token := jwt.NewWithClaims(jwt.SigningMethodHS256, claims)
            tokenString, err := token.SignedString(secretKey)
            if err != nil {
                w.WriteHeader(http.StatusBadGateway)
                w.Write([]byte(err.Error()))
            }
            response := Response{Token: tokenString, Status: "success"}
            responseJSON, _ := json.Marshal(response)
            w.WriteHeader(http.StatusOK)
            w.Header().Set("Content-Type", "application/json")
            w.Write(responseJSON)
        } else {
            http.Error(w, "Invalid Credentials", http.StatusUnauthorized)
            return
        }
    } else {
        http.Error(w, "User is not found", http.StatusNotFound)
        return
    }
}
func main() {
    r := mux.NewRouter()
    r.HandleFunc("/getToken", getTokenHandler)
```

```
        r.HandleFunc("/healthcheck", HealthcheckHandler)
        http.Handle("/", r)
        srv := &http.Server{
            Handler: r,
            Addr: "127.0.0.1:8000",
            // Good practice: enforce timeouts for servers you create!
            WriteTimeout: 15 * time.Second,
            ReadTimeout: 15 * time.Second,
        }
        log.Fatal(srv.ListenAndServe())
    }
```

This is a very lengthy program to digest. First, we are importing jwt-go and its subpackage called request. We are creating a REST API for two endpoints; one for getting the access token by providing authentication details, and another one for fetching the health check API that authorizes the user.

In the getTokenHandler handler function, we are comparing the username and password with our custom defined user map. This can be a database too. If authentication is successful, we are generating a JWT string and sending it back to the client.

In HealthcheckHandler, we are taking the access token from a header called access_token and validating it by parsing the JWT string. Who is writing the logic of validating? The JWT package itself. When a new JWT string is created it should have a claim called ExpiresAt. Refer to the following code snippet:

```
        claims := jwt.MapClaims{
          "username": username,
          "ExpiresAt": 15000,
          "IssuedAt": time.Now().Unix(),
        }
```

The program's internal validation logic looks at the IssuedAt and ExpiresAt claims and tries to compute and see whether the given token is expired or not. If it is fresh, then it means the token is validated.

Now, when a token is valid, we can read the payload in the HealthCheckHandler where we parse the access_token string that passed as part of the HTTP request headers. username is a custom private claim we inserted for authorization. Therefore, we know who is actually sending this request. For each and every request there is no need for the session to be passed. Each API call is independent and token based. Information is encoded in a token itself.

`token.Claims.(jwt.MapClaims)` returns a map whose values are interfaces, not strings. In order to convert the value to a string, we should do `claims["username"].(string)`.

Let us see how this program runs by making requests through the Postman tool:

This returns a JSON string that has a JWT token. Copy it to the clipboard. If you try to make a request to the health check API without passing that JWT token as one of the headers, you will receive this error message instead of JSON :

```
Access Denied; Please check the access token
```

Now, copy that token back and make a `GET` request, adding an `access_token` header with a token string as the value. In Postman, the headers section is available where we can add headers and key-value pairs. Refer to the following screenshot:

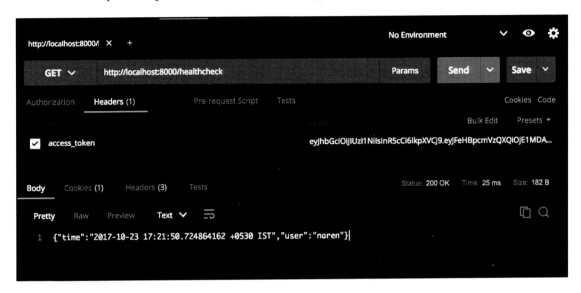

It returns the time properly as part of the API response. We can also see which user's JWT token this is. This confirms the authorization part of our REST API. Instead of having the token validation logic in each and every API handler, we can have it as a middleware and make it applicable to all handlers. Refer to `Chapter 3`, *Working with Middleware and RPC*, and modify the preceding program to have a middleware that validates the JWT token.

> Token-based authentication doesn't usually provide a log out API or API for deleting the tokens that are provided in session based authentication. The server gives the authorized resources to the client as long as JWT is not expired. Once it expires, the client needs to refresh the token—that is to say, ask the server for a new token.

Summary

In this chapter, we introduced the process of authentication. We saw how authentication usually works. Authentication can be of two types: session-based or token-based. Session-based authentication is also called simple authentication, where a session is created when the client successfully logs in. That session is saved back in the client and supplied for each and every request. There are two possible cases here. In the first case, the session will be saved in the server's program memory. This kind of session will be cleared when the application restarts. The second case is to save the session cookie in Redis. Redis is an in-memory database that can act as a cache for any web application. Redis supports storing a few data types such as string, list, hash, and so on. We explored a package called `redistore` that replaces the built-in sessions package for persisting the session cookies.

Next, we saw about JWT. A JWT is a token string that is the output of performing a few steps. First, create a header, payload, and signature. A signature can be obtained by combining both header and payload with `base64URL` encoding and applying an encryption algorithm such as HMAC. In token-based authentication, a client needs a JWT token for accessing server resources. So, initially, it requests the server to provide the access token (JWT token). Once the client gets this token, next time it makes API calls with the JWT token in the HTTP header and the server returns the response.

We introduced OAuth 2.0, an authentication framework. In OAuth 2, the client first requests for a grant from the resource owner. Once it gets the grant, it then requests an access token from the authentication server. The authentication server gives the access token, which client can use to request an API. We implemented the second step of OAuth 2 with JWT.

We tested all our APIs with a tool called Postman. Postman is a great tool that helps us to test our APIs quickly on any machine. CURL is limited to Linux and macOS X. Postman is a wise choice for Windows because it has all the features of CURL.

We came a long way from the first chapter by learning how to create HTTP routes, middlewares, and handlers. We then linked our applications with databases to store the resource data. After the basics, we explored the performance-tuning aspects such as microservices and RPC. Finally, we saw how to deploy our web services and also secure them using authentication.

Index